DISCARDED BY

PLU Library

MAO'S GENERALS

Chen Yi and the New Fourth Army

Lanxin Xiang

University Press of America,® Inc.
Lanham • New York • Oxford

Copyright © 1998
University Press of America,® Inc.
4720 Boston Way
Lanham, Maryland 20706

12 Hid's Copse Rd.
Cummor Hill, Oxford OX2 9JJ

All rights reserved
Printed in the United States of America
British Library Cataloging in Publication Information Available

ISBN 0-7618-1129-X (cloth: alk. ppr.)

♾️ The paper used in this publication meet the minimum
requirements of American National Standard for information
Sciences—Permanence of Paper for Printed Library Materials,
ANSI Z39.48—1984

To the legendary "Old First Regiment" of the New Fourth Army

Contents

Dedication		iii
List of Photos		v
List of Maps		vi
Preface		vii
Acknowledgements		viii
Chapter 1	The Making of a Red Bandit	1
Chapter 2	Origins of the New Fourth Army	33
Chapter 3	Strategies for Expansion	55
Chapter 4	"Experts of Friction"	77
Chapter 5	Politics of Conformity	109
Chapter 6	Struggle for Mastery in Shandong	135
Chapter 7	The Showdown	161
Chapter 8	From Yangzi to Shanghai	183
Concluding Remarks and Epilogue		199
Appendix	Evolution of the New Fourth Army	205
Bibliography		211
Index		221

List of Maps

Map 1: The Battle of Huang Qiao (October,1940), between p.82 and p.83

Map 2: The Southern Anhui Incident (January, 1941), between p.92 and p.93

Map 3: The Battle of Laiwu (February, 1947), between p.138 and p.139

Map 4: The Battle of Menglianggu (May, 1947), between p.142 and p.143

Map 5: The Campaign of Huai-Hai, stage 1 (November, 1948), between p.172 and p.173

Map 6: The Campaign of Huai-Hai, stage 2 (December, 1948), between p.176 and p.177

Map 7: The Campaign of Huai-Hai, stage 3 (January, 1949), between p.180 and p.181

List of Photos   p.107-108

Photo 1: Marshal Chen Yi in 1955
photo 2: The Chen brothers in Shanghai, 1929
Photo 3: The "bandit" leaders in 1938
Photo 4: Zhou Enlai's trip to Cloud Hill, 1939
Photo 5: The wedding, 1940
Photo 6: The First Mayor of Shanghai, 1949

The Anti-Japanese War, the longer the better. The civil war, the shorter the better --- Mao Zedong

Preface

I was prompted to explore the People's Liberation Army's history by my own admiration of the Chinese military establishment that had grown in me. Fascinated by the official history of the PLA while growing up, I did not ask many questions until the vast amount of documentation available in China---either published or just for internal circulation--- began to appear at breath-taking speed in the past fifteen years. I have spent four years working on this book, which turns out to be a story that would, inadvertently at least, run counter to the story lines of the official history of the Chinese Communist Party.

My curiosity grew also because this appears to be a relatively unknown subject in the West. Previous studies of Chinese communism have focused on politics and international relations. Little attention has been given to the role of the military in the communist system, even though it was the military that had brought the Communist Party to power in 1949. Neither the internal thinking on military strategies of the communists nor the personal contributions of many key military leaders has attracted much attention. The study of Chinese communist military thinking and practice in English language is far from adequate. The lack of original research on this subject has long been attributed to the lack of the first-hand materials. Indeed, before China's opening to the West, the only sources were some short personal reminiscences, often presented in literature form, in official series such as "The Red Flag Flying." However, since China's dramatic opening to the West, a large amount of new documentary materials began appearing in various forms more than a decade ago.

It is critical for us to sort out the military aspect of Chinese communism for at least two reasons. First, among all communist systems in the world, China has the closest and most symbiotic tie between the party, the state and the military. Unlike the Bolsheviks who created the Red Army after the Revolution of 1917, the Chinese military establishment immediately manned the state machine after 1949. Hence it has always functioned as a powerful "state within the state." It is no accident that in its 47-year history, the head of Communist Party of the People's Republic has changed hands five times, the head of the powerful

"Central Military Commission" only three and a half (Hua Guofeng). Therefore, the nature of the Chinese party-state cannot be understood without unveiling its military history. It may be said without exaggeration that the military is both the Party and the State. Second, military factionalism has always been a decisive factor in intra-party power transition. The traditional western dichotomy of the civilian versus the military seems to make little sense in this connection. The study of the evolution of the Chinese military will provide us with a fresh insight into the inner dynamics of the Chinese communism.

The Chinese communist military has been a fragmented institution. A general study of the military establishment would yield far fewer results than studies based on factionalism. History and geographical developments of the Chinese military have decreed that it has always been a factionalized organization consisting of four major elite groups: the First Field Army under Peng Dehuai; the Second Field Army under Liu Bocheng and Deng Xiaoping; the Third Field Army under Chen Yi and the Fourth Field Army under Lin Biao.[1] Factional loyalty has always been extraordinarily intense and the factional languages are very different. Among the four, Lin Biao and Chen Yi's factions were undoubtedly the strongest and had contributed more than the other two to breaking Chiang Kai-shek's backbone in China. While Lin is relatively well known, Chen Yi and his elite troops are far less so. This study therefore focuses on this particular faction and its unique character to indicate that it was, perhaps, the most successful story in Chinese communist military history since its inception in 1927.

This project also intends to explore the relationship between Mao's high command and his top generals in the field in order to determine the actual military contribution by Mao both in theory and in practice. Two myths have made this kind of study difficult in the past. First, Mao has long been presented as invincible and infallible. He is credited with all the military successes associated with the communist victory. Second, before 1985, biographical information was too inadequate to allow us to obtain a clear picture about actual happenings on the battlegrounds. The new information available now indicates that field commanders in the front had perhaps contributed far more than has been commonly thought.

As a military theorist, Mao was far more limited in scope than it is commonly believed. His understanding of Sun Zi's *Art of War* and Clausewitz's *On War* had been tutored and nurtured by some best-known

---

[1] One may also add Nie Rongzhen's North China Field Army to the list.

communist theorists at Yanan (General Guo Huaruo, for example) whose credit has yet to be acknowledged. As a military practitioner, Mao had often made critical misjudgments which could have cost the communists dearly, but were opposed and corrected by brilliant commanders. Many legendary military commanders played a key role in the Communist victory. From "bandit" years of peasant guerrillas to the large-scale regular warfare during the Civil War that consumed millions of Chiang Kaishek's troops, these generals were innovative and decisive in comparison with the communist high command that was sometimes muddle-headed and lacking directions. Their military professionalism was especially critical in the communist victory in Manchuria, East China, and the Yangzi Valley area. The latter two were Chen Yi's territories.

In four aspects Mao and his commanders were very often at logger heads. The first point of contention was the principle of "luring the enemy deep into a pre-planned pocket" (*You Di Shen Ru*). This was Mao's favorite strategy. Although successful during the Red Army period, many commanders rejected this principle during the civil war that required modern military thinking and tactics. Su Yu, Chen Yi's brilliant longtime deputy, for example, had challenged Mao many times and executed brilliant frontal attacks on many occasions in defiance of Mao's instructions. The second point of contention was the principle of concentrating superior troops to seek the destruction of weaker enemy wings (*Yi Duo Sheng Shao*). Mao often held to this principle very rigidly. Field commanders, Chen Yi and Peng Dehuai, for example, were often skeptical that this principle could be applied under all circumstances. A third area of disagreement between Mao and his generals was the timely grasp of the strategic turning point in a specific war zone. In this area Mao seemed to have made many wrong yet stubborn decisions that could have cost the communists far more than that it did. Mao's penchant for guerrilla warfare often prevented him from grasping strategic links between one battle and another, between one theater and another. This "win-and-run" attitude particularly vexed Mao's generals under Chen's command. On many occasions they were frustrated by Mao's irrational orders that demanded a shift of operations from interior to exterior lines at a premature moment. Nevertheless, the generals managed to maintain considerable military professionalism in battle planning and execution. The fourth, and perhaps the most important, is the constant clash over Mao's favorite "political commissar system." This, according to Mao, was a life and death issue determining the relationship between the Party and the gun. Many top generals like Chen Yi, Peng Dehuai and

He Long were known to dislike this system intensely throughout their military careers.

Strictly based on historical materials, this attempt at studying Chinese military on its own terms intends to unveil the mystery of a unique military elite group that centered on Marshal Chen Yi's remarkable career. Poet, French literature lover, former Deputy Premier and Minister of Foreign Affairs, Chen was both a founder and the leader of the New Fourth Army faction. Deriving from scattered guerrilla troops, it evolved under Chen's adroit direction from a hodgepodge of peasant irregulars into one of the largest military field armies at 600,000 men in strength by 1949. It was Chen's group that broke Chiang Kai-shek's backbone in Central and Eastern China where Kuomintang power was traditionally based. The focus of this study will be on Chen and his best generals who had worked with him since 1938. Four major aspects will be explored in the process: first, how the Chinese communist military factions generally evolved; second, the extent to which Mao and his generals contributed to the communist victory in 1949; third, to what extent the Chinese communist leaders including Mao were able to deal with the tendency toward military factionalism rampant in Chinese peasant societies; fourth, the historical character of the Chinese officer corps and the military establishment in general. Although I cannot deal with these issues completely, I hope to break some new ground and inspire further studies.

In the process of obtaining a clear picture of PLA history, I occasionally found the "selective" nature of the Chinese communist document compilations rather frustrating. Nevertheless, because of the enormous amount of materials that exist in many different forms, I was able to gather scattered materials to reach a conclusion that may grind harsh to the ears of both Beijing and Taipei---that is that: the major Chine anti-Japanese forces during the war were far more preoccupied with civil strife than with the fight against Japan. The subsequent civil war therefore seems inevitable. This conclusion may be surprising to none of the well-informed in the West, but it has so far been unacceptable on both sides of the Taiwan Straits.

This work is primarily aimed at entering a debate with the official Chinese historians based on the materials available. I realize the fact that nobody can write a definitive history on this subject without the complete opening of the communist archives. But I would feel gratified if my work should trigger a further release of some key documents. As an ancient Chinese saying goes, you throw out a brick, but get back a jade!

Acknowledgements

I must thank all the New Fourth Army veterans who had granted me interviews. Since most of them preferred to remain anonymous, I quote the interviews only sparingly. But they have provided me with a strong sense of "how" if not "why" things went the way as they did in the past. The lives of my generation seem rather prosaic in comparison with theirs.

I must also express my gratitude to the National Endowment for the Humanities in Washington, D.C., which provided me a generous grant for field researches in China.

I would also like to thank my dear friend Thomas Row for his enthusiasm and unflinching support in reading through the whole manuscript.

Finally, I must thank Zhong Delu for preparing the photos. His father, the late General Zhong Qiguang, was Chen Yi's top aide since 1938 and was among the best loved New Fourth Army leaders.

Chapter 1

The Making of A Red Bandit

Chen Yi was born on August 26, 1901 in Lezhi County in central Sichuan Province, at a village called Zhang An Jin. According to the Chinese calendar, this was the Guangxu Emperor's Twenty-Seventh year of the Qing Dynasty. It was the most humiliating year for China. The Manchu Court had to sign the Boxer Protocol after the rape of Beijing by the allied forces during the war of 1900. The Chen ancestors were not originally Sichuanese. They moved to Sichuan from Hunan Province during the early years of the Qing Dynasty, when the new regime forced many residents from Hunan and Hubei to emigrate into Sichuan because of the rapid drop of its population, resulting from bloody wars between the dynasty, Wu Sangui and the Three Feudatories.[1] Five generations before Chen Yi was born, one of the ancestors passed a lower level Imperial Examination, which had brought prosperity and respect to the family. For quite a while the Chen family became substantial landlords with eight hundred *mu* (some one hundred and thirty acres) at its peak. By the end of the nineteenth century, the Chen fortune declined rapidly, partly due to bad luck at imperial examination tables, mainly due to economic difficulties caused by agricultural recession and persistent natural disasters. At Chen Yi's birth, his paternal grandfather shared only forty *mu* (less than seven acres) with his five sons. All family members had to work in the fields, for they could afford to hire but one farm hand during the year. A second son to Chen Changli who was also a second son in the household, Chen was given the name Shijun, meaning "handsome," a name Chen seldom used in his life after acquiring Yi as his formal name, which meant "perseverance," during his teenage years.

Although born in the countryside, unlike his uncles and elder brothers, Chen Yi did not have much experience in the fields. At the age of seven, he was brought to Hubei Province where his rich maternal grandfather had just purchased a position as a county magistrate. He hired Chen Yi's father to do paper work for him. The grandfather was a strict, no-nonsense type. He was very tough with criminals who were mostly debt-ridden poor peasants. Chen later claimed that he hated the two years spent in Hubei, because of his sympathy with those who were tortured and imprisoned by his grandfather. This may be a little far-fetched, for there was hardly any evidence of rebellious behavior after that experience.[2]

What really influenced his views of the world was his own family's continued decline. He deeply resented his maternal grandfather's constant mocking remarks about the Chen family's misfortune. Seeing no future in the countryside, the Chens tried their luck in an urban area. Before Chen Yi returned with his father from Hubei to Sichuan two years later, his paternal grandfather had already sold all their land holdings and moved to a suburban area of Chengdu, the capital city of the province. The Chens were literate and ambitious, determined to return to the family's old status. But they had acquired no substantive skills to survive other than farming. So they continued to do so in suburban Chengdu by renting two hundred *mu* (over thirty acres) of land.

The social environment at Chengdu for the children was, however, a far cry from that in the backwater of the Lezhi countryside. The Imperial Examination system was abolished by a Court decree in 1908, and the Manchu Empire was on its last leg. The immediate liberating effect was that the children were no longer required to recite everything in the Chinese classics, and in Chengdu the "New Study" (*Xinxue*)---modern science and technology---became popular day by day. For the first time the Chen brothers were sent to a "new school" with a modern curriculum, instead of an old school (*Sishu*) taught by private tutors of Chinese classic literature.

In the fall of 1910, the first major blow to the family came. An unusually huge flood devoured all crops on their rented land. Unable to collect the rent, the landlord sued the Chen family for a rent strike. Chen's oldest uncle was chained in public and was thrown in jail after the family had lost the case at a county court. The grandfather died in humiliation shortly afterwards. The next year, the Chen brothers left school since the family could no longer pay for their tuition, and returned to the Lezhi countryside. Without land, the family found it hard to re-adjust to country life. Chen Yi's father, Changli, who was well trained in classics, managed to find a job at the Chongqing Salt Administration. But he could not afford to sustain the family in urban Chongqing at six silver dollars a month working as a junior clerk. Chen's strong-willed mother brought the Chen children back to suburban Chengdu, where they had relatives. With a little money sent from the father each month, the family was supplemented by income from a small plot of land the mother rented to grow and sell vegetables.

Fortunately, the two brothers were hardworking students. In early 1913, the twelve-year old Chen Yi and his elder brother Chen Mengxi were accepted by a modern elementary school where the top three in the class could get a tuition waiver. The Chen brothers were always at the top of the class. Science and technology fascinated the brothers. Chengdu had a giant abandoned arsenal equipped with German technology. It was an ironic legacy of Li Hongzhang's modernization program started in the 1860s. The brothers often spent a lot of time hanging around the arsenal admiring those strange machines rusting away under the sun. They also enjoyed watching in awe foreign steamships roaming on the Yangzi River. The Manchu Dynasty had finally been swept away two years earlier. A Chinese republic was in its very amorphous form. Politics were chaotic and social conditions were appalling. But many educated Chinese began to explore ways to halt China's degeneration. The most popular view of the day was the belief in science and technology as the only salvation for the country. Chen was naturally influenced by this trend of thought.

At school, the thirteen-year old boy often argued with conservative teachers, a behavior considered taboo in Chinese schools. One of the teachers often regretted in class that Sichuan had never produced an emperor in any dynasty. Chen retorted that, "Now we have a republic, and no need for emperors, it's better to produce just a few more scientists."[3]

True to his words, after graduation, Chen decided to apply for Chengdu Grade-A Industrial School. He got accepted in 1916. This was a new-type professional school funded by the provincial government under the control of a warlord who had a penchant for portraying himself as being progressive. Chen chose textiles as his major. But he found literary study more to his taste. While at the school Chen acquired a reputation as an effective student organizer. He was also known as an excellent soccer player with an English nickname "Chen Forward."

Because the family had chronic financial problems, Chen dropped out after spending only two years at the school. Meanwhile, another opportunity appeared to be attractive in the horizon. Some radical intellectuals in Beijing, such as Wu Zhihui and Wu Yuzhang, had been organizing work-study programs for Chinese students to study in France. Why were the radical intellectuals fascinated by France? There were two main reasons. Firstly, most modern Chinese intellectuals at the time admired France for being the home country of the principles of "Liberty, Fraternity and Equality." Secondly, there was a widespread misperception that France was much stronger than it actually was. According to Wu Yuzhang, who was the chief organizer for sending students to France in

Sichuan Province, "France is the center of European civilization. Most of the scholarly inventions are from France. Recently it has defeated Germany and Austria.... The character of its people is similar to ours."[4] The social and political decline of the "decadent" Third Republic, reflected by such chaotic events as the Dreyfus Affair, was of course beyond the ken of the radical intellectuals in China who preferred a wholesale transplant of French civilization to the fragile republic.

At the end of 1917, the Chen brothers entered a program sponsored by Wu Yuzhang to prepare for work-study in Europe. It was tuition-free, but each student must pass a final examination to obtain the very competitive overseas opportunity. Many old classmates of Chen Yi at the Chengdu Grade-A Industrial School did not see any future in "work-study" abroad. They tried hard to persuade Chen to apply for military academies because the widespread warlordism around the country would surely provide unlimited opportunities for a military career that was known to be rewarding politically as well as financially. Chen considered this idea appalling. He was too much absorbed with literary studies to enter a profession that treasured obedience, but did not, in his view, require much imagination.

Two years later, the brothers both passed the examination with flying colors. This qualified them, along with thirty other top students, for government support for travel to France. Arriving at Shanghai in June, 1919, the brothers were excited by the massive demonstrations against the Versailles Treaty on the streets. China was a member of the Entente during the War, but the post-war settlement at Versailles rewarded Japan for its participation on the Entente side with the German-controlled Chinese territory in Shandong. This blatant power politics angered radical Chinese intellectuals and ordinary citizens alike. On May 4, 1919, Beijing students revolted against the warlord government. Under heavy domestic pressure, the Chinese government representative at the Versailles Conference refused to sign the treaty on the second day of Chen's arrival at Shanghai. There were wild celebrations everywhere. Known later as the May Fourth Movement, this event had a tremendous impact on Chen. Unlike in Sichuan backwaters, where local issues were the only concern, Shanghai was an international city, bustling and prosperous, connecting old China and the new. For the first time, Chen Yi was exposed to the radical publications such as the *New Youth* magazine founded by Chen Duxiu, the leader of the May Fourth Movement who would later become the founding father of the Chinese Communist Party. Another favorite book for radical youth at the time was a biography of George Washington. While in Shanghai, Chen spent a lot of time collecting radical books and magazines.

In October, the Chen brothers reached Marseilles. But they were more impressed with Paris a few weeks later. They were shocked by the success of western civilization. Although Shanghai was known as the "Paris of the East," it paled in comparison to the real Paris. As Chen recalled years later: "Paris was like a paradise. The social order was stable, the city so clean, I almost knelt down in front of French civilization and began to think that Chinese civilization is worthless, and decided never again to read Chinese classics and compose Chinese poems."[5]

But the realities for Chinese students in France soon hit him very hard. After a few months studying French at a lycee in a small town in suburban Paris, Chen entered a plant of the Le Havre-Schneider Company to begin his work-study program. The Le Havre-Schneider Company was one of the biggest companies producing automobiles, heavy machines and armored vehicles. Chen was awed by the fact that, Li Hongzhang's Chengdu arsenal, his favorite hanging-out spot in his earlier childhood, was no match at all to the plant where he reported to work. He imagined that the civilization he saw outside the plant must have been translated into the same reality within the plant. He was wrong. The tension and conflict resulting from blatant inequality in pay and racial discrimination hurt him deeply. Assigned a menial job at little pay, Chen was shocked to discover that the "civilized" French "treated the Chinese no better than the Negroes."[6]

Under exposure to various European social and political thoughts, Chinese work-study students quickly split into three main camps. One group were anarchists, worshiping Bakunin and Krupotkin; another the opposite---statists, disciples of the radical European nationalists. Both had large groups of followers. But the third, a relatively small group, known as "socialists" seemed fresh and new to Chen. Led by Cai Hesen and Zhou Enlai, who had been very conspicuous during the May Fourth Movement and who had become well-versed in Marxist theories, this group began to openly embrace the Russian Revolution of 1917. Chen knew nothing about *Das Kapital* and the class-struggle concept. He was impressed by Cai Hesen's enthusiasm about European socialism, but was somehow skeptical of the Russian Bolshevik revolution.

But things began to have a better turn for him three months later, when the capitalist system rewarded his hard work with a promotion. A daily wage of twelve francs increased to eighteen, and he began to have some savings at the end of each month. It seemed to him that some of his radical friends did not care much about study, and hardly needed to work in industrial plants to make ends meet. Zhou Enlai, for example, was among those who had financial backing of their own. They could afford to be professional radicals. Chen had a different perspective. He had dreamt that his savings may enable him to enter a serious university, and obtain a doctoral degree. This would be his "last victory." Disappointed with industrial exploitation in the West, Chen shifted his interest from technology to French literature. He spent all his spare time at the Le Havre-Schneider Company devouring French romantic literature. Although fascinated by Balzac, Hugo, and Rousseau, Chen was more taken by Alfred de Musset and Alfonse de Lamartine, the romantic poets. His French reading ability was enhanced rapidly during this period.

Once again, financial circumstances destroyed his "French literature-doctor" dream. His brother Mengxi got a promotion, too, at the same plant, but the French economy was in deep recession. Foreign workers naturally bore the brunt of massive unemployment. Living in constant fear of being laid off, their problems were compounded by the family crisis back in Sichuan. After years of decline, the Chens had become so poor that a sister's wedding expenses were beyond its means. A wedding ceremony was an important part of a Chinese family's social status. Abandoning the idea of entering a serious university, the brothers decided to send their savings home. Chen Yi was quickly radicalized as a result. At the end of 1920, the politically aloof Chen participated for the first time in a radical student organization called the "Work-Study World Association." Openly advocating Marxism and the Russian Revolution, this organization would later become the first Chinese communist branch in Europe led by Cai Hesen and Zhou Enlai.

The Chinese government became concerned with the radical students who they believed to have hardly studied at all. Even Wu Zhihui, one of the original founders of the Work-Study Program publicly declared that these students were unfit for staying in France. According to Wu, these students who "have neither the work skill, nor the will to study,"[7] should be sent back home immediately. Chen participated in protests organized by Zhou Enlai at the Chinese Embassy in February, 1921, but was quickly fired by the Le Havre-Schneider Company due to his absences at work. He was pushed into a desperate corner, for he had to live on a meager government stipend, issued on weekly basis depending on good behavior.

Chen began to drink heavily with his friends and became increasingly more restless. In June, the students discovered a godsent opportunity to vent their spleen. The Chinese government had sent a special envoy to Paris to negotiate a secret loan with the French government. In exchange for two hundred million francs, the Chinese offered railway concessions to the French. Chen Yi and Zhou Enlai were among the first to learn of the deal. They at once organized an "Anti-Loan Conference" whose impact spread quickly back to China. Offering railway concessions to foreign governments belonged to the era of the imperial past. The popular anti-government sentiment on this issue was so strong that the warlord government in Beijing had to back off the deal in August. In retaliation, the Chinese Embassy in Paris announced the termination of all stipend issued to the work-study students in September.

The relationship between the government and the students further deteriorated when the government announced a plan to recruit students in China, instead of those already in France, into a well-endowed school named Institut Franco-Chinois. Funded by the Boxer Indemnity money at Lyon, this Franco-Chinese joint venture was the last hope for the work-study group to pursue their studies in France. Apparently the government was fed up with the extremely agitated and thousand-member strong work-study group. In protest, Cai Hesen, Chen and the other radical students decided to occupy the Lyon campus. The Chinese Embassy called in French police force, who detained over a hundred students at an old military barrack in suburban Lyon on September 21. A few weeks later, on October 14, the armed French police escorted one hundred and four detainees to Marseilles and immediately deported them back to China.

Chen's less than two-year sojourn in France thus ended in misery. His dream of obtaining serious education had melt away like a snow flake in hot summer. Aside from acquiring the reputation as a radical student leader, Chen had nothing---money, degree or skill---to show off. But his serious study of French literature had had a tremendous impact upon his character. Unusual for a student leader at the time, he did not join any political parties, not even the communist youth league founded by his friends Cai and Zhou. French romantic literature had, perhaps, instilled in him the firm belief in "Liberty, Fraternity and Equality." He was not keen to affiliate himself with any political organization that may restrict his personal freedom. He preferred to be a free soul, a liberal writer, and an independent social reformer. Cai Hesen also returned to China at the same time and became Chen Duxiu's right-hand man. Chen Duxiu, the spiritual leader of the May Fourth Movement had just become the first General Secretary of the Chinese Communist Party, founded the same year with the help from the Soviet Russia. Cai persuaded Chen to join the party and even offered to send him to study in Moscow. Chen declined offhand.[8]

He was more concerned with helping the other Sichuanese work-study students in France. For a moment, Chen was able to gain a sympathetic ear from a Sichuan warlord, who promised to help financially. But soon a war broke out among the warlords themselves, and the hope of getting money from the warlord was dashed. Having achieved nothing for six months lobbying the warlords, Chen returned to the Lezhi countryside in the fall of 1922. The family situation further depressed him. All the family property was sold, and one uncle had just died of hunger. The other uncles together with Chen's mother had no place to live and were temporarily allowed to settle in a kinship temple normally used for ancestral worshiping rituals. Psychologically, Chen was hurt even more deeply by sneering villagers who laughed at the Chen brothers for their failure in France and more so for Chen's deportation by the French government. He could not even get a job. As Chen recalled bitterly that, he was usually "rejected for a position I wanted, because the employer would say I was over-qualified for being a returned student from abroad. And I refused to sink so low" as to take a menial job.[9]

The communist leader Cai Hesen continued to write him that fall, and finally Chen agreed to join the Communist Youth League (the CY), the front organization of the party. The traditional Spring Festival was hard for him and the family. At his mother's request, he wrote the family-scrolls pasted on the temple door. On the right side it said, "It is difficult to live through the Spring Festival, yet you have to endure it year by year." On the left, "I have achieved nothing, but I will succeed eventually." The conclusion at the middle: "Wait for the next spring."[10]

Indeed the spring of 1923 did bring Chen some luck. He was hired as a lead columnist by a radical newspaper, *The New Sichuan Journal*, published in Chongqing where his father had been working as a low-paid clerk. After his return from France, Chen had already published a few articles defending the work-study students' cause in France. A columnist job provided him with a better opportunity to develop his talent as a writer and a poet. He published a first poem while still in France. Titled "She," it was an emotional yarn about a young man caught between the love of an old-fashioned girl and the new cultural wave against the traditional values the girl held. It was not at all radical even by the standard at the time. But in December 1921 upon arrival at Shanghai from France, Chen published a totally different one titled "To Work-Study Fellow Students." The influence of French romanticism was at once apparent. Like his first poem, it was typically in the Baihua (spoken language) style developed during the May Fourth Movement. In great pains, Chen asked: "Are we criminals? No! Are we parasites? No! Are all the human beings dead? Is life so hopeless? Let's bear it all, the unreasonable punishment!"[11]

Although Chen was very happy working for the small newspaper with a circulation of a few hundred only, he soon became a thorn in the side of General Yang Sen, a Sichuan warlord who controlled the province. After several sharply-worded crusading articles against warlord politics, Chen was "paid to get out of Sichuan" (*Li Song Chu Chuan*) by the general in October 1923. With a little money in his pocket, Chen decided to pursue his dream of getting a college degree by entering the Institut Franco-Chinois in Beijing. This was a new college founded by several leaders of the work-study movement such as Cai Yuanpei, Li Shiceng and Wu Yuzhang. Originally this was the Beijing prep-school for work-study in France. It was named the School of [Auguste] Comte in 1917 and was changed in 1920 into the same namesake as its counterpart in Lyon. What attracted Chen most to this school was its policy that the top five of each graduating class would go to Lyon to continue study, all expenses paid. While there, although he had already been a communist youth league member, he joined the party in November. In the same month, Dr. Sun Yat-sen, the founder of the Kuomintang Party decided to cooperate with the Communists. Thus began the First United Front period. The enemy was warlord-controlled politics.

Chen apparently kept a busy schedule. He was soon appointed communist party secretary for its branch at the institute. Aside from party work, he began to publish poems, essays, fiction, translations and commentaries in large quantities. In 1925 he and several close friends organized a literary club called "The West Hill Literary Association." In one short story titled "Revenge," Chen relished the idea of killing the enemy with his own hand. It shocked the readers.[12] At one point, Chen and two of his best literary friends were hired to edit the literary supplement of a reputable newspaper, but the negotiation on financial terms did not work out. As one of the friends, named Jin Mancheng, recalled years later, "I wonder if Chen would have become a famous literary figure instead of a soldier, had the deal come through."[13] Indeed, Chen proved to be most creative in writing short stories and poems during this period. He apparently had a long novel in mind, too, based on his experience in France.

But upon graduation at the end of 1925, Chen became a professional party functionary. His party career during this period was highlighted by his appointment to the Kuomintang Beijing Special Branch, a secret united front organization, since both the KMT and the communists were outlawed by the warlord regime in Beijing. Chen began working together with Kuomintang luminaries such as Wu Zhihui, an old enemy of Chen's who refused to allow the work-study students in France to enter Institut Franco-Chinois in Lyon. His communist colleagues included two influential leaders, Li Dazhao and Zhang Guotao.

Juggling between party operation and literary self-satisfaction became increasingly more impractical and unbearable. In a sentimental essay titled "Burial at the West Hill" published in June 1925, Chen declared that he had had enough of literary life, for he had been buried alive for four years, because of his literary preoccupation. Now it was the time for him to "go out of the coffin and return to the mass population."[14] One event in particular destroyed his literary ivory tower. The Beijing government was then under the control of a warlord, General Duan Qirui. The western embassies were agitated by the widespread mass movement aimed at ridding China of foreign influence. In the spring of 1926, the government under General Duan opened fire on a mass student demonstration against loans provided by foreign countries for the explicit purpose of "preventing Reds." Chen was a key organizer of the demonstration. After surviving the incident, the communists went underground completely.

But in Guangdong, the situation for the United Front was upbeat even after Dr. Sun Yat-sen's untimely death in 1925. The Kuomintang party, with the help from the communists had begun the military Northern Expedition for the purpose of wiping out once and for all warlord politics in northern China. The communist leadership decided to send representatives to various provincial warlord headquarters to persuade them to collaborate with the Northern Expedition forces, or at least to keep a neutral position between Guangdong and Beijing. One day Chen met a work-study fellow student named Yu Zhengheng on the street. Yu was working for General Yang Sen, the Sichuan warlord who had paid Chen to get out of the province a few years before. He was now General Yang's personal secretary, and his mission to Beijing was to establish connections with representatives from the Guangdong Revolutionary Government. Chen at once volunteered to go back to Sichuan. With Li Dazhao's handwritten letter of introduction in his pocket, Chen arrived at Wanxian City where Yang's headquarters were stationed. A small-time warlord, Yang was a consummate opportunist. He owed his appointment as Sichuan provincial governor to his mentor, warlord general Wu Peifu, who was a big player in warlord politics at the time. Yet Yang also pretended to be progressive and, while claiming to be a good friend of Li Dazhao, received Chen with full arms and immediately offered him a senior advisor position.

But Chen was more surprised when the general, in a cryptic manner, introduced him to a "representative from the Third International"---the Moscow-based mother organization of all communist parties around the world. His name was Zhu Yujie, a middle-aged professional soldier well known in Sichuan military circles. Although Chen had doubts about Zhu's alleged identity, for he knew nothing about this assignment, he liked this honest elder man. Several days later, the local communist party organization informed Chen to meet a secret party contact at a tobacco company compound, he found out that the man was none other than Zhu Yujie, whose formal name was Zhu De. Zhu had been a famous general in a warlord army and an old friend of Yang Sen. Disappointed with warlord politics, he went to study in France and Germany in 1922 after Chen had already been deported by the French government. He became a communist member in Germany, introduced by Zhou Enlai in the same year. Fate decreed that the two met in Wanxian and that their friendship and partnership were to become decisive in Chen's career. Zhu laughed at the idea General Yang had of him as a representative of the Third International. He was really sent by Chen Duxiu in person. He came to

Yang's headquarters for the same purpose as Chen's: lobbying for Yang's neutrality. Chen and Zhu were both in an advisory capacity. A few days after Chen's arrival, they prompted General Yang to make a tough yet costly decision to engage the British gunboats cruising the Yangzi River near Wanxian City. The event was triggered by an incident which occurred on the river when a commercial steamship owned by a leading British firm, the Jardine Company, overturned by accident three wooden sailboats carrying a large amount of silver dollar and rifles belonging to Yang's headquarters. Over eighty thousand silver dollars and fifty eight crew members were sunk to the bottom of the river. Emboldened by Chen and Zhu's encouragement, Yang ordered detention of two Jardine steamships and asked for compensation and a formal apology. The British authorities refused to accept any responsibilities.

The crisis deepened, when on September 5, three British gunboats opened fire, shelling the downtown area of Wanxian. Yang returned shots immediately. Zhu De joined Yang's command during the battle. Chen was busy raising troop's morale in the rear. This was his first military, though noncombat, experience. At one point, when a French Catholic church was hit by British cannon shots, Chen boarded a French gunboat anchored nearby to expose the British behavior, and, with his French speaking ability, was able to gain some sympathy from the French officers.

Although Yang repelled the British gunboats, thousands of people and houses perished. As a result, General Yang was reprimanded by his boss General Wu Peifu for reckless action. In the meantime the Guangdong-based Northern Expedition forces had conquered Wuchang, Yang decided to turn his back on the marching Kuomintang forces in order to remain loyal to his mentor. Chen and Zhu's work at Yang's headquarters thus ended quickly. Zhu went to Wuhan for a new mission. The communist party assigned Chen to Chongqing to organize a mutiny in another warlord army.

On April 12, 1927, however, the communists and Kuomintang fell out in occupied Shanghai. The Kuomintang General Chiang Kai-shek, commander in chief of the Northern Expedition forces, began to eliminate all communists within territories under his control. Chen narrowly escaped from the warlord army which had become pro-Chiang. He fled to Wuhan where he hoped to reconnect with the party organization. Wuhan was still under the influence of left-leaning Kuomintang leaders led by Wang Jingwei. The split initiated by Chiang between the two parties had not yet put an end to an existing United Front there. The communists continued working within the Kuomintang-controlled organizations. In May, Chen found Zhou Enlai, his fellow student in France. Zhou was now a senior party leader in charge of the Central Committee's military activities. He assigned Chen to work at Wuhan Central Military Political Academy, formerly Whampoa Military Academy in Guangdong. The school's political division had always been under the communist influence. Zhou Enlai, for example, had once served as its political director. Chen's party identity was supposed to be secret. He could therefore obtain only a junior position as a clerk handling day to day paper work at the political division of the academy. Yet within the secret party organization at the school, Chen was supposed to take charge. But like any military establishment, a person's rank counted. Being just a warrant officer, Chen was often frustrated when cadets and officers alike showed no respect of him. This made his party activities extremely difficult. Soon the left-leaning Kuomintang leaders began to turn right. Wang Jingwei decided to dissolve the Red-infested military academy altogether. Chen's work once again ran into trouble.

While in Wuhan, the Chen brothers were united for the first time in many years. His elder and younger brothers had both been cadets at the Whampoa Academy. They also united with their respected eldest cousin, the first son of the Chen clan, also a cadet. The Chens were always a close family, but their political views began to diverge among the brothers. The elder cousin was determined to enter a manufacturing industry, Mengxi, the elder brother who was together with Chen Yi in France, decided to maintain his faith in the Kuomintang and was sent to work for a progressive warlord. The younger one had no idea what to do.[15] None of the brothers knew for sure what was in Chen Yi's mind, for he had to be cautious not to reveal his true identity. In private, he was unsure. On one occasion, one of his close friends remembered years later, Chen, while drunk and depressed, claimed he would rather become a bandit, a statement that shocked his friends. Three of the brothers made remarkable careers. Chen Yi would eventually become a top general of the communist military, while his cousin, ironically, was to be Chiang Kai-shek's top aide in charge of national military industries. Elder brother Mengxi would turn out to be a general at a warlord army.

The Communist Party Central Committee was preoccupied with other, more urgent issues. It paid no attention to Chen's work. After the dissolution of the academy, cadets and officers were reorganized into a special regiment. Chen hid in one of its companies, working again as a junior clerk. In early August 1927, the regiment was ordered to depart for Nanchang, Jiangxi Province, where Chen first learnt that the party Central Committee had, on August 1, organized a failed uprising aimed at establishing a communist regime. It was, in fact, a mutiny staged by Zhou Enlai, who, through government commanders affiliated with the party, such as He Long, Zhu De and Ye Ting, successfully controlled several Kuomintang divisions. But the mutiny failed to gain support from the other generals. Therefore, the communist-controlled force at twenty thousand strong had to abandon Nanchang and flee to the south. Chen immediately deserted the company where he was hiding and went after the fleeing communist troops. In Wuzhou city in Jiangxi, he finally caught up with the communist headquarters commanded by Zhou Enlai. The retreat was extremely chaotic and Zhou could not find a suitable position for Chen except the relatively insignificant job as a political director of an elite regiment known for its bravery during the Northern Expedition period. This was the regimental home of the famous general, Ye Ting, who had become a household name during the heroic fight against the warlords. Ye's Fourth Army had acquired national fame as the "Iron Army" during all the toughest campaigns against the warlords, though nominally under the overall command of Chiang Kai-shek. Ye was a card-carrying communist party member and one of the most respected military leaders who organized the Nanchang Uprising.

Thus, by accident, Chen formally entered the profession he had always despised and stayed there until the last day of his life. Chen had never seen battle action in real life. As a political officer and a college graduate, Chen's position was rather embarrassing. The hard-boiled soldiers under Ye Ting were especially disgusted by talkative political officers who always appeared well-dressed and arrogant. In Wuhan, political officers had a notorious image of the so-called "three golds and five leathers (*San Jin Wu Pi*)." The "three golds" referred to gold teeth, gold belt knuckles, and gold rings; the five leathers were leather jackets, whips, shoes, belts and briefcases. These were said to be the typical outfits of political officers. Although Chen hardly wore those things, most officers considered him a fraud. A few days later, Chen participated in his first battle at Huichang. This was an experience he would never forget. Years later he admitted honestly that his mind was at the time full of death and blood, the knees were weak and the heart pounding. But he managed to stay in the front line, and thus passed the first test with flying colors and won respect from the rank and file.

Breaking through the enemy's encirclement, the leadership made a major mistake at a place called San He Ba in splitting the troops in two. Chen's division and another regiment commanded by Zhu De, his old acquaintance in Sichuan during his work with warlord Yang Sen, were left to cover the main force to retreat. Within a few days of bloody battles, the rear-guard force now under Zhu's overall command were reduced to two thousand. But worse still, as soon as they had finished the cover action and began to retreat in order to join Zhou Enlai's headquarters, the sad news came that the main force left earlier under Zhou Enlai's command had been mostly wiped out. The twenty thousand troops gathered by the communist party during the Nanchang Uprising had all but vanished. Zhu's rear-guard troops at two thousand in strength now became the only regular armed force controlled by the communists in the nation. Nobody knew what to do next. Desertion increased on a massive scale. When Zhu finally decided to bring the troops to the mountain area at the border of the Jiangxi Province, only a thousand soldiers followed him. What struck Zhu and Chen hardest was the desertion of the two top leaders---Chen's division commander and its political director, both were veteran communists.[16]

The situation turned desperate. Zhu was the only high-ranking commander bent on carrying on the cause; most others hesitated. Chen also wavered for a while. But after weighing all the options, he decided to stay. Years later, Chen would admit: "I was only 26 years old, just a kid. I wanted to go abroad, but had no money. Big cities were too dangerous for me. There was really no choice."[17] Because of the desertion of the division commanders, Chen's position as a regimental leader became critical, for he was the only senior officer left in charge of what was left of Ye Ting's "Iron Army" which made up the bulk of the remaining troop under Zhu's command. Zhu made a great effort to win Chen over, for the latter's support would be a decisive factor in Zhu's cause. Talking to the troops gathered at a village, Zhu passionately compared their defeat with the Russian Revolution of 1905, raising the expectation of a successful 1917. According to the recollection of one young officer named Su Yu, who would become an important partner of Chen's career for years to come, Zhu's speech was sensational and effective and Chen immediately seconded Zhu's view, and declared his willingness to accept Zhu's leadership.[18]

Chen had thus become second in command of this defeated force. The troops morale was low. Desertion continued. One of the company commanders named Lin Biao deserted once but returned shortly thereafter.[19] The soldiers were hungry and exhausted. After taking over a small town, Xinfeng, the troops ran amuck. Soldiers ate in restaurants without paying bills. Some even pawned hand-grenades for money, then decided to rob the pawnshop. Only after Zhu and Chen executed the offenders on the spot, was discipline restored.

In November, 1927, the troops arrived at the border area of Hunan, Jiangxi and Guangdong. They had been constantly on the run and chased relentlessly by the government forces. There was an apparent need for a home base. But the idea to occupy a mountain and become traditional bandits never occurred to them. This force derived after all from a famed regular army unit. Nobody knew much about guerrilla warfare. They were unaware of another communist force active in the nearby Jinggang Mountains at the time. This was the peasant troops led a Party Central

Committee member named Mao Zedong. After the failed Nanchang Uprising, the Central Committee held an emergency meeting in Wuhan and decided to send Mao back to Hunan, his native province, to organize a "Harvest Uprising." After the quick defeat by government troops, Mao brought the remnants into the mountains and founded the first of what was later known as the communist base areas.

One day in mid-November, the Zhu-Chen troops met a unit from the Jinggang Mountains, and decided to connect with Mao whom they did not know in person. It just so happened that Mao's younger brother Mao Zetan was a political officer working with Zhu and Chen, he was dispatched immediately to the Jinggang Mountains. While waiting for Mao's response, Zhu found a better alternative to the bandit life. He discovered that General Fan Shisheng, one of his old army buddies, with whom he had sworn a blood relationship a long time ago, was now stationed in a nearby area. General Fan commanded a Yunnanese unit, which was nominally a government force assigned to chase the communists. But Fan was never keen to engage the Reds for the satisfaction of Chiang Kai-shek who never trusted provincial armies beyond his control. After several negotiations, Zhu's old friend agreed to provide him with the much-needed supplies under the condition that the troops must, in name only, be part of his. Zhu and Chen jumped at this offer.[20]

The troops soon obtained a generous offer of supplies, as Zhu would recall years later, "A hundred thousand rounds of bullets and ten thousand silver dollars a month ... in our Red Army history, [Fan] should be praised for the help he offered to us."[21] They were also provided with brand new winter uniforms. The collaboration did not, however, last long. Pressured by Chiang Kai-shek, Zhu's warlord friend asked them to leave in December. In the meantime, Mao Zedong sent a special envoy to see Zhu and Chen, whose name was He Changgong. He was Chen's fellow student in France. But the thought of becoming bandits still could not attract Zhu and Chen. Like most of the communist leaders at the time, they were preoccupied with the idea of attacking cities. Well fed, clothed and equipped, Zhu and Chen decided to strike in southern Hunan where the government forces were the weakest. This idea was enthusiastically embraced by the local party organization, for it always considered Mao's hiding in the mountains a defeatist behavior.

In early 1928, they indeed succeeded in taking over a few cities. The troops were expanded to eight thousand and renamed "The Workers and Peasants Revolutionary Army First Division." Soon, however, the strategy of attacking cities ran into trouble. Because once they took a city, they had to spare troops to hold it. The forces had to split, and were compelled to adopt a defensive posture all the time. Moreover, when dictated by defense strategy, the Zhu-Chen troops paid little attention to the interests of city dwellers. The party functionaries were often hot-headed, advocating an all-out defense strategy of "Burn, Kill, Engage (*Shao, Sha, Gan*)." One of most bizarre incidents occurred at Chenzhou City, where the communists openly pursued a "burn-all" policy, and strangely still, the party functionaries justified their action by evoking the image of Kutuzov, the Russian general who burnt Moscow to thwart Napoleon's advancing troops. It was apparently a rehash of the story learnt by some communist leaders during their training in Moscow. To the uncouth peasants and city-residents, who could not figure out who Kutuzov was, this was simply a nightmare. The "burn-all" policy backfired when an angry mob killed communist leaders at a mass meeting. Chen Yi had to take personal control over Chenzhou and after apologizing to the city dwellers, the riot was somehow quieted down.[22]

Overwhelmed by constant attacks by the government forces, Zhu and Chen had to abandon cities one after another and in late spring 1928 fled once again to the Jinggang Mountains area. For the second time Mao sent his right-hand man He Changgong to persuade them to join him. This time He succeeded. In April, 1928, Zhu, Chen and Mao met for the first time to discuss the plan of combining forces. Zhu was the oldest at forty-two, Mao was thirty-four and Chen was the youngest at twenty-seven. But a power struggle started as soon as the troops were reorganized. Mao was senior to Zhu and Chen within the party, for he was one of the original twelve delegates at the first party congress in 1921 and a member of the Central Committee. But his force in the Jinggang Mountains was a hodgepodge of untrained peasants, regular soldiers and genuine bandits.[23] Less than two thousand in strength, they were badly trained and poorly equipped. When the two units met, Mao's soldiers could not but envy the Zhu-Chen force. At ten thousand strong now, they had all sorts of new weapons Mao's men had never seen before. Short of supplies, Mao's soldiers mostly dressed themselves in typical bandit style---rags, worn-out uniforms and animal skins---in sharp contrast to the gray, solemn uniforms worn by their new partners. The superior number and quality of the newly-arrived force allowed Zhu and Chen to retain control of their units. The combined force was renamed, at the insistence of the new partner, "The Red Fourth Army," after Ye Ting's "Iron Fourth Army."[24] Thus at the very beginning, Zhu and Chen controlled the bulk of this combined force. It had three regiments. The new units were divided into two regiments. Mao, though nominally the top political officer, headed only one, his mixed irregular force.

In June 1928 the first crisis developed when the troops under Zhu and Chen decided not to return to the Jinggang Mountains after a skirmish with the government forces outside the base area. The main reason for this decision was that the local party organizations began to criticize Mao's guerrillarism rooted in the mountains, and instructed the Red Fourth Army to establish a southern Hunan guerrilla base. Mao was deadly set against this instruction, arguing that only the mountains could provide the best chance for the Red Fourth Army to survive. Since the majority of the Zhu-Chen force were recruited from southern Hunan before they hooked up with Mao, the soldiers were naturally longing for returning to the home base. At a party conference convened by Zhu and Chen, the decision to move out of the mountains was taken against Mao's will. Moreover, Chen was elected party secretary, a position held so far by Mao since 1927, who had thus been deprived of official authority.[25] Mao and his men returned to the Jinggang Mountains and Zhu and Chen departed for southern Hunan. But after taking over a city, the soldiers deserted on large-scale, carrying with them war booties---considerable amounts of silver dollars and other valuables. One of the two original regiments under Zhu and Chen's command had only one company left. The disaster almost cost Zhu and Chen's party membership.[26]

In September, the crestfallen remnants returned to the Jinggang Mountains. Delighted that he was right, Mao appeared conciliatory, but he warned Zhu and Chen that it was a principle that the party should control guns, not vice versa.[27] In December, the Jinggang Mountains Red Army was reinforced by another communist troops led by Peng Dehuai. Peng was a government officer and secret party member. While serving a government army, Peng organized the Pingjiang Uprising in Hunan. Thus, to the Red Army was added a third component. The power struggle became further complicated.

The Party Central Committee was far away in Shanghai. It held its Sixth Congress in Moscow. During the conference, Comintern leader Nikolai Bukharin believed that the Chinese communist movement was at its low tide. He demanded that the Red Army should split into smaller units. More importantly, he suggested that Zhu and Mao leave the Red Army in order to avoid attracting a concentration of government forces. Mao was not at this conference, but he disputed this judgment, insisting on the concentration of troops and retention of his hold of the Red Army. By this time, however, Mao was in a disadvantageous position. He had trouble getting along with commander in chief, Zhu De. Zhu preferred that military strategy have priority over party work. Many soldiers under Zhu, Chen, and Peng were regular army men. They longed for opportunities to move around, to seek battles, and to take cities to replenish their supplies. At Zhu's insistence, the Red Army left the Jinggang Mountains base while leaving only a small force under Peng Dehuai to hold on to it. Mao reluctantly agreed, and, as the top political officer, he had to take overall responsibility for the operation. A few months later, news came that Peng had lost the mountain base forever. The Red Army had become homeless again. It moved around in Jiangxi to seek opportunities for survival. The Zhu-Mao dispute had been dormant for some time. In the face of the recent defeat, it erupted with gusto. The conflict centered on Mao's leadership as exerted through the party "Front Committee" with Mao as its secretary. While Zhu, Chen and Peng shared some common background, either service in regular army or travels abroad,[28] they had little in common with Mao, who had done neither. Moreover, the three shared a penchant for regular, mobile warfare which was at odds with Mao's unflinching faith in peasant guerrilla tactics. Mao also had a petulant and revengeful character, and was hard to work with. Zhu, Chen and Peng were known to be honest men, uncomfortable with Mao's extraordinarily conniving mind. By all accounts, Zhu had never stabbed anyone in the back throughout his life. Chen and Peng were frank and known for their unguarded mouths. Mao was different. Every step must be well-planned and each calculation must be always to his own advantage. Mao typified a Chinese saying that "a clever rabbit must have three caves (*Jiao Tu San Cao*)."

Another opportunity for replacing Mao came when the Central Committee sent a military representative named Liu Angong to Jiangxi. A fellow Sichuanese with Zhu and Chen, Liu had a perfect track-record in his party career. Having participated in the Nanchang Uprising, Liu was sent to Moscow to study military strategy. He was therefore another fanatic for regular warfare. Zhu and Chen were especially taken by his charm and experience. Liu's first move was to supplement the "Front Committee" with a "Military Committee" headed by him in order to destroy Mao's power base. The idea was not, however, accepted by the majority party committee members who were already fed up with a number of committees created by Mao. But the tide began to turn against Mao personally. Zhu and Mao began to fall out over the real issue: whether the party committee should control military affairs. Zhu apparently supported Liu's view that the party organization should limit its authority. This view was not without support from the Central Committee which had sent a directive to Mao and Zhu a year before, suggesting the abolition of the "party representative" system in the Jinggang Mountains troops.[29] The dispute became open in June, 1929 when Zhu and Mao had to defend their respective views at numerous internal meetings. What was devastating to Zhu was that Lin Biao, one of his best commanders, decided to side with Mao. In a rather vicious letter to Mao, Lin pointed out that "Some people ... have strong ambition to become top leaders of the Red Fourth Army and ... have formed invisible factions through feudal methods."[30] The Red Fourth Army held its seventh party congress chaired by Chen. The delegates severely attacked the work of Mao's Front Committee, calling it "secretary dictatorship" while rejecting Mao's criticism of Zhu's "pure militarism." Supported by Mao, Lin Biao once again attacked Zhu in person, calling him "warlordist." But a majority of the participants backed Zhu. It was critical that Chen, as chair of the meeting, stated that while both Zhu and Mao were responsible for losing the Jinggang mountains base, but Mao should accept the main blame.[31] For the second time in less than a year, Mao's position was taken over by Chen. More importantly, Mao was also relieved of all military responsibilities. At the same time, the party Politburo, secretly based in Shanghai, requested a representative from the Red Fourth Army to discuss their future. Chen, as the new party chief, departed for Shanghai in August, 1929.

The key Politburo members at this time were Li Lisan and Zhou Enlai. Both were Chen's old fellow students in France. They worked well together for two months drafting the Central Committee's directive to the Red Fourth Army. Chen could have had the opportunity to vent his spleen against Mao personally, but he was too decent to do so. More importantly, the Politburo began to have second thoughts about Bukharin's judgment at the party's Sixth Congress held the previous year in Moscow. The Comintern leaders had suggested that the Chinese Red Army should be split into smaller units. Li and Zhou turned against Bukharin, not least because the latter himself was in political trouble with Stalin.[32] Li Lisan and to a lesser extent Zhou Enlai went so far as to have reached the opposite conclusion that, since Bukharin was very pessimistic about the Chinese Revolution, the Red Army should be concentrated as one force to attack major cities. Li advanced the theory that the Chinese Revolution could achieve its initial success in one or a few provinces. Under the circumstances, Mao's inherent anti-Bukharin tendency fitted in perfectly with Li Lisan and Zhou Enlai's mindset.

Mao had already been keen to find an area where he could build a Soviet base. In his view, Jiangxi was the perfect place. According to a letter he wrote to Lin Biao, Jiangxi possessed three conditions ideal for the communists to take control: 1. the capitalist economy was weak and the landlords lacked armed forces; 2. the government troops were in most cases not native Jiangxi recruits; 3. it was far away, unlike Guangdong which was facing colonial Hong Kong, from the influence of the foreign imperialism. Therefore, Mao suggested the possibility of winning victory in one province first, then spread the impact nation-wide. This thinking anticipated Li Lisan's well-known "Struggle for One or Several Provincial Victories" resolution a year later, though official Chinese communist history refuses to admit this connection, because Li's resolution was later judged to be "adventurism."[33] Mao, of course, differed from Li in his lack of enthusiasm for attacking big cities.

The Politburo's position on the dispute between Zhu and Mao was thus in favor of the latter. Instead, Mao's original argument gained upper hand with the top leadership. After hearing Chen's honest and detailed report, the Politburo reached a conclusion: Mao was mostly right.[34] Chen must have endured great pains in helping draft an important Politburo directive, later known as the "Central Committee's September Letter," criticizing himself and Zhu De. Chen later recalled that his stay in Shanghai was like "taking an intensive training course for two months."[35]

Although the directive also criticized Mao's leadership style, it suggested that he remain party secretary of the Front Committee. Upon return to the base area, Chen found Mao was even more petulant and uncompromising than before. He refused to attend the eighth congress of the Red Fourth Army organized by Chen to reinstate him, claiming he would never return if "Chen Yiism was not destroyed." Eventually Mao agreed to take over his old position, but, as it would turn out, he would never forget the humiliation of being twice replaced by Chen. Feeling awkward to work with Mao at the top level, Chen accepted a demotion suggested by Mao a few months later to become a chief political officer at a newly formed Red Army unit under the command of Huang Gonglue. He would never re-enter the top decision-making mechanism for years to come.

From 1930 to 1934, Chen worked only at the second echelon of the Red Army establishment. The Party Central Committee was turning more and more adventurous after 1930. Li Lisan's resolution calling for attacks on big cities was vigorously implemented. The results were disastrous. Unable to return to the mountains, Mao decided to establish a Soviet regime in Jiangxi. In the summer of 1930, Chen married for the first time. The bride was a political officer working at his unit, Xiao Juying. He was twenty-nine, she was just seventeen. Xiao was a pretty girl from a middle-income family at Xinfeng city in Jiangxi, where she first heard that Chen and Zhu had executed the pawnshop robbers under their command two years ago.

Unfortunately, their married life had never been easy. Shortly after the wedding, Mao who had by now dominated the Jiangxi Soviet issued a major purge instruction, claiming the widespread existence of an AB (Anti-Bolshevik) Clique within the Red Army. The AB-Clique was a Jiangxi-based organization encouraged by Chiang Kai-shek during the 1927 Northern Expedition. It hardly existed after the Red Army took over control of the province. In May 1930, Mao's Front Committee claimed to have busted a secret AB-Clique branch in southwestern Jiangxi, and the impact immediately spread within the party. The truth was that Mao's political machine was never happy with the party leadership in that region. For months, the local party organization opposed Mao's idea of establishing local communist administration. More importantly, they disagreed with Mao's land reform policy which was aimed at achieving absolute equality through distribution of land on a per capita basis. The local party organization favored distribution of land according to the labor force, i.e., how many competent farm hands a household had. They argued that absolute equality would only result in waste and a decline in productivity. In the long run, the lowering standard of living that would result would destroy popular support for the party. Mao, however, vehemently criticized these views, claiming that "increasing production is not our first policy criterion, 'winning over' the masses is the number one criterion." In effect, Mao sacrificed the long-term foundation of popular support for the short-term gain through satisfying the desire of the landless poor peasants. Calling the labor-based distribution of land a "rich farmer policy," Mao started the first wave of brutal purge under the pretense of ferreting out the bogus AB-Clique. The irony is, Mao himself came from a rich farmer family.

It was apparent that Mao's method was inspired by Stalin's massive campaign to destroy the Russian rich farmers---the Kulak class. Evidence indicates that the purge leadership under Mao had always likened the AB-Clique to the rich farmers. In a report to the Central Committee dated October 14, 1930, Mao stated that, "Recently there appears to be an extremely serious crisis of the party organization in southwestern Jiangxi. The whole party is completely under the control of the rich farmers." In a subsequent resolution worked out by Mao, it demanded transforming all party and government organizations and "not allow a single rich farmer counterrevolutionary (the AB-Clique) to stay in either the party or the Soviet regime."[36]

For quite a few months, terror reigned in the Jiangxi Soviet. The level of brutality surpassed any brutality committed by government forces. There were massive arrests, suicides and executions everywhere. Kangaroo courts mushroomed to cope with the increasing number of the bogus cases. The executions were typically carried out swiftly and often in summary style. The number of people killed may never be known. The methods often bordered on barbarity. This was a practice undoubtedly inherited by Mao's favorite campaign, the Cultural Revolution, thirty-five years later.

According to reminiscences of the Red Army veterans, a special anti-AB Clique task force was formed in October 1930. The chief executioner was a man named Li Shaojiu, a trusted Mao protege. Li and his men used torture, kangaroo courts and forced confessions to execute Red Army officers who were more often than not Mao's opponents. Sometimes, Li simply lined up the suspects, threatened them with loaded pistols and executed whoever shook and sweated under pressure.[37] Another bizarre practice was to execute those who could write beautiful calligraphy with ink brush, which was thought to have belied a better education, affordable only in rich families.[38] High-ranking communist leaders were no exception. One sensational incident involved Chen's political director, a veteran communist named Cai Huiwen. Cai's land-owning mother and a sister were detained right under his nose during one of the attacks on rich farmers (*Da Tu Hao*). To avoid Li Shaojiu's suspicion, Cai decided to ignore their fate. Unable to bear the humiliation of imprisonment and her son's stiff rebuff, the mother simply threw herself into a river.[39]

Chen was ambiguous about the purge. He was disgusted by massive executions, but shied away from opposing Mao's method, perhaps because of his painful experience in dealing with Mao in the past. This ambiguity was reflected in his attitude towards an incident when a Red Army unit revolted at Futian against Mao's leadership. The mutiny leaders arrested Li and his execution team, which also included Mao's wife He Zizhen. Believing that Mao was behind the purge campaign, the rebellious Red Army officers openly declared "Down with Mao, Support Zhu (De), Peng (Dehuai) and Huang (Gonglue)." Chen was naturally sympathetic with this view since the three men supported by the officers were all his closest associates. But he decided to follow Mao's order to take over the command and released Li and his execution team. But Chen did not treat the rebel officers harshly just because of their anti-Mao behavior, which would later become a heavy political liability for years to come. Chen's rather lenient attitude toward the case was supported by Mao's superior at the time, Politburo member Xiang Ying, who, as chairman of the central military committee, decided after an investigation that the incident was not related to the AB-Clique.[40]

Mao was far from satisfied. After the Futian Incident, Li Shaojiu began to investigate Chen, and for the next three years Chen became a potential target. At one point, the swashbuckling Li told Chen face to face: "You are a member of the AB Clique, if you want to survive, you must make confessions." But Li did not arrest and execute Chen, knowing that he was too important to be executed without Mao's explicit approval. On another occasion, Li boasted to his men that he would soon possess Chen's horse and his new pistol. Upon hearing the story, Chen immediately wrote a letter to Mao asking for protection. The latter apparently decided to relent.[41]

Chen was fortunate to survive the purge. But his young wife could not take it any more. As Chen's colleagues were being executed one after another, the eighteen-year old Xiao Juying lived on the verge of a nervous breakdown. Whenever Chen left for a meeting, she thought about Chen's execution. One day when Chen did not come back as it was expected, the poor girl threw herself into a well. This was a devastating blow to Chen.

A passionately romantic man, he had never imagined that his love would be destroyed by the cause he had believed in. Xiao was well educated, romantic and an occasional poet herself. They enormously enjoyed each other's company. Chen fell into deep depression. He began to collect her poems and read them again and again. In a cold, lonely and moonlit night, Chen wrote a poem apparently in tears: "I still see your icy figure leaning against the door, I am numbed while reading your poems. You disappeared without my knowledge, where are you now in the heaven?" Returning to the grisly reality, Chen continued, "One says a revolutionary career is a good life, and one will be honored if he dies at the battle front. I don't mind hardship in life, but the thought of having lost a life companion at middle age cannot stop my tears."[42] Years later, Chen in a rare interview pointed out that the Anti-AB Clique movement was the number one issue disgusted by the peasant population in Jiangxi.[43]

At the height of the purge campaign, Mao's own luck began to have a downturn. The Party Central Committee finally decided to take over the Jiangxi Soviet directly, for its secret existence in Shanghai was all but destroyed by defections at the top level. Since Mao was never enthusiastic about attacks on cities, he became a thorn in the side to the new leadership, which was first under Zhou Enlai and Xiang Ying, both Politburo members, and later under the "Muscovites," the so-called "Twenty-Eight and A Half" returnees from Moscow.

But Mao's guerrilla strategy seemed to have been effective after three successful campaigns against the encirclement launched by the government forces. Yet, at the end of 1932 Mao was relieved of military command and severely criticized by the new Central Committee. One accusation was his factionalism. In early 1933, the fourth anti-encirclement campaign was organized by Zhou Enlai and Zhu De. For the first time in the Red Army's history, the high command used large-scale mobile war strategy, unbeknownst to Mao. But it succeeded in wiping out three divisions of the best government troops. The Central Committee was delighted. The anti-Mao campaign further escalated. Mao's guerrilla tactics were now called "opportunism" and the Mao cronies were purged one after another. One of the victims of this purge was Chen's fellow student in France, Deng Xiaoping. Although a relatively junior officer, Deng was a best friend of Mao's younger brother Zetan who had served with Chen and Zhu in 1928. The new leadership claimed to have ferreted out a small pro-Mao group known as the "Deng-Mao-Xie-Gu Clique," which included Deng Xiaoping, Mao Zetan, Xie Weijun and Gu Bai, all close associates of Mao. The official communist history often suggests that Mao was purged simply for his "correct" military strategy, this is only a half truth. Mao's character as it was reflected by the Anti-AB Clique Campaign had already alienated the rank and file of the Red Army.

Meanwhile the situation in the Jiangxi Soviet began to deteriorate after a Comintern military advisor arrived at the scene. In October 1933, Moscow sent Otto Braun, a German-born military strategist, to Jiangxi just before another round of the government encirclement campaign started. Braun knew nothing about China and his military expertise derived from textbooks of the Soviet military academy where he had been trained. Contending that the Chinese Red Army must be regularized, he was determined to transform it into a serious copy of the Soviet Red Army. Braun quickly took over the overall command. His military orders throughout the disastrous campaign were based on so-called"Two-Fists Strike" tactics, i.e., meeting the enemy at all points. This was anathema to Mao and also to the Zhou-Zhu joint command in the previous campaign. While Mao was not in a position to influence military decisions, Zhu and Zhou were too timid to challenge the Comintern strategist. After a crushing defeat in early 1934, Braun decided to abandon the Jiangxi Soviet altogether, thus a hasty preparation for retreat was begun as early as in the spring of 1934. Such a general exodus was later euphorically called the heroic "Long March." The Communist International in Moscow approved Braun's plan at once.[44]

The plan for retreat was so secretive that only three persons knew it: Otto Braun, Zhou Enlai, and Bo Gu. Bo was a young Moscow returnee and the head of the party. He was personally sponsored by Stalin. In July and August 1934, the Big Three dispatched two advanced troops out in two different directions. The first unit was ostensibly sent out on an impossible mission to north China to engage the Japanese who had invaded China two years before. With all the fanfare and publicity, the expedition force was designed to attract the government attention away from the actual retreat route of the Central Committee. This first mission was therefore meant to be suicidal. But the top leaders did not yet know where to go, except for an vague idea of building another base area in western Hunan and Hubei. The projected retreat route for the Central Committee was therefore to the southwest aimed at joining He Long's red army active in Hunan-Hubei border area. Thus a second advance column was dispatched to that direction.

One of the leaders of the first mission, Su Yu, who would later become Chen Yi's closest confidant,was not given the full picture even until as late as the 1970s when he confronted a reluctant Zhu De with the question. Su's troops, at six thousand strong, were hastily formed and poorly equipped even for the purpose of strategic diversion. They in fact became the sacrificial lamb of the escapist Central Committee.[45]

Besides the troops for the suicide mission, there were two other kinds of people who were to be abandoned by the Central Committee: the physically unfit, and the politically incorrect. The Big Three in charge of the retreat plan rejected many who begged to participate in the Long March. Prominent among the abandoned were Qu Qiubai, Chen Yi, He Shuheng and Liu Bojian.[46] Qu, for example, had been accused of "extreme adventurism" during his brief tenure as the party leader. He Shuheng, a founding member of the first party congress was too old to endure the march. Chen Yi perhaps fitted into both categories. He was wounded in the leg during the last campaign and was a demoted political outcast, Chen had no chance to join the retreat. His fate was thus sealed. But Zhou Enlai did come to see him upon his request at the hospital shortly before the Central Committee's departure. Chen complained bitterly to his old friend that "Why don't you tell me you are leaving? I have sensed it for some time."[47] Nevertheless, Zhou gave him a consolatory appointment as the director of the care-taking government of what was left of the Jiangxi Soviet regime. Xiang Ying, a Politburo member, was left to take overall control of the party work. Xiang, an earlier Moscow returnee, was Mao's former boss and *bete noire*. He was very much trusted by Zhou.[48]

In late October 1934, the Central Committee and an eighty-thousand strong Red Army force left Jiangxi. The government troops immediately closed in to finish the job of annihilation. Chen's care-taking Jiangxi Soviet government decided to withdraw women from the base area, among them was Chen's second wife Lai Yueming.[49] Mao's younger brother Zetan had not been allowed to join the main force. His wife He Yi was also Mao's wife He Zizhen's younger sister. Chen made a special effort to arrange for He Yi to go underground in Ganzhou city.

The situation was increasingly more severe day by day. To mislead the government forces, the Central Committee instructed Xiang to hold on to the base area at whatever cost. But Xiang and Chen had only just over ten thousand troops, certainly not the best, at their disposal. Within a month, this force was all but crushed by the overwhelming government attacks. The Central Committee did not order them to abandon the base until the end of the January 1935, but it was too late to organize meaningful guerrilla warfare and to repeat the Jinggang Mountains experience.

The difficulty was compounded by the fact that the communist command under Xiang did not know much about war strategy. Xiang had always been an effective party functionary. Chen was wounded and stayed mostly in bed. Moreover, according to a communist insider, it was a mistake to leave these two men in charge of the base area, for none of them was a Jiangxi native, capable of mobilizing strong local support for building a guerrilla base.[50] In February 1935, they decided to break the tight enemy encirclement by splitting the Red Army remnants in several directions. At the end of the month, they received, for the last time, a telegram from the Central Committee detailing a conference held at Zunyi in Guizhou Province, which relieved all the power held by Otto Braun and catapulted Mao, for the first time, into the top decision-making position. In March, Xiang and Chen led the last group of soldiers, at only two hundred in strength, to try to break through the last line of the government encirclement. In the meantime, all communications with the Central Committee were cut off, for the new leadership began to use a different code. After smashing the radio, Xiang and Chen finally joined another troops at Dayu Mountain area bordering Jiangxi and Guangdong.

From this time on, they began a three-year period of primitive life as "red bandits," hunted all the time by the government. The government forces returned to the Jiangxi Soviet area with a vengeance. For three years, according to one estimate, over seven hundred thousand people, about twenty percent of the population under communist control, were executed.[51] The government, however, apparently obtained cooperation from many local people who had suffered years of economic and physical deprivation, as a result of a land policy that destroyed productivity and the terror caused by widespread persecutions such as the dreadful Anti-AB Clique Campaign launched by Mao. The official communist history has never admitted this fact, though Mao later in the 1940s summarized "ten major mistakes" made by the communists in Jiangxi in an internal telegram.[52]

For Chen Yi, the return to guerrilla warfare was nothing new. Xiang Ying found it hard to adjust but managed to endure the grim conditions. Although Xiang and Chen were left to take overall control of scattered guerrilla units, they had in fact no means of communication with the other units except for their own until 1937. At the end of the year, the government continued to close in at the mountain area, and established three lines of encirclement. After all the supplies were cut off, the "red bandits" had to live under extremely primitive conditions. But the ever romantic poet Chen still found time to humor himself. In one poem he wrote in 1936, it said: "We have no food, and have tasted no meat for three months. But we manage to eat plums in summer and bamboo shoots in winter.... We hunt wild hogs everywhere, and catch snakes in the mid-night. We hide when chased by the enemy, we strike when the enemy is resting. We sit calmly on the fishing boat, the enemy will take the bait."[53]

The worst, however, came in the winter of 1936. Tipped off by a communist defector, Chen was cornered in a hill called Meiling. He was surrounded by four battalions of government troops for twenty days. The enemy burnt everything flammable. This was the first time Chen realized that the end had come. Writing on his shirt, he left a poetic will: "What do I think if I die today? I have fought hundred battles, so I am going to the heaven to recruit my old troops, and will lead ten thousand soldiers to

kill the monster king in Hell."[54]
But the final blow did not come. Something odd happened: the government troops suddenly disappeared. Chen had no radio and newspaper to determine what was going on. A few days later, he sent a guerrilla down the hill, which brought back the shocking news: Chiang Kai-shek, the Kuomintang leader had been detained on December 12 by his subordinates in Xian, so the government troops were hurriedly recalled.

The Xian Incident was staged by a former warlord from Manchuria, General Zhang Xueliang. Angered at Chiang's unwillingness to resist the Japanese who had overrun his home base in Manchuria, Zhang and another general named Yang Hucheng, whose power base was in Northwest of China, decided to force Chiang's hand. They obtained immediate cooperation from the communists now based in northern Shaanxi. Exhausted by the Long March, the communist Central Committee found the Xian Incident a godsend for their much-needed period of consolidation.

The communists now had less than ten percent of the original eighty thousand troops as a result of the Long March. The Central Committee decided in 1936 to regain popular support which they had lost in Jiangxi. The Communist International in Moscow had initiated a policy of another united front under the name of fighting the Japanese. Throughout early 1936, the Chinese communist leadership had worked out deals with General Zhang's Manchurian army to stop the fight with the communists. Zhou Enlai in particular used his talent as a consummate deal-maker to influence another government troops, the Northwestern Army led by General Yang Hucheng. None of these government armies were considered elite troops under Chiang's direct control.

The initial communist strategy was to persuade Zhang to fight the Japanese while opposing Chiang (*Fan Jiang Kang Ri*). Zhang hesitated and indicated various difficulties. The communist leadership quickly changed its attitude. At a secret meeting between Zhou Enlai and Zhang Xueliang, the communists expressed willingness to associate with Chiang in the fight against Japan (*Lian Jiang Kang Ri*). But Chiang was still bent on eliminating the communists, his attitude indicated that no change of heart was forthcoming. Zhou and Zhang agreed in September on a common strategy approved by the Communist Central Committee known as "Force Chiang to Fight Japan" (*Bi Jiang Kang Ri*).[55] General Zhang would work from the "inside" while the communists on the "outside." For the communists, the strategy was aimed at destroying Chiang's leadership credibility by an open appeal to the government for stopping the civil war. But the impatient General Zhang decided to stage a mutiny while taking the opportunity of Chiang's visit to his headquarters at Xian to arrest him in order to force his hand.

As soon as the Xian Incident occurred, Zhou Enlai went to Xian in person and persuaded Zhang and Yang to release Chiang under the condition of signing an agreement to legitimize the communists. This arrangement was carried out shortly afterwards, but Chiang would never later regain his reputation as respected national leader. Under the circumstances, the communists turned out to be the only winners in this twisted and unexpected incident.

Living like wild men for three years, Chen, Xiang and their colleagues had learnt to survive under any circumstances. Even Xiang the former Muscovite had realized the need for abandoning the facade of Marxist-Leninist dogmatism. Throughout the three years, they were painfully aware that the Red Army's excesses in land policies and other issues had destroyed a popular base for support during the Jiangxi Soviet years, which made their survival all the more precarious. Chen in particular began to undergo a tremendous transformation in his views on many fundamental issues. In one heated debate with his colleagues, Chen stated that he thought he could compromise with at least fifty out of each one hundred landlords, although only a few supported his view.[56] Xiang was, however, generally in agreement with Chen. Therefore, when the news of the Second United Front came, though shocked as they were, they were psychologically at ease with the turn of events. This attitude proved to be a far cry from the mindset of many communist survivors hiding elsewhere, and spreading across several southern provinces. It would soon turn out that the idea for Chen and Xiang to recruit their old subordinates in the mountains was no less a stressful task.

Notes

1. Chinese generals who rebelled against the Manchu Dynasty in its early years.
2. Chen told this story for the first time in 1942 in a letter to a medical doctor named Jakob Rosenfeld from Austria who was then working at the New Fourth Army headquarters . See *A letter to Dr. Rosenfeld*, in *Chen Yi Shi Ci Xuan* (Selected Poems of Chen Yi, Beijing 1978), p.359.
3. *Chen Yi Zhuan* (Biography of Chen Yi, Beijing 1992), p.5. There are two valuable biographies of Chen Yi. The one published in Beijing is an official biography. Hereafter it will be referred to as "official." Another was published in Shanghai in 1992 by Jiang, Hongbin, hereafter it will be referred to as "Jiang."
4. *Biography of Chen Yi* (Jiang), p.29.
5. Chen, Yi, *Choosing the Revolutionary Road*, in *Chen Yi Zao Nian de Hui Yi yu Wen Gao* (Chen Yi's Early Reminiscences and Writings, Sichuan 1981), p.25.

The Making of A Red Bandit   29

6. Chen Yi, *My Two-year as Work-Study Student*, Ibid., p.47.
7. *Biography of Chen Yi* (Official), p.14.
8. Ibid., p.21.
9. Ibid., p.21.
10. This is a typical form of Chinese scrolls, Ibid., p.22.
11. This poem was apparently influenced by French Romantic poets, especially Alfred de Musset. Chen later would publish a translation of de Musset's poem. See *Chen Yi Shi Ci Quan Ji* (Complete Collection of Poems of Chen Yi, Beijing 1993)
12. Published in *Chen Bao Fu Kan* (Morning News Literature Supplement), April 25, 1925, Beijing.
13. Qiu, Yang (alias Jin Mancheng), *Chen Yi: Cong Shu Sheng Dao Jiang Jun* (Chen Yi: from Scholar to General), *Ta Kung Pao*, May 30 to June 4, 1949, Shanghai.
14. Qu, Qiu (Chen Yi's pen name), *Xi Shan de Mai Zang* (Burial at the West Hill), *Morning News Literature Supplement*, June 25, 1925, Beijing.
15. Luo, Yingcai, *Tien Jun Dang Dai Biao* (Iron Army Party Representative, Beijing 1992), p.128.
16. Zhou Shidi and Li Shuoxun. Zhou later rejoined the Red Army. Li, father of Li Peng, went underground and was captured and executed by the government a few years later.
17. Luo, op.ct., p.144.
18. Su, Yu, *Zhan Zheng Hui Yi Lu* (War Memoirs, Beijing 1988), p.133-135.
19. Lin Biao's desertion was not known until his death in 1971. Lin would become a top general in the communist establishment.
20. This episode would cost Zhu and Chen dearly. At the peak of the Cultural Revolution, both were labeled by the Red Guards as "warlords."
21. Jin, Chongji and Huo, Xiguang, *Zhu De Zhuan* (Biography of Zhu De, Beijing 1993), p.98-99.
22. Luo, op. ct., p.232-233. See also Huang, Kecheng, *Huang Kecheng Hui Yi Lu* (Memoirs of Huang Kecheng, Beijing 1989), vol.1, p.58-59.
23. The bandit leaders who were pacified by Mao were Wang Zuo and Yuan Wencai.
24. It is interesting to note that the same namesake would stick to Chen's career for years to come.
25. This was the first of the two occasions when Chen replaced Mao as party secretary. Mao would never forgive him for this.
26. *Biography of Chen Yi* (Official), p.80-81.
27. Mao actually wrote this down in an article, see *Selected Works of Mao Zedong* (Beijing 1991), vol.1, p.?
28. Zhu had studied in Europe and Russia.
29. *Zhong Gong Zhong Yang Wen Jian Xuan Ji* (Selected Documents of

the CCP Central Committee, Beijing 1989), hereafter it will be referred to as WJXJ, vol.4, p.253.

30. *Biography of Zhu De*, p.177-178.

31. According to Gong Chu, who was at the meeting and he would defect to the government a few years later, Chen severely criticized Lin's attitude. See Gong, Chu, *Gong Chu Jiang Jun Hui Yi Lu* (Memoirs of General Gong Chu, Hong Kong 1978), p.233-235.

32. The political assassination of Bukharin was started in August 1929; it had a strong impact on foreign communist parties around the world. See Bullock, Alan, *Hitler and Stalin---Parallel Lives* (New York 1992), p. 214.

33. For Mao's letter to Lin Biao, see *Selected Works of Mao Zedong*, vol.1, p.106. For a rather defensive discussion, see Gai, Jun, *Mao Zedong He Zheng Qu Jiangxi Shou Xian Sheng Li Lun* (Mao and the View of Winning Victory in Jiangxi First), in *Materials of the CCP History*, vol.44, p.118-127.

34. There is a good reason to believe that Chen had made an honest report in Shanghai. For details of the "September Letter," see *WJXJ*, vol.5, p.473-490.

35. *Biography of Chen Yi* (Official), p.107.

36. Wu, Guoyou, *Lun Su AB Tuan Wu Qu de Xing Cheng* (On the Formation of the Wrongly-targeted Area during the Purge of the AB-Clique), in *Zhong Gong Zhong Yang Dang Shi Yan Jiu* (Studies of the CCP History), vol.6, 1994, p. 50-53.

37. Interview with Red Army Veterans in Nanjing, August 1994.

38. *Biography of Chen Yi* (Jiang), p.345-346.

39. Liu, Puqing, *Cai Huiwen Jiang Jun Zhuan* (Biography of General Cai Huiwen, Beijing 1987), p.168-169.

40. Wang, Fuyi, *Xiang Ying Zhuan Lue* (Brief Biography of Xiang Ying), in Materials of the CCP History, vol.37, p.119-120.

41. *Biography of Chen Yi* (Official), p.126.

42. *Complete Collection of Chen Yi's Poems*, p.32.

43. Chen, Yi, *Several Issues of Jiangxi Revolutionary Struggle---Interview with Chen Yi*, in *Chen Yi Zi Liao Xuan* (Some Materials on Chen Yi, Shanghai 1978), p.223.

44. Braun decided to abandon Jiangxi in the spring of 1934 and the party secretariat approved this decision in May, though no detailed plan was made at the time. See Jin, Chongji, *Zhou Enlai Zhuan* (Biography of Zhou Enlai, Beijing 1989), p.277.

45. Su, Yu, *War Memoirs*, p.133-135.

46. Liu Bojian had begged several times but to no avail. He died shortly after. See *Ye Jianying Zhuan* (Biography of Ye Jianying, Beijing 1987), p.66.

47. Chen, Yi, *Interview*, see note 43.

48. Xiang had worked for years in Moscow as Chinese Trade Union Representative to the Comintern Executive. He was sent by Zhou Enlai to take control of the Jiangxi Soviet in 1931. His judgment on the Futian Mutiny had sowed the first seed of mutual distrust between him and Mao.
49. Little is known about this marriage. Lai was a party functionary. After the Long March, she left the party and married a local peasant.
50. In his memoir, General Huang Kecheng frankly thought that the decision to leave Xiang and Chen in charge was a mistake. See *Memoirs of Huang Kecheng*, vol.1, p.216.
51. *Biography of Chen Yi* (Official), p.135.
52. Chen, Yi, *Interview*, see note 43.
53. *Complete Collection of Chen Yi's Poems*, p.41. For a detailed description of the bandit life, see Chen, Pixian, *Gan Nan San Nian You Ji Zhan Zheng* (Three Years of Guerrilla War in Southern Jiangxi, Beijing 1982).
54. *Complete Collection of Chen Yi's Poems*, p.46.
55. *WJXJ*, vol.11, p.89-91.
56. Chen, Yi, *Interview*, see note 43.

Chapter 2

The Origins of the New Fourth Army

Official Chinese communist history has long insisted that the formation of the New Fourth Army, which was based on the scattered guerrilla forces left behind by the Communist Party Central Committee, was a brilliant idea of the new party leadership under Mao. The evidence suggests otherwise. Xiang and Chen had lost contact with the Party Central Committee for almost three years now. Without any instructions from Yanan, where the communist headquarters were located, they decided on their own initiative to appeal to the local government for negotiations. One of the most important conditions Chen listed in a proposal for truce was to concentrate all scattered guerrilla forces and organize them into a single army unit. The Jiangxi local government responded. First a local county magistrate who was also a "returned student" from Japan struck a personal rapport with Chen through letter communications and who in the end pushed for a serious negotiation between Chen and the provincial government.

On September 23, 1937, Chen arrived at Ganzhou. At the same time, his colleague Xiang Ying went to Nanchang, the capital city of the province. Ganzhou was an ancient city surrounded by three rivers and thick high walls. Because of its strategic location, Ganzhou had always endured attacks throughout history. But the city was easier to hold than to take. The "red bandits," the former Red Army remnants of the Jiangxi Soviet knew it all too well, for they had failed to overcome its defenses three times in the early 1930s. Eventually the Red Army was driven out of Jiangxi in 1934, but the city dwellers in Ganzhou were aware of a small communist guerrilla band that had been hiding in nearby mountains for the past three years.

But the communists came today not for attack. Chen, whose head had been sought by the government at a fifty-thousand silver dollars reward, now arrived as representative for the red guerrillas in southern China. Estimated at about ten thousand strong, these guerrillas were spread in mountainous areas bordering eight provinces. The troops under Xiang and Chen's direct control were merely four hundred and fifty. After a three-year long primitive life, the communist negotiators were tired, haggard, and malnourished. But their spirit seemed very high.

The Party Central Committee a thousand miles away in northwestern China knew nothing about this. Having been kept virtually incommunicado for three years, Chen and his comrades only recently learnt through government newspapers of the formation of the Second United Front---the official rapprochement between the communists and the Kuomintang-controlled government. Chen knew little about what the new Party Central Committee had wanted, much less about its new power structure emerging from the Long March. He did know, however, that his one time *bete noire*, Mao Zedong, had risen to the top of the party leadership.

While in Ganzhou, Chen met a woman who was sent by him to work underground in October 1934. Pressured by the government attack, the communist leaders who stayed behind in Jiangxi decided that all males should retreat into the mountains, while women go underground in government-controlled areas. Chen had lost touch with her ever since. She was more than just an old acquaintance. Her name was He Yi, whose elder sister, He Zizhen, was the wife of Mao Zedong. She herself was married to Mao Zetan, Mao's younger brother who died in Jiangxi after being excluded from the Long March and his brother at the time not being in a position to help him. Chen must have learnt quite a lot from her while staying in Ganzhou. He immediately decided to take her on board of the negotiation team.[1]

In fact, the Party Central Committee in Yanan did not know what to do with these guerrilla units. Chen's meeting with He Yi was not the official re-connection with the Central Committee after a three-year lapse. His guerrilla colleague Xiang Ying went to Nanchang and was able to connect with Yanan for the first time. But specific instructions were still not forthcoming for quite a while.

The first effort to establish the United Front against Japan was carried out in early August, 1937. According to an agreement between the communists and the government, the Red Army troops that had survived the Long March, which were now under Mao's direct control, were re-organized into the National Eighth Route Army, which was nominally under government command, but was subordinated only to the communist headquarters. Xiang and Chen thought it only natural to follow the same format. By October, Chiang Kai-shek had realized that he had made a mistake in giving a green light to communist expansion of its power base through government finance. Afraid of repeating similar arrangements with the red guerrillas in southern China, Chiang Kai-shek was determined to adopt a different formula. He preempted Mao in September, when the communist leadership was still indecisive at the time, by offering a new format to get the guerrillas out of the mountains. The idea was to gather all the red guerrillas to form a new army and to appoint a non-communist general as commander acceptable to both sides. The choice was Ye Ting. General Ye was a communist leader during the 1927 Nanchang Uprising. He had quit the party after being brutally snubbed by the Communist International in Moscow because of his role in the failure of the communist-staged Nanchang and Guangzhou uprisings in 1927. For years he had lived a life of voluntary exile in Hong Kong and Macao. Since Ye was a soldier with national fame during the Northern Expedition period when Chiang was his commander in chief, many people had persuaded him to volunteer for service to fight Japan after years of retirement. Chiang was delighted. To please Ye, Chiang accept the request by Ye that the concentrated guerrilla forces could be called the "New Fourth Army," which was named after his old regimental home---the "Iron Fourth Army" during the war against the northern warlords. This army happened to be the main communist troops that participated in the Nanchang Uprising, whose remnants were brought to the mountains by Zhu De and Chen Yi in 1928. Besides, General Ye was more than enthusiastic about the chance to regain his reputation after many years of humiliation.

The Communist Party Central Committee was panic-stricken about Chiang's idea. It did not trust Ye, the deserter of the party. In an earlier instruction dated August 1, the Central Committee asked the guerrillas to stay where they were to build up local power structures in existing base areas. It requested the guerrilla leaders to fulfill seven tasks:

1. To change the local Soviet regime into a popularly elected local administration; 2. To stop land policies that are aimed at confiscating land from the landlords. 3. To join local government forces but retain vigorous independence. 4. to continue the efforts to mobilize the masses; 5. to befriend the government troops that are against the Japanese; 6. to turn party organizations into secret branches; and, 7. to explain to the members of the party the necessity for establishing the United Front.

This was an outlandish instruction. It reflected Mao's penchant for scattered guerrilla warfare, but at the same time, it also indicated how far he was out of touch with reality. After three years of bloody struggle for survival, there was hardly any base area or local Soviet regime left, apart from unpopulated mountains where the guerrillas were hiding. Most importantly, the instruction never mentioned the word "concentration" of the troops.[2] Thus the idea of gathering the guerrillas to form a unified command was out of the question.

As events began to spin out of Yanan's control in September, the Party Central Committee began to issue explicit warning against the concentration of guerrilla troops. Mao was greatly frustrated by Chen and Xiang's behavior in Jiangxi and apparently thought that they had been tricked by the government, since there was some indication that they seemed to be more than enthusiastic about the idea of regrouping guerrillas under a single government command.

Indeed, both Xiang and Chen had already made such a proposal. At Ganzhou, Chen presented his eight-point plan to the government, which included immediate cessation of hostilities as well as "concentration" of guerrillas at certain geographical point, "waiting for reorganization."[3] Xiang went even further to publish an "Open Letter to Southern Guerrilla Comrades" in Nanchang. It stated that, "I have formally declared an end to guerrilla war [against the government], and urged the reorganization of all the guerrilla troops under the unified command of the national government .... Please start concentrating your troops and wait for official roll call after reading this open letter."[4]

Under the circumstances, the discord between the guerrilla leaders and the Party Central Committee started almost immediately. After an incident occurred in Fujian when a communist guerrilla unit was completely disarmed while waiting for reorganization by the government, Mao's distrust of guerrilla leaders, especially Xiang Ying who was a Politburo member, deepened greatly. On October 1, 1937, the Party Central Committee issued an important secret instruction. It stated pointedly that, "These southern guerrilla base areas are the result of ten-year bloody warfare .... The government is trying to destroy them by using Ye Ting." Therefore "it will be to our disadvantage to concentrate these troops." Although Mao admitted that, "in principle we should not reject troop concentration," since it would appear rather impolitic in view of the formation of the Second United Front, he listed several important conditions. The most crucial of all was that the guerrilla units must not take any action and wait for several months until receiving clear instructions from the Party Central Committee. In addition, "Ye Ting must come to Yanan and, after he completely agrees with the political and military principle of the Party Central Committee, he may be allowed to proceed ... to take over command of either the unit under Zhang Dingcheng or the unit under Liu Ying." In other words, Yanan initially intended to try Ye Ting out by assigning him a small unit instead of all communist guerrilla troops in southern China. But Mao's criticism of Xiang Ying was extremely severe, "Comrade Xiang Ying does not seem to understand the principle of maintaining independence within the United Front. Even less does he understand the principle of maintaining strategic fulcrums without the necessity of unconditional concentration of the southern guerrilla troops. His activities in Nanchang are dangerous. He should be informed to come to Yanan immediately."[5]

But this instruction came too late. To Mao's chagrin, a few days later, Chiang Kai-shek officially announced Ye's appointment. This embarrassment could be considered the first painful challenge to Mao's personal authority coming from the leadership of the future New Fourth Army. On October 8, the Communist Party's official representatives at Chiang's capital, Bo Gu and Ye Jianying, suggested the immediate acceptance of the format proposed by Chiang, pointing out that it would be difficult for the guerrillas to stay where they were and there was no meaningful base area to speak of. And in any case, Bo and Ye reported, it was too late to reject Chiang's offer, which was made with great fanfare and publicity, for an open rejection on the communist side would support Chiang's claim that the Red Army in northern China was fundamentally different from the one in the south. The former could be considered regular army but the latter were simply the bandits. Thus the delay of reorganization would render the communist control of these troops even less likely. In response to Mao's constant concern about whether communists could exert absolute control over the New Fourth Army, Bo Gu and Ye Jianying suggested that the New Fourth Army be put under the command of the Eighth Route Army. They also reported that General Ye Ting had indicated his willingness to resign if the communists disapproved his appointment. It is interesting to note that, according to Bo and Ye, General Ye Ting had actually claimed that it was Zhou Enlai's idea for his appointment in the first place. But the Central Committee seemed to know nothing about this.[6]

Chiang was determined that Ye Ting should command all red guerrilla forces. In a secret internal instruction dated October 6, Chiang specified that troops under Gao Jingting, Zhang Dingcheng, Xiang Ying and Liu Ying, etc. must fall under Ye's overall control.[7] In desperation, Mao asked whether General Ye was willing to rejoin the party and every effort should be made to ensure that the new army would be part of the Eighth Route Army in the north.[8] As late as on October 30, Mao's doubt about Ye Ting remained strong. In another telegram to Bo Gu and Ye Jianying, Mao warned, "Whether or not Ye Ting can become the commander will depend on the guarantee you provide." Willy-nilly, Mao agreed to make certain concessions to Chiang but he continued to insist on partial concentration of the guerrilla troops. Mao's new idea was to allow three-fifth of this force to be commanded by Ye, while the remaining two-fifth would stay where they were. Mao added that in the latter case, no government appointees would be accepted.[9] Only after General Ye privately expressed his unequivocal willingness to accept the Communist leadership exclusively, did Mao begin to change his mind. Pressured by the government for a positive response, Mao finally requested General Ye and Xiang Ying to report to Yanan at once.

On November 3, 1937, General Ye arrived at Yanan. Both sides were very cautious at first, trying to fathom each other's real intention. To Mao's chagrin, Ye was not keen to rejoin the Communist Party. But Mao was quickly put at ease when Ye began to use the communist jargons freely, declaring that "Revolution is like climbing a mountain, most comrades have reached top, but I turned back at the middle of it." This, to Mao, was a clear sign that Ye remained enthusiastic about the communist cause.

On November 6, Mao informed Bo Gu in Nanjing that the Central Committee had decided to accept Ye Ting, but the new army must belong to the Eighth Route Army commanding system. Chiang Kai-shek flatly rejected this proposal.[10] The communists had no choice but to accept the Chiang formula. A few days later, Xiang Ying also arrived at Yanan. After an absorbing and passionate report by Xiang that took seven straight hours on the hardships he and Chen had endured for the past three years, the Politburo was so moved as to announce in an internal resolution dated December 13 that Xiang and the southern guerrilla forces had been "basically correct" in adopting party lines and should be "models" for the whole party to learn and admire.[11]

Having made the decision to accept Chiang's format, the Politburo decided to set up a Yangzi River Party Bureau to direct the New Fourth Army affairs. However, the head of the bureau was not Mao's choice, but Stalin's favorite Muscovite, whose name was Wang Ming. Zhou Enlai, Bo Gu, and Xiang Ying were also appointed leading members of the bureau. Moreover, Xiang was concurrently the head of its Southeastern Sub-bureau to manage day to day affairs of the new army. His official military capacity was specified as Lieutenant General and deputy commander of the New Fourth Army, a position that put him in *de facto* charge of all the military and political affairs of this newly formed force. The rank of "deputy commander" was deliberately designed to deceive the government, for its real function was that of party secretary and political commissar during the Red Army years. Thus at the outset, General Ye Ting, the government choice, became a figure-head of the New Fourth Army.

But the feeling of being preempted by Chiang, Ye, and the guerrilla leaders on the issue of concentrating troops had sown the first seeds of mutual suspicion between the Communist Party Central Committee controlled by Mao and the New Fourth Army leadership controlled by Xiang. At the end of September, the Central Committee had already agreed to establish a General Liaison Office at Nanchang to start the process of recruiting guerrillas. Chen Yi was placed in charge of the task. But the concentration of troops was easier said than done. These scattered guerrilla forces had endured the most horrible conditions in fighting with the government, and like Chen and Xiang, they were unaware of what had been going on outside the mountains for three years. For the most hard-boiled guerrilla leaders, the Second United Front appeared to be an open surrender to the government. Officially, after the Party Central Committee's departure in October 1934, Xiang and Chen had been appointed leaders in charge of party and military works in the former Jiangxi Soviet. But for three years they had neither *de facto* control over nor any communication means to contact these guerrillas. As a result, persuading the guerrilla leaders to come out of the mountains to accept the government-sponsored reorganization program proved to be a very dangerous affair for the communist recruiters.

Within months, several communist envoys, including such well-known veteran Red Army officers as Ming Anlou, a former division commander, were executed in the mountains upon arrival. In one endeavor to look for the guerrillas in Hunan and Jiangxi border area, Chen Yi was almost tortured to death by the guerrilla leaders who were convinced that Chen was a traitor working for the government. They put Chen on trial for days. The head of this force, Tan Yubao, was a Jinggang Mountains veteran who had led a guerrilla force in this area since 1934. Tan blasted constantly at Chen who was tightly tied up on a bamboo shoulder-pole, "In Jinggang Mountains, you talked all the time about revolution and history, now you don't even remember what you had said then!" Chen was repeatedly harassed and tortured. Tan used his copper tobacco pipe to hit Chen's forehead frequently while haranguing in front of him. Before Chen's scheduled execution, Tan decided to send a guerrilla down the hill to make sure that the government troops were not led in by Chen's footsteps. The soldier, however, brought back some publications a few days later. Realizing that he had made a terrible mistake, Tan was all in tears when turning loose the tight ropes that were on Chen for four days.[12]

Tan's mountain base was just one of the several that had been kept completely incommunicado for three years from the outside world. Like the peasant-born Tan, many guerrilla leaders not only hated the government deeply but also chafed at the fact that they had been dumped by the defeatist Party Central Committee in 1934. Moreover, the turn of events had seemed too good to be true and the complicated political arguments behind the party's decision to form the Second United Front were often beyond the immediate ken of their understanding. But there were several types of guerrillas, whose attitude toward "Zhong Yang"---the Party Central Committee---varied according to their origins. First of all, those guerrilla troops who originated from the former Jiangxi Soviet were more receptive to the idea of concentration and reorganization. Most of their leaders were Xiang and Chen's former subordinates. In the mountainous area between Fujian and Zhejiang provinces, one such guerrilla force at about five hundred in strength had already taken the initiative to negotiate with the government. Led by Su Yu and Liu Ying, whose troops in 1934 were sent by the Central Committee to engage the Japanese, an effort to divert the government attention away from the retreat route for the Long March by the main Red Army forces. Su came from a family that belonged to the ethnic Dong minority. He was a junior officer with Zhu De and Chen Yi in 1928. Rising steadily through the ranks, Su was appointed the chief of staff of the newly organized, but ill-fated decoy army in 1934. After fighting many heroic battles, Su's troops were joined by a local communist leader in northeastern Jiangxi named Fang Zhimin. But their joint command did not save the fate of the troops. Within months they were crushed by government forces in northeastern Jiangxi. Fang was captured and executed, but Su was able to escape and survive. His six thousand troops were reduced to five hundred. It finally dawned upon Su that such a mission was clearly meant to be suicidal. He naturally held strong grudges against the Party Central Committee. Throughout the three years in the mountains, Su had only organized small-scale ambushes against the government troops. In October 1937, Su negotiated with the local government and formed an "Anti-Japanese Guerrilla Column" with government's full blessing. Since Su was Chen's long time subordinate, he answered Chen's call in the most favorable manner. His troops were certainly not among the most difficult to accept the government reorganization program.

In Western and northern Fujian province, two other troops which historically had a connection with the Jiangxi Soviet were the remnant units that broke through the government encirclement and split with Xiang and Chen in 1935. Led by Chen and Xiang's subordinates Tan Zhenlin, Zhang Dingcheng and Deng Zihui, these guerrillas had been very successful in retaining their strength and even managed to maintain a small guerrilla base with limited number of population under their control. By the time Chen Yi called upon them, they had also started negotiations with the government on their own initiative. They, too, proved to be a much easier task for Chen to recruit and reorganize.[14]

The second type of guerrillas had been totally independent. They had developed their own base areas without the Central Committee's knowledge. Feeling beholden to none, they had total freedom of action. The largest such force was led by Gao Jingting, who in 1937 commanded some three thousand troops belonging to Zhang Guotao's *Er-Yu-Wan* (Hubei-Henan-Anhui) Soviet Regime. Zhang Guotao, Chen's colleague in Beijing back in the mid-1920s, was a Politburo member who had had a major conflict with Mao and had intended to take over control of the party during the Long March. He was the last substantial challenger to Mao's authority before the latter's position was totally secured.[15] As early as in July 1937, Gao was the first guerrilla leader to begin negotiations with the government without any authorization from the Party Central Committee. Among all guerrilla units at the time, Gao's troops were the best trained and equipped. Moreover, they, like all the troops under Zhang's command, had substantial experience in regular mobile warfare. Many commanders of Zhang Guotao's *Er-Yu-Wan* Red Army, such as Xu Xiangqian and Chen Geng, were trained at the Whampoa Academy, whose military successes had outshone Mao's escapist "Central Red Army" during the Long March when the two troops met for the first time in 1935. For obvious reason, Mao's Central Committee never trusted Gao, for his troops were totally immune from the brutal internal purge campaign against Zhang Guotao in Yanan. Gao's men were not receptive to the Central Committee's negative verdict on Zhang Guotao's attempt at the party leadership during the Long March. In order to control this force, Mao sent Gao's former subordinates who had been converted into Mao cronies to work for Gao. Mao specifically instructed them "not to criticize them in the way we criticize Zhang Guotao."[16] Gao, on his part, often showed signs of insubordination, an attitude that would cost him dearly in the next few years. Gao was to be wrongly accused of being a traitor and executed in June 1939. The real problem was his insubordination. It was not until 1980 did the Party Central Committee admit this execution to be a mistake.[17]

A smaller force of the independent type, about one thousand, was active in eastern Fujian area. It was led by a twenty-three year old communist leader named Ye Fei. Ye was an unusually gifted party organizer and guerrilla leader. Born near Manila, the Philippines, Ye was half Chinese with a Filipino mother and a Chinese father. Well-educated and young, Ye started his party career by organizing urban workers in manufacturing plants. He was sent by the party, at the age of eighteen to organize a peasant uprising in eastern Fujian in 1932 and had stayed there ever since. Having endured countless harsh conditions and, having almost died twice, Ye rose to the top echelon of the base area and became its undisputed leader. Ironically, the durability of Ye's leadership and his troops in this base area was helped by the fact that his small base had been kept incommunicado for years, which meant that the constant internal purges and external excesses by the Party Central Committee had had little effect on this particular base. In fact, it was fortunate that this base had all but been written off by the Party Central Committee. Ye's guerrilla base had little to do with the Jiangxi Soviet and his troops were all recruited from local peasant families and the fiercely combative "mountain people"---the She minorities. The party central authorities only had a vague idea through government newspapers that there was some red guerrilla activities in this region. More remarkably, few of the leaders, including Ye, had any formal military training. They had learnt to fight guerrilla war not from the Soviet or the Whampoa Academy textbooks, but entirely through practice. Yet this base was maintained for five years and was perhaps the only guerrilla base that was built entirely by local party workers, largely free from outside interference as had often been common in many other communist base areas throughout the nation.

During the five years, only one attempt was made by Ye at cooperating with "Central Red Army" forces. These were Su Yu's remnants in nearby mountains. But Ye was soon disgusted with the overbearing "Central Red Army" officers under Su, who in turn tried to kidnap and kill Ye and take over his guerrilla command. This brief and disastrous encounter with Mao's Red Army ended with a bloody feud that would have a lasting impact on Ye for years to come.

As late as August 1937, Ye and his men were still engaging in constant skirmishes with the government troops. But they were shocked to read in newspapers captured after attacking a small town that the Party Central Committee had reached an agreement for cooperation with the government. Therefore, Ye hurriedly decided to negotiate with local government authorities. In December, Chen Yi's General Liaison Office in Nanchang finally managed to contact Ye and invited him to meet the New Fourth Army leaders such as Xiang and Chen for the first time.[18] The meeting turned out to be a fruitful one. Ye was destined to become one of the best generals under Chen's command.

All in all, there were twelve isolated guerrilla bases in existence in 1937. Although the total strength was at some 10,000, the red guerrillas had no more than 4,000 weapons at their disposal and most of these weapons were old models. This indicates the fact that the guerrillas hurriedly expanded their troops in great numbers only after the Central Committee's call for cooperating with the government.[19]

One of the direct results of negotiations between the communists and the government was the release of a large number of former Red Army prisoners of war. Since the red guerrilla forces lacked training and discipline, these former Red Army officers became invaluable assets for the party. Upon their release, most of them were immediately assigned to the New Fourth Army headquarters. Among them, the most valuable were

The Origins of the New Fourth Army 43

the former members of Zhang Guotao's *Er-Yu-Wan* Red Army. After the Mao-Zhang falling-out during the Long March, they were dispatched to conquer the northwestern province of Gansu, an operation aimed at setting up a new Soviet regime. But it ended disastrously. Thousands Red Army soldiers were rounded up by the government-affiliated Muslim cavalry men. Most had perished in the deserts. Many were captured by the enemy. Another group of the POWs were from Su Yu's suicide army that tried to divert the government attention away from the Long March and was destroyed in 1935 in northeastern Jiangxi. The most important was a small, trusted group of senior Red Army officers belonging to the "Central Red Army" under Mao. They were sent directly by the Party Central Committee in Yanan to reinforce the New Fourth Army leadership. They, together with the former POWs became an important outside component of the New Fourth Army.

Therefore, the New Fourth Army consisted of a hodgepodge of people from various places and backgrounds. Ridden with factionalism (it was aptly called "mountain-toppism") and provincialism, it was a very difficult army to lead. But the majority of these people did share something in common: a general apathy towards "Zhong Yang"---the Party Central Committee in Yanan. This was a new Central Committee. For the first time in the party's history, it began to fall under the tight control of a single man---Mao Zedong, who previously had occupied much lesser status within the party. This apathy derived above all from the fact that they were mostly abandoned by the defeatist Central Committee in 1934.

To be sure, the New Fourth Army leaders were staunchly communist. But this does not follow that they were comfortable with a new Central Committee which they knew very little about and from which they had got little help therefrom for several years. Few of the top leaders of the New Fourth Army had got along with Mao in the past. Xiang Ying and Chen Yi both knew Mao's character very well and quarreled with him constantly throughout their earlier career. Xiang Ying was Mao's boss in the Jiangxi Soviet as head of both the government and the party before the arrival of other Central Committee heavy-weights, including Zhou Enlai, and later the "Moscow Returnees." Xiang had always been disgusted with Mao's style and ruthlessness. Mao in turn was determined to make sure that Xiang's power at the new army would be curbed. In one instance, Xiang demanded that he be privy to the decision of selecting all officers sent by Yanan to the New Fourth Army. Mao rejected his proposal offhand.[20]

Chen Yi was Mao's equal and colleague in the Jinggang Mountains base area. Having replaced Mao's position twice, Chen had never regained Mao's full trust. Mao was widely known in the Jiangxi years as being cruel, narrow, petulant and revenge-minded. General Huang Kecheng, a communist insider, daringly recalled many years later that, even though he and the other Red Army officers in Jiangxi recognized that "Mao was often wise in his political judgment," his personal character was "a far cry" from that of the more honest and open-minded Zhu De, the Red Army commander in chief. Mao trusted those who were subservient to him. Sycophants were assigned important duties no matter what the qualification they had. Li Shaojiu, the dreadful chief executioner in internal purges during the Anti-AB Clique campaign was just one of the numerous examples. But to suppress his opponents, Huang added, Mao was "relentless and decisive." Thus in addition to the role played by the "Moscow Returnees" who had demoted Mao several times in Jiangxi, Huang Kecheng believed that Mao's personal character also contributed to his own downfall in the Jiangxi Soviet's later years, for he was hated by the Red Army rank and file because of his role in radical land policy as well as mass internal murders.[21]

By the end of 1937, Mao held, as the result of the Zunyi Conference in 1935, almost the undisputed leadership position within the party. Although the party general secretary's position remained in the hands of Luo Fu (Zhang Wentian), a "Muscovite," Mao obtained the chairmanship of the Party Central Military Committee, through which he could exert *de facto* control over decision-making process. Hence, the reign of "Chairman Mao" period truly began. This was a different Party Central Committee. Ironically, at the same time the Chinese Communist Party started to enter the period of Stalinization in terms of one-man dictatorship, it also became Sinicized as a result of Mao's penchant for fierce party independence and freedom of action from the Communist International in Moscow. Never before in its history, had the party had one man enjoying such an undisputed authority. It was hard enough for the communist rank and file in Yanan to comprehend, not to mention those who were a thousand miles away such as Xiang and Chen.

Even some top leaders at Yanan doubted at the time that the Chinese Communist Party had finally discovered a Stalin in any one person. Nor would Stalin himself relish this notion. In an interesting letter to Luo Fu, the party general secretary, on March 4, 1937, Politburo member Liu Shaoqi stated that, "I remember Comrade Wassiliev[22] told us [in Moscow] before we departed for China, 'the Chinese Communist Party does not have a Stalin yet. It cannot independently lead the revolution without the help from the Communist International.' The experience of the last few years indicates that Wassiliev was right. We do not have a Chinese Stalin, anyone who wants to become one is doomed to failure."[23] Although Liu would later become one of the leading Mao cronies in the process of creating a Chinese Stalin, he would have to pay with his life for it, suffering the same fate as other Stalin cronies in Moscow. He would be

The Origins of the New Fourth Army   45

brutally purged and tortured to death. Liu's turn would come, however, in 1967.[24]

Throughout the last two months of 1937, the communist Yangzi River Bureau had engaged in tough negotiations with the government over every detail of the new army. Chiang Kai-shek personally summoned General Ye Ting to Nanjing, telling him flatly that he would not appoint key officers based solely on the communist list. He warned Ye pointedly that "You are not a communist, your life will be in danger in the future."[25] But the communists refused to budge an inch on key personnel issues. In retaliation, Chiang in early January of 1938 granted an exceedingly low rate of monthly expenses for the New Fourth Army, a rate usual for maintaining one C-rank government division. Moreover, Chiang firmly refused to allow the new army to join forces with the communist Eighth Route Army in the north. Instead, he placed it directly under the control of the government Third War Zone commanded by his protege, General Gu Zhutong. Xiang reported to Yanan in January that the funds he had received could hardly accommodate the need for food, not to mention the purchase of weapons.[26] Despite the difficulties, Xiang Ying's organizational skill, preeminent since his early career as a trade union leader, proved to be remarkable and indispensable. Within a short period of three months, Xiang was able to assemble some 13,000 troops from various mountain bases. From January to March 1938, the scattered guerrillas were finally concentrated at Yansi, a small scenic town in southern Anhui province where the New Fourth Army headquarters were temporarily located. Lacking modern communication and transportation means, many troops simply marched on foot to Anhui.

After the concentration, problems began to mount day by day. The number one problem for this new army was its factionalism or "mountain-toppism" derived from geographical origins. The new force at a strength of ten thousand were divided into four columns, three of the columns commanded two regiments each, but Gao Jingting's three thousand men were given three regiments plus a handgun unit. Moreover, Gao's troops were the only column allowed to stay where they were and did not need to come to Yansi for training sessions.

At the outset, the efforts to dilute geographical loyalty were not successful. Many key members of the guerrilla troops were immediately sent to Yanan for extended "study" sessions at the central party school known as the Anti-Japanese Military and Political School (*Kang Da*). But the Yanan communist headquarters quickly found it hard to break up geographical affiliations when reorganization process started. Regional leaders seemed to resist any such attempt while the rank and file were not receptive to any outside leadership. In order to maintain control of the troops and to prevent massive desertion, the regiments were eventually formed more or less along geographical lines. The guerrillas from Fujian province consisted the largest group, four of the nine regiments were Fujianese, a fact that Fujianese communist veterans were most proud of.[27] The second largest group were Gao Jingting's Hubei-Henan-Anhui force. The four columns were designated as follows: the First Column were mostly from guerrillas in Hunan and Jiangxi, which included the force under Chen Yi and Xiang Ying. Chen naturally became its commander. The second and third columns were mostly Fujianese. But Su Yu's small troops from southern Zhejiang were combined with the Second Column with Su as its deputy commander, subordinate to Fujianese commander Zhang Dingcheng. Tan Zhenlin's western and northern Fujianese troops formed main part of the Third Column. But Ye Fei's eastern Fujian guerrilla troops were able to retain integrity as a single regimental unit --- the soon-to-be legendary Sixth Regiment of the Third Column. Gao Jingting's troops consisted of the entire Fourth Column with three regiments of their own. This regionally based troop formation was to have profound impact upon the character, troop cohesion and battle spirit of the New Fourth Army for years to come. While it certainly retained "mountain-toppism," it also, ironically, promoted fierce competition among the regional commanders and units.

The second problem for the new army was its lack of discipline and military training. The guerrilla members had seldom slept under roofs for years, or to use Xiang Ying's word, they had "said goodbye to houses since 1934."[28] Formal military training such as early morning drill, tactical exercise and sharp-shooting sessions became a dreadful routine that was extremely hard for these hard-boiled "red bandits" to adjust. The Party Central Committee sent a group of outsiders---the former Red Army officers from Yanan to redress the guerrillarism and to help regularize this poorly trained army. Since they were mostly chosen from Zhang Guotao's *Er-Yu-Wan* forces, these officers were heavily influenced by military professionalism promoted by Zhang and his top commanders who were graduates from the Whampoa Academy. Throughout the Red Army years, these officers had acquired a reputation of being the best Red Army soldiers familiar with mobile warfare and professional training.

The tension between the outsiders and region-based guerrilla troops developed almost immediately. Accustomed to regular warfare and strict discipline, the former regular Red Army officers were disgusted with guerrillarism prevalent in the New Fourth Army. Moreover, they had never been enthusiastic about the job in the first place. Many held their personal grudges against this assignment. Most of these officers would have preferred to work in the better trained Eighth Route Army in the north. Their *Er-Yu-Wan* comrades had staffed one of the three elite divisions of the Eighth Route Army---the 129th Division, which would become Deng Xiaoping's original power base, for Deng was its chief political officer. But upon their release from the government jails, there was no place for them in the 129th Division. The New Fourth Army in the meantime had a severe shortage of supply in the officer corps. This unpleasant assignment became inevitable. Worse still, the small troop strength of the new army could not accommodate their previous ranks. Thus almost all the former Red Army officers were in fact demoted from the positions they had previously held under Zhang Guotao to work for this poorly trained irregular mess in the south.

These officers were further hit hard when in April 1938, their beloved "Chairman Zhang (Guotao)" defected to the government side, when taking the opportunity of participating in a rather archaic ritual of worshiping the "Yellow Emperor" of prehistoric China. The Party Central Committee's response to the somewhat rebellious attitude of the former Red Army officers was swift and ruthless. One of the noted cases reflecting widespread dissatisfaction involved a hard-boiled Red Army officer named Ye Daozhi. Disgruntled about his demotion and the new job, Ye decided to go back to Yanan to join his old buddies in the north. To set an example, Xiang Ying was authorized to execute him on the spot. The execution was based on the most severe accusation of "counterrevolutionary betrayal," not simple desertion (It was not until forty years later, Ye Daozhi's execution was declared a mistake by the Central Committee). Very soon, these newly arrived outsiders were silenced.[29]

But the rank and file of the new army remained wary of these seasoned officers because they often appeared to be strict and arrogant. The New Fourth Army was manned by an overwhelming number of southern China's peasant guerrilla soldiers. They did not understand their trainers' dialects, hated the early morning drill, and felt uncomfortable with their overbearing demeanor. An interesting case involved Wu Kun, a former Red Army officer whose dislike of the job was complicated by his infatuation with a young New Fourth Army recruit. The young girl took care of him aboard the same ship when they were traveling together to the headquarters. Wu had a severe case of nausea. Wu considered this as love, showering the girl with dinners and cash. Upon arrival, Wu was severely rebuked in person by Xiang Ying. He was demoted from a division commander post when under Zhang Guotao to deputy commander of Ye Fei's sixth regiment from eastern Fujian. A Sichuan native, Wu's encounter with the Fujianese soldiers was difficult. The soldiers simply called Wu and the other outsiders "two-voices," meaning they could not speak the Fujianese dialect. The regiment commander Ye Fei was bombarded by complaints from both sides day after day. It took a long time for Wu and the outsiders to gain respect from the rank and file. But these hard boiled former Red Army officers were very impressive once at the front. They appeared to be true warriors and afraid of nothing.[30] A year later the unfortunate Wu would, however, seek his own reckless death to release himself from the psychological complex caused by love and job stress.[31] In an internal report dated March 16, Xiang Ying pointed out that guerrillarism, desertion, and poor training were among the most urgent issues facing the new army.[32]

The third, and more subtle problem concerned relationship with the government. From the very beginning, the cooperation between the government and the communists was on a very fragile basis. After ten years of bloody civil war, the mutual distrust and hatred were understandably deeply-rooted. The central issue was whether or not the communists should be able to maintain independent command of their troops during the war against Japan. Chiang Kai-shek had made it very clear that any troops that failed to obey government orders would be considered rebellious. But he had only one leverage over the communists: the reduction of government financial and material supplies.

The communist leadership itself had split on this issue. On the one hand, the Muscovites led by Wang Ming, head of the Yangzi River Bureau, advocated unified command with the government. Wang, a Politburo member, was more than just a regional party bureau chief. He was a member of the Comintern Executive whose authority, theoretically at least, went beyond that of the Chinese Communist Party's Central Committee. At the outset, Mao's attitude was unequivocal. He would never allow the United Front to hinder communist expansion. In northern China, the communist-controlled Eighth Route Army was establishing numerous base areas ostensibly for the purpose of fighting Japan. By 1938, the Eighth Route Army had expanded by 500 percent in actual strength. In his personal interview with General Ye Ting, Chiang Kai-shek complained bitterly that the Eighth Route Army even refused to let government officers make roll calls. Chiang stated that he would not repeat the same mistake with the New Fourth Army.[33] Chiang's concern was not totally without foundation.

With no restrictions in the north, Mao preferred that the Eighth Route Army should only perform the function of "strategic support" to the government forces in the war against Japan. After a spectacular yet costly ambush commanded by Lin Biao against the Japanese troops at Pingxingguan, Mao decided to stop this practice. To conserve the troop strength, Mao chose to avoid costly frontal engagement with the Japanese as long as the communist territorial expansion could be legitimately carried out. In September 1937, Mao wrote several instructions to Peng Dehuai, the Deputy Commander of the Eighth Route Army, urging him to explain to the government the communist strategy of avoiding "hard battles." Mao stressed the need for relying on mountain terrains to survive. He told Peng who was a fanatic for mobile war that he had better "not be nostalgic about the past [i.e., the regular war during the Red Army years]." Since, Mao continued, the number one task was to mobilize the masses, "concentrating troops for war is not compatible with the task of mass mobilization." Euphorically, Mao defined his strategy for troop conservation as "independent mountain guerrilla warfare."[34] To Mao, the Second United Front was doomed to failure.

But Wang Ming would have nothing of this. He had good reason to take most of the credit concerning the establishment of the Second United Front, which was after all first proposed by the Communist International. His contribution was duly acknowledged by a Politburo resolution dated December 13, 1937. It stated, "We ... think that the Chinese delegation [to the Comintern] led by Comrade Wang Ming and under the leadership of Comrade Dimitrov [the Comintern leader] ... have provided extremely important help in setting up the new policy about the anti-Japanese United Front."[35]

Two weeks after this resolution, Wang published an important article titled, "The Key to Saving the Current Situation." According to Wang, "some people" from both Kuomintang and the communist parties had misunderstood the United Front. First, they "have forgotten the simplest truth---whoever fight the Japanese are our friends and the vice versa." Second, they "do not understand the fact that the weakening of the other party in the United Front will weaken themselves, too." Third, one should abandon the widely held view that "The failure of the anti-Japanese war will mean the Japanese control of China. But the victory of this war will mean the communist Soviet's control of China." According to Wang, a complete victory of the communist party was not possible. In conclusion, Wang proposed that every effort should be made to maintain the unification of the country and the military forces.[36]

There is hardly any doubt that Wang's view ran counter to that of Mao's. Wang's article was not just for public consumption. At a December Politburo meeting, Wang declared a policy of "everything should go through the United Front," a policy seconded by Stalin who was cautious not to alienate Chiang Kai-shek. It should be noted that Wang's attitude was shared by many top leaders historically associated with Moscow, such as Bo Gu and Xiang Ying. Even Zhou Enlai was a fan of the United Front. At a Politburo meeting, Wang told the participants that the Comintern was not happy about the Chinese Communist Party's over-emphasis on independence and guerrilla war. Zhou seconded his view, stating that the penchant for expanding communist influence everywhere would hinder the work of the United Front.[37]

From the very beginning, Zhou and his colleagues at the Yangzi River Bureau also differed with Mao on the military strategy which the reorganized communist troops should adopt. Zhou Enlai, Zhu De and Peng Dehuai seemed to lean toward the view that the main communist forces must engage the Japanese actively through combined tactics of mobile and guerrilla war. They believed that the communists could bear main strategic task of fighting Japan. But Mao insisted on playing the "supporting role" based on unflinching guerrilla tactics alone. As a result, Zhou often found it hard to convince Chiang of the sincerity about the United Front on the communist side.[38]

Although somewhat isolated, Mao had manipulated skillfully Lo Fu's figure-head party leader position to rally support at the top. In particular, he was able to obtain staunch support from a key Politburo member, Liu Shaoqi. As early as in May 1937, Liu, in an internal speech, explicitly expressed the view that the success or failure of the United Front would depend on who was in charge of the war against Japan. According to Liu, if the Bourgeois class, referring to the power base of the government, should control the United Front, it would be impossible for a complete victory against Japan. Moreover, the struggle with the Bourgeois class "remains not only complicated, but also cruel." Yet "for the moment there is no need for picking up weapons to start a fight."[39] Like Mao, Liu was preoccupied with incessant conflict with the government. The Liu-Mao partnership had already started at this time, even though Liu was still unsure of Mao's qualification to become a Chinese Stalin. It was natural that Mao would soon choose Liu to be his hatchetman to destroy another Politburo member whose loyalty was always in question. The target was none other than the United Front-prone Xiang Ying at the helm of the New Fourth Army.

But Mao's preferred policy for relentless territorial expansion did not work well because of the different reality in the south. The status of the New Fourth Army was quite different from that of the Eighth Route Army in the north, for the New Fourth Army was very much restrained in its freedom of action by the agreement with the government. In the first place, the area of operation was clearly specified and limited. At the time the New Fourth Army was assembled at the mountain resort town Yansi, the Japanese had already conquered numerous cities in the Yangzi Valley where the communist operation zone was designated. In other words, to expand, the New Fourth Army had to operate within the enemy zone in the Yangzi plains. They enjoyed no such luxury as the Eighth Route Army did to be able to stay in the mountains.

Secondly, by mutual agreement, the New Fourth Army did not fall under the commanding system of the Eighth Route Army as Mao and the top communist leaders would have hoped. After many rounds of difficult bargaining, the government rejected the communist proposal of combining the two command systems. Therefore, it fell under the command of the government Third War Zone whose headquarters were in Jiangxi, with the exception of Gao Jingting's Fourth Column, which was put under the jurisdiction of the government Fifth War Zone headquarters in Anhui. Thus nominally at least, the New Fourth Army was a separate military unit, equal in status with Mao's Eighth Route Army command. Its decision-making process was far more complicated than the simple fulfillment of party directives. As a result, the New Fourth Army leadership would often be caught between the excessive demands made by the expansionist Mao and the need for abiding by the original agreement with the government in order to maintain the existence of the United Front. It would turn out, however, to be an impossible position between the devil and the deep sea. The conflict between Mao's Central Committee who knew little about the conditions in the south and the New Fourth Army high command was inevitable.

Thirdly, the possibility of an internal conflict within the Communist Party was further increased by the fact that the top man in charge was Xiang Ying, who had never been Mao's political favorite. The first hostile encounter between Xiang and Mao was over the Futian Mutiny in 1931. Xiang, as Mao's boss, deliberately toned down the significance of the mutiny which openly advocated "Down With Mao Zedong." Mao had not trusted him since. Under the circumstances, Chen Yi's attitude became critical from Mao's point of view. It was unfortunate that Chen was frequently caught between Mao and Xiang. On the one hand, he was generally in agreement with Mao as far as the durability of the United Front was concerned. Mao was not sincere about the Second United Front from the very beginning. This vision was echoed by some New Fourth Army leaders as well. Chen Yi, for example, was more skeptical than Xiang Ying about cooperation with the government. This was clearly reflected in a poem written shortly before the Ganzhou negotiations in 1937, in which he was determined "never to become another Chen Duxiu."[40] Chen Duxiu was the first party general secretary whose excessive reliance on cooperation with the Kuomintang was believed to have cost the Communist Party a great deal in 1927, when Chiang turned his troops against the unprepared communists.

On the other hand, Chen found it hard to stab his colleague and a dear friend in the back. Together they had endured the harshest conditions in life. Chen's official position was commander of the First Column at 2,300 in strength. But within the party, he was deputy secretary of the military committee of the New Fourth Army, a position that put him at the top leadership echelon where he could not avoid making a clear position concerning the Mao-Xiang dispute. Yet, because of their conflict during the Red Army years, Mao was also concerned about Chen's loyalty. It seemed that Mao was always keen to know Chen's activities.

Through Zhou Zikun, deputy chief of staff of the New Fourth Army who was sent directly from Yanan, Mao learnt occasionally what Chen was up to and apparently paid intense attention to it.[41]

Under the circumstances, since the method, policy and key personnel involving the formation of the New Fourth Army were largely beyond Mao's direct control, the leadership under Xiang Ying was at the outset treated somewhat like an illegitimate child by Mao's Central Committee. It is thus not surprising that, as soon as the New Fourth Army started operations, a struggle for decision-making power would erupt. In a few months, a major conflict indeed came to a head, ostensibly over strategic differences. The Xiang-Mao dispute involved all the factors ranging from personal dislike to fundamental views of the New Fourth Army's expansionary strategies. This conflict, which would affect many critical decisions, was to be kept smoldering for the next few years. In the end, Mao was able to undercut Xiang's power and personal authority at the new army. Xiang Ying was no match to Mao's scheming character and he lacked ruthlessness and decisiveness. Predictably, the Xiang-Mao dispute would end with tragedy for this veteran communist leader and the final control by Mao of the New Fourth Army affairs in 1941.

Notes

1.*Biography of Chen Yi* (Official), p.180-181.
2. *WJXJ*, vol.11, p.300-304.
3.*Biography of Chen Yi* (Jiang), p.427-428.
4. *Xin Wen Bao* (The News), September 30, 1937, Shanghai.
5. *WJXJ*, vol. 11, p.362-364.
6. Ma, Hongwu et al, *Xin Si Jun Zheng Tu Ji Shi* (A Chronology of Events Related to the New Fourth Army, Nanjing 1988), p.23. According to Jin, Chongji, Zhou did meet General Ye Ting in August 1937 and tried to persuade him to "participate in guerrilla organization." This contact was not authorized by the Central Committee. There was no evidence that Ye was formally asked to command all guerrilla troops in southern China during this meeting. See, *Biography of Zhou Enlai*, p.438.
7. Ye, Fei et al, *Xin Si Jun Can Kao Zi Liao* (Reference Materials of the New Fourth Army, Beijing 1992), vol.2, p.39.
8. Ye, Fei et al, *Xin Si Jun Wen Xian* (Documents of the New Fourth Army, Beijing 1988) p.53.
9. Chen, Xing, *Xin Si Jun Dan Sheng Shi Shi Kao Zheng* (A Study on the Birth of the New Fourth Army), in *Da Jiang Nan Bei Magazine* (Shanghai 1992), vol.42, p.50.
10. Ye, Fei et al, *Documents of the New Fourth Army*, p.58 and p.60.

11. Ma et al, op. ct., p.24.
12. *Biography of Chen Yi* (Official), p.184-185. See also Chen, Pixian, *Three-year Guerrilla War in Southern Jiangxi*, p.140-141.
13. The Dong people in Hunan often preferred to hide their ethnic identities. Su did not admit his identity until his death in 1984.
14. For detail, see Jiang, Weiqing et al, *Tan Zhenlin Zhuan* (Biography of Tan Zhenlin, Hangzhou 1992), Chapter 6.
15. Zhang Guotao, Chen Yi's colleague in Beijing in 1925, had been head of the Er-Yu-Wan Soviet and a chief contender for power with Mao during the Long March. For the Central Committee's resolution on Zhang, see *WJXJ*, vol.11, p.164-168.
16. Ye, Fei et al, *Xin Si Jun Hui Yi Shi Liao* (A Collection of Memoirs of the New Fourth Army, Beijing 1990), vol.1, p.13.
17. Wang, Fuyi, *Xin Si Jun Shi Jian Ren Wu Lu* (The New Fourth Army: Personnel and Events, Shanghai 1988), p.414.
18. For detail, see Ye, Fei, *Ye Fei Hui Yi Lu* (Memoirs of Ye Fei, Beijing 1988), Chapters 1 to 4.
19. Ye et al, *A Collection of Memoirs of the New Fourth Army*, vol.1, p.1-2.
20. Ye et al, *Documents of the New Fourth Army*, vol.1, p.88.
21. A Comintern leader.
22. Huang Kecheng, *Memoirs of Huang Kecheng*, vol.1, p.165-166.
23. Liu Shaoqi to Luo Fu, March 4, 1937, *WJXJ*, vol.11, p.817.
24. In 1967, Liu was tortured to death after being stripped of his position as President of the People's Republic of China.
25. Duan, Yusheng et al, *Ye Ting Jiang Jun Zhuan* (Biography of General Ye Ting, Beijing 1989), p.276.
26. Ye et al, *Documents of the New Fourth Army*, vol.1, p.71.
27. Interview with a Fujianese general in Nanjing, August 1994.
28. Wang, Fuyi, *Brief Biography of Xiang Ying*, p.131.
29. For detail of this case, see Cui, Xianghua et al, *Tao Yong Jiang Jun Zhuan* (Biography of General Tao Yong, Beijing 1989), Chapter 1.
30. Ye Fei's Sixth Regiment was to develop into the legendary First Regiment under Chen's command. For this period, see *Memoirs of Ye Fei*, p.98-104.
31. Wang, Yugeng, *Chang Jiang de Nu Er---Ji Nian Yang Ruinian*, in *Da Jiang Nan Bei Magazine*, vol.37, p.4-14. The late Madame Wang was Ye Fei's wife. In Ye's own memoirs, he chose not to mention this unhappy episode.
32. Ye et al, *Documents of the New Fourth Army*, vol.1, p.84-85.
33. Duan et al, *Biography of General Ye Ting*, op. ct., p.276.
34. *WJXJ*, vol.11, p.338-340.
35. Ibid., p.402.

36. Ibid., p.826-834.
37. A few years later, Zhou admitted that he was wrong to support Wang Ming. See Jin, *Biography of Zhou Enlai*, p.422-423.
38. Ibid., p.336-337.
39. Liu, Shaoqi, *Liu Shaoqi Xuan Ji* (Selected Works of Liu Shaoqi, Beijing 1981), vol.1, p.72-79.
40. *Complete Collection of Chen Yi's Poems*, p.53.
41. *Biography of Chen Yi* (Jiang), p.447-448.

Chapter Three

Strategies of Expansion

The New Fourth Army was officially under the command of the Third War Zone of the National Government. After the concentration and intensive training, Xiang and Chen decided to start their activities to the mountainous border area of Zhejiang, Anhui and Jiangsu where it would be safer for the troops. Chen was Deputy Party Secretary of the New Fourth Army Military Committee headed by Xiang, and thus was in effect second in command within the party.[1] It turned out that Mao would have nothing of this. In a telegram to Xiang and Chen dated February 15, 1938, Mao pointed out that the best place for the communist expansion was in southern Jiangsu Province and instructed them to move the main force there to establish a base in *Maoshan*(the Mao Mountain). Southern Jiangsu was the enemy zone where the Japanese had been active and well fortified. Moreover, it was in the Yangzi Valley plains, a terrain hardly suitable for hiding the troops. The so-called Mao Mountain specified by Mao was, as Chen Yi would discover later, nothing more than a barren hill, no mountain or thick forest to speak of.

More importantly, the New Fourth Army's operation in the enemy zone would have to obtain government approval. Therefore, Xiang was somewhat reluctant to follow Mao's order, but he agreed to send a "reconnaissance column" to the area designated by Mao. Led by Su Yu, this small unit consisted partly of the troops under Chen and Su's command, i.e., the First and the Second Columns of the New Fourth Army. Su's small-scale operation went smoothly.

But Mao's appetite was getting bigger after reading reports that the government did not interfere with Su's reconnaissance unit. On May 4, 1938, Mao wrote a personal letter to Xiang, making his point more clearly that the true purpose of this operation should be to avoid collaboration with the government Third War Zone. According to Mao, although guerrilla activities in the enemy zone could be difficult, it would still be better than working together with the government and putting the New Fourth Army under its command. Therefore, "After the reconnaissance, main force should follow .... Once you reach there, you will have total freedom [to expand]." More importantly, Mao at this time had already begun to consider the possibility of expanding into the forbidden area north of the Yangzi River, as he suggested splitting one part of the main force to cross the Yangzi River into northern Jiangsu.[2]

Xiang had, however, no intention whatsoever of following Mao's directive to move his main force there. He considered guerrilla warfare in the plains suicidal. Meanwhile Xiang was also pressured by the Third War Zone command under the nationalist general, Gu Zhutong, to move his troops in the same direction to engage the Japanese. So he argued with Mao that this was exactly what the government wanted, since the Third War Zone could "use the Japanese knife to kill us."[3] Realizing Xiang's objection, another directive from Mao arrived ten days later. This time it was signed by the party secretariat, the powerful organ handling day to day party affairs. It stated forcefully that it would be "extremely convenient for our guerrilla activities and the setting-up of guerrilla bases within the enemy zone," because the possibility to expand in the plains instead of mountains was much stronger. It further pointed out the fundamental principle that the New Fourth Army was to expand "in any place where the government troops dare not enter." More significantly, it stressed for the second time the need to move north of the Yangzi River in Jiangsu.[4] In effect, this directive called for blatant violation of the agreement with the government, which had already specified areas of operation for the New Fourth Army in southern Jiangsu.

Chen Yi was impressed by this strategy. Unlike Xiang, Chen had no illusion about the United Front. Determined not to become another Chen Duxiu, as he wrote in 1937, he felt that the enemy zone was the only place where the New Fourth Army could compete with the government troops. Loathing the dilemma of being caught in the middle of the unfolding Mao-Xiang dispute, he volunteered to lead his First Column into southern Jiangsu to establish, as was ordered by the party secretariat, a guerrilla base in Maoshan. In June 1938 his column and Su Yu's reconnaissance unit met in Lishui, not far from Nanjing. A few days later they organized the first ambush of the Japanese at Wei Gang near the city of Zhenjiang. Although a small battle which succeeded in killing thirteen Japanese soldiers and destroying four trucks, it was widely publicized to be the first communist battle against Japan in Jiangsu. Nonetheless it was important for local residents who had been angered by government troops' inaction for a long time after the spectacular resistance in 1932 near

Shanghai. Southern Jiangsu was one of the most prosperous areas in China. The population saw little incentive in accepting any communist ideology. It was not like poverty-ridden Jiangxi, where the communists were able to build a strong base. During the early 1930s, at the peak of the communist base-building fervor, only one such attempt was made by the communists in this area and it failed miserably. Chen quickly recognized the fact of lacking popular support and decided at the outset to adopt a moderate policy concerning land reforms in communist-dominated areas.

The Japanese were in a favorable geographical position. They controlled railways and water transportation routes through the Yangzi River, the Grand Canal and numerous lakes in southern Jiangsu. Their defense lines were also facilitated by close distances between cities. Chen's base in Maoshan was therefore a small "isolated island." According to Chen, the only possibility for him to hold on to this base would be "popular support" (*Ren He*), in order to destroy the "geographical advantage" (*Di Li*) enjoyed by the Japanese enemy.[5] Arriving at Maoshan, Chen immediately started busy socializing activities. The most important targets were local business and political luminaries. One of the top businessmen in this area was Ji Zhengang, who owned a major tea production and trading company. Chen sent one of his top aides to work Ji. In his instructions, Chen foresaw three possible options. First and the best would be the acceptance by Ji of the communist-sponsored position as head of the local anti-Japanese association. If this did not work, Chen hoped for the second best result, which was to win Ji's material support behind the scenes, while allowing him to appease the Japanese ostensibly. The worst option was to prepare for eliminating Ji if he should decide to work for the Japanese. Chen believed that the demise of Ji would achieve nothing for his consolidation at Maoshan.

Fortunately, Chen's second best option was realized. Ji set a precedent for active covert collaboration between the New Fourth Army and the local business community in the Yangzi Valley. The supplies obtained through the local business community proved to be crucial for Chen to hold on to his isolated base. More importantly, such close cooperation helped reduce popular fear about the communists whose reputation was all but tarnished during the 1930s. Years later, Chen considered the success in winning over Ji's support to be "a crucial chess move."[6]

A more complicated issue was the existence of numerous guerrilla troops in southern Jiangsu. Some were directly related to the government, some were plainly bandits, but more were secret societies who had taken the opportunity to fill a power vacuum left by both the Japanese and the government. There were self-appointed "commanders" everywhere. To expand into these territories, Chen had to make *ad hoc* arrangement to avoid harassment by these irregulars. But there were opportunities, too. Because of the complicated origins and affiliations of these local forces, the government usually turned a blind eye to their activities.

Among these self-appointed "commanders" was a man called Guan Wenwei. Guan was an ex-communist who had been imprisoned by the government for years. Out of jail only recently, he returned home in Dan Yang of southern Jiangsu Province and organized a local self-defense force against the Japanese. Guan was a southern Jiangsu native, whose father was a local luminary. After learning about Guan's background, Chen immediately made an effort to contact him and persuaded him to work for the New Fourth Army. Guan's cooperation was critical for Chen's expansion plan, since, according to the agreement with the Third War Zone, the New Fourth Army was given a sixty-square-kilometer area for their activities in southern Jiangsu. But the government had no way to exert control over various native forces such as that of Guan's. After a lengthy conversation, Chen re-admitted Guan into the party and sent his best men to work in Guan's native troops.

Since the previous Central Committee directives had urged Chen to move to north of the Yangzi River where the power vacuum had not been filled yet, Chen instructed Guan's troops to occupy Yangzhong, an island critically located in the middle of the river, rich in resources. Guan at once organized an attack on the local irregulars who controlled the island. Chen was thus guaranteed a strategic springboard between the south and the north of the river.

Another opportunity for bypassing government observation came when another self-defense force active near Shanghai began to contact with Chen's headquarters. Although less reliable, since the leaders of this force were wavering between the government and the communists, Chen managed to persuade them at the end of 1938 to accept reorganization into a communist-affiliated column called "Anti-Japanese Braves of Southern Yangzi River" (*Jiang Kang*). This force also proved to be an important instrument for Chen's expansion plan in southern Jiangsu.

On both accounts, Chen had in fact violated the agreement with the Third War Zone. Even the New Fourth Army headquarters thought it had gone too far. Xiang Ying in particular criticized Chen's actions, calling it "manpowerism, weaponism, and moneyism."[7] Xiang was, of course, afraid of provoking a violent government reaction. But Chen's activities seemed to gain support with the Party Central Committee in Yanan. In October 1938, the Central Committee held an important conference which provided Mao with an opportunity to settle scores with the Muscovites Wang Ming and Bo Gu. The debates were so fierce that the conference lasted over a month. In a major speech, Mao elevated guerrilla warfare to the level of communist party's long-term strategy to compete with the government for national leadership role in the future. According to Mao, the war against Japan was a "protracted war," similar to the prolonged trench warfare of the *Entente*'s Western Front during World War I. The policy advocated by Wang Ming was labeled "right-wing surrenderism." Mao criticized severely Wang's "Everything through the United Front" policy.[8] It was critical once again that Zhou Enlai turned about to support Mao. The result of the conference was disastrous for the Muscovites. The Yangzi River Bureau, Wang's power base, was abolished. The Politburo set up instead three regional bureaus, the Central Plains, the Southern and the Southeastern. Mao's trusted aide Liu Shaoqi was dispatched to central China to take over the Central Plains Bureau in charge of the northern Yangzi River party and military activities. But the Southern Bureau was only given the area of Guangdong, Guangxi and the other southern provinces, no longer being responsible for the affairs of the New Fourth Army. The original Southeastern Sub-bureau under the dissolved Yangzi River Bureau was expanded into Southeastern Bureau, with Xiang still at its helm. But it was clear that Xiang's power had been curbed, for he had to compete with Liu's Central Plains Bureau whose turf overlapped that of Xiang's in Jiangsu. The Muscovites had by this time, of course, lost all the control over the New Fourth Army activities.[9]

After the Yanan conference, Zhou Enlai was dispatched to the New Fourth Army headquarters which had now been moved to a place called Cloud Hill (*Yun Ling*) in southern Anhui. Zhou's mission had two objectives. On the one hand, he had to explain to his one time protege Xiang Ying the new policy which was aimed at active expansion in spite of violating the agreement with the government. On the other, Zhou tried to solve the tension which had been building up between Xiang and General Ye Ting, who, as an outsider of the party, had been constantly ignored by Xiang since the founding of the new army to which Ye was its *de jure* commander.

The personal dislike between the two was so intense that General Ye had tendered resignation twice by early 1939.[10] The first time was in June 1938. Ye complained to Zhou Enlai in person that he wished to establish a committee to which he would be a member to participate in decision-making process. The actual decision-making was usually done through Xiang's party committee to which Ye was barred from attending. Yanan immediately agreed. But the tension did not subside easily. The Central Committee had long expected this tension and sent a veteran communist officer named Li Yimang to serve as buffer between the two, but Li apparently did not know how to do this job.[11] Having little say at the headquarters because he was not a party member, Ye spent most of his time taking scenic photographs, hunting, partaking gourmet meals and reading books. Xiang was a strict working-class party functionary. He could not stand Ye's proud show-off of his well-cut lieutenant general uniform and ownership of a private kitchen for exquisite Cantonese dinner parties. But the conflict went beyond personality differences.

Xiang did not trust Ye also because the commander appeared to support more aggressive operations in Jiangsu. At this time, Xiang had a strategy of his own. He was not averse to expansion of the New Fourth Army, but this must be done within his control, and in the place he considered having the best chance to succeed. Slowly developed for some time, Xiang's strategy was to bank on the scenario that the Japanese might soon move southward to the Zhejiang and Jiangxi area. If this should occur, he could bring the bulk of his troops into the high mountains in order to avoid what he had considered to be the dangerous adventure in the Yangzi Valley plains. Despite the fact that he had allowed a small force under Chen Yi to go to southern Jiangsu, he always insisted on the need for guarding his base in the mountains so as to buy time and to conserve his main forces. In a personal letter to Chen Yi dated June 23, 1939, Xiang confided to his friend the thought that he intended to build a long-term base area in southern Anhui, because, "If future war conditions should change, we can expand from this base ... into the mountains ... therefore the main force should not move [to Jiangsu]." Apparently Xiang's idea, later labeled the "Southern Strategy," ran counter to Mao's eastern and northern expansion strategies.[12] This waiting strategy was to cost him dearly two years later, since the Japanese would not strike to the south as Xiang had expected. Instead, they concentrated their strategy in northern China. Jiangsu for the moment was as far south as the Japanese would go.

Zhou Enlai arrived at Cloud Hill, the New Fourth Army headquarters, in February 1939. After lengthy debates with Xiang, Zhou was able to work out a fixed strategy with the New Fourth Army leadership: "Consolidate in the south, fight in the east and expand in the north." Although this strategy has long been hailed to be brilliant by the Chinese communist official historiography, it appeared rather vague at the time, because it did not demolish Xiang's "Southern Strategy" altogether. Nevertheless it stressed the preferred priority: to expand in the north and the east, both in the Jiangsu territory. Strategically it was meant to link up with the Eighth Route Army in the north, since Mao had always expected armed conflicts within the Second United Front. Should another civil strife start, the two communist troops would be placed in a favorable position for crucial strategic coordination. Xiang accepted this strategy only halfheartedly. Chen participated in these deliberations and was of course delighted, since this would mean the further expansion of his power base and the increase of the troops at his disposal in Jiangsu.

While at the headquarters, Chen's personal life was also changed. After years of bachelor life, he was quickly infatuated with a seventeen-year old girl, a new recruit from Wuhan. Her named was Zhang Qian. Pretty and well-educated, Zhang was also very talented in acting. The guerrilla leaders were by this time all in their late thirties or early forties. Few had the opportunity to settle down to raise families because of the extreme hardship they had endured in the past few years. Chen had married twice but none of the marriages lasted. His first wife committed suicide, scared by Mao's purge campaign. His second wife simply disappeared after the Long March. Now that the New Fourth Army life became relatively stable, and with a constant flow into the headquarters of patriotic students, the blood of these hard-boiled former guerrilla leaders was set aboil. All were overawed by elegant city girls whom they had no chance even of meeting in the past. But, in order to avoid chaos, girl-chasing was reserved for the middle-aged veterans. No one under twenty-five, with less than eight years with the communist cause and below the regimental rank, according to an unwritten rule[13], was allowed to fall in love and marry. Only top leaders in the Party Central Committee enjoyed unrestrained privileges in this area. One unrecorded purpose for Zhou Enlai's mission at Cloud Hill was to scout pretty southern, urban girls, who were remarkably short in supply in the backwater of Shaanxi Yellow Earth Plateau. Ostensibly they were to be recruited to "work" for top leaders.[14]

Most guerrilla leaders with peasant or coolie background knew nothing about romance and modern urban culture. Thus the permitted massive girl-chasing activities at Cloud Hill often bordered on farce. In one instance, Tan Zhenlin, a Jinggang Mountains veteran and the commander of the Third Column, expressed his unrequited affection for a pretty Shanghai girl. To help him succeed, the girl's comrades simply forced a date by somehow locking him and her up in a straw hut.[15] The well-educated Chen Yi adopted a far more subtle approach. He was rejected by Zhang Qian several times. Fresh from a big city, Zhang was appalled at being chased relentlessly by a thirty-eight-year old man who had married twice. Chen used all the charm embedded in his French literature training by sending poems and pictures, and eventually captured the girl's heart. One passionate poem declared,"I am dazzled by the spring light [you emit], I am ashamed to be a commander of an elite unit. Where is my courage, I am defeated by a girl and don't even know it."[16]

Chen's deputy commander Su Yu was less fortunate. His target was a teenage girl from Jiangsu who had thrown Su's love letter and personal snap shot straight into the trash can. The thin-skinned Su did not know what to do. Eventually the party organization found a way to transfer the girl to work for Su, but she remained uninterested in his marriage proposal. Su was patient enough to wait for three years before his unrequited love was finally answered.[17] The party often interfered to ensure the success by providing extra incentives. Among them were good job assignments, the promise of fast admission into the party or a promotion, and extra supplies of food. In fact, the Party Central Committee at the time had a special policy to provide twenty-six top leaders with extra ration of eggs, chicken, meat, sugar and other nutritious food. Xiang Ying, Chen Yi and Tan Zhenlin were among them.[18]

Returning to Jiangsu, Chen immediately began to carry out Zhou's strategic plan to move to the east and the north. Neither direction had been authorized by the government. The Japanese troops in southern Jiangsu were largely on defensive. Tokyo at this time was preoccupied with taking central China and the city of Wuhan. According to Chen's observation, the lack of Japanese troops in this area rendered any large-scale "mopping-up" (*Sao Dang*) campaign against the communist forces impossible. Therefore the communists could seize the opportunity to expand in a vast territory both in the east and the north.[19]

In the east, the area near Shanghai, the situation was becoming severe. The native "Anti-Japanese Braves of Southern Yangzi River" which had been reorganized by Chen at the end of 1938 began to tilt toward the government. Chen decided to send a regular New Fourth Army unit into that area. His choice was the Sixth Regiment under Ye Fei. This was the regiment that had the strong troop cohesion and less internal conflict, for they were almost all the original guerrilla members in eastern Fujian communist base. Largely free from the brutal internal purges that had been common in the other Soviet bases, there was little legacy of lasting wounds that remained unhealed since the Red Army days.

Chen acquired this regiment only by accident. In October 1938, Xiang Ying decided to pull one elite regiment under Chen's command back to southern Anhui. In replacement, he sent to Maoshan Ye Fei's troops which at the time belonged to Tan Zhenlin's Third Column. But Chen soon fell in love with this regiment and was greatly impressed by its toughness and ability to endure any hardships. In an affectionate letter to Ye's regiment shortly before the latter's departure for the new task in the east, Chen praised them to be the toughest survivors, "Smoking tea-leaves, having two meals a day and wearing cotton wool instead of shoes ... yet you are able to maintain low desertion rate and good discipline ......"[20]

At the end of May 1939, Ye's regiment was ready and was instructed by Chen to move eastwards in disguise as part of the local "Anti-Japanese Braves." For the purpose of deceiving the government Third War Zone, the mission was a top secret one. Ye Fei and his other commanders even changed their names. Ye called himself "Ye Chen." The day before their departure, Chen Yi received Xiang's urgent telegram from the headquarters

Strategies of Expansion

at Cloud Hill, ordering him to cancel this mission on two grounds; one, it would be a blatant violation of the agreement with the government; two, it was too dangerous for a whole regiment to move to Shanghai area right under the Japanese nose. Chen immediately summoned Ye who was all set to go, asking him whether or not he could guarantee success, Ye replied affirmatively. Chen decided to disobey Xiang's order. This was the first open split between the two erstwhile guerrilla colleagues.[21]

Ye's mission turned out to be a very successful one. Within three months, their manpower and weapons were expanded several times over. The weapons were mostly captured during battles with Japanese puppet forces and the government-supported guerrilla forces. It was remarkable that this mission succeeded without leaking its true identity. Both the Japanese and the Third War Zone had no idea that this was a regular New Fourth Army unit until much later.

However, Shanghai was too important for the Japanese to ignore. Ye even attacked a Japanese airport at Hongqiao, the close suburbs of Shanghai, which caused great alarm on the enemy's part. The government troops also began to pay attention to this area. After a while, however, Ye's position was becoming increasingly more difficult, because he had to fight constant battles with the Japanese, the government-supported forces and the local pro-government guerrillas. Under the circumstances, Chen decided to withdraw Ye's regiment from the east and gave it another important assignment, to move northward across the Yangzi River. In order to deceive the government again, since the expansion into northern Jiangsu was also forbidden, Ye's troops were combined with Guan Wenwei's native guerrillas that had been reorganized by Chen a few months earlier and stationed at Yangzhong island. This time Ye assumed the name of "Nie Yang," and the troops maintained the title of Guan's guerrilla force known to the government, "the Anti-Japanese Advanced Column (*Ting Zong*)."

The "Northern Strategy" was part of the overall strategy decided by the Communist Central Committee to expand the New Fourth Army power base. The Japanese paid little attention to the area north of the Yangzi River, not only because it was poor, but also because it was strategically insignificant. Japan's main concern was south of the Yangzi River in order to defend Nanjing, Shanghai and the transportation network. Northern Jiangsu was close to none of these. As a result of this neglect, even Chiang Kai-shek was able to maintain an official Jiangsu provincial government and a regular army there. Moreover, there was a pro-government guerrilla force at thirty thousand in strength. Commanded by Li Mingyang and Li Changjiang, known as "Two Lis," this force was only nominally under government control. The Jiangsu provincial governor was General Han Deqin, a Whampoa Academy graduate and

Chiang Kai-shek's protege, who controlled some seventy thousand regular army troops. While none of these forces were keen to engage the Japanese, they had their own share of conflict over local taxes, military supplies and territories of control. With the help of the communist leaders born in northern Jiangsu, Chen analyzed the situation carefully and designed a strategy for Ye Fei's advancing troops, "Fight the Japanese, befriend Two Lis, and isolate Han [Deqin] (*Ji Di, Lian Li, Gu Han*)."[22] This strategy was consistent with the Central Committee's intention of taking north Jiangsu away from the government in order to prepare for strategically linking up with the communist Eighth Route Army in the north.

As early as in April 1939, the Party Central Committee's secretariat had decided to beef up the expansionary efforts in Jiangsu by establishing a Northern Yangzi River Headquarters in central China and transferred several Eighth Route Army units to that area. In a directive dated April 21, it suggested that Xiang or Chen leave the New Fourth Army and take over the new command. Both apparently refused and did not report to work at the new post.[23]

The tension between the Central Committee and Xiang Ying continued to build up throughout the year of 1939. Chen was again caught in the middle. On the one hand, he was interested in expanding into northern Jiangsu, a move consented by Xiang so long as it was under his control. On the other, Chen disagreed with Xiang's "Southern Strategy" aimed at retreating to the mountains. Determined to stay out of the conflict, he focused on political maneuver in northern Jiangsu where he was at his best.

Meanwhile the tension within the Second United Front also became high. At first, armed clashes between the government and the Eighth Route Army escalated in northern China. The largest of such skirmishes ended with over four hundred communist casualties. In fact, since the founding of the fragile Second United Front, sporadic civil fighting had never really stopped throughout China. Euphorically called "friction (*Mo Ca*)" instead of the "civil war," these bloody armed conflicts between the government and the communists were the natural extension of the deeply rooted antagonism that had evolved over a decade. Chen's expansion into northern Jiangsu would expectedly trigger another round of major "friction." In order to secure Two Lis' neutrality in the event a major conflict between the government and the communists should occur, Chen went to see them three times in person. The Two Lis had their own problems. Not taken seriously by Governor Han Deqin, their troops were poorly equipped and always short of supplies. To test Chen's sincerity in cooperation, they secretly asked Chen to help smuggle a large quantity of ammunition obtained through private channels. The escort mission required a dangerous crossing of the enemy zones. Chen jumped at this request and immediately organized a unit commanded by Zhang Daoyong, a brave former Red Army officer under Zhang Guotao, to carry out this mission. Like Ye Fei, Zhang changed his name to Tao Yong for deceptive purposes. Tao crossed the Yangzi River with the Two Lis' blessing. After having successfully completed the task, Tao Yong's troops were instructed to stay in the northern Yangzi River area so that Chen now had two regular units at his disposal in an area he had been forbidden to enter in the first place.

Alarmed by these developments, Chiang Kai-shek decided to focus his attention on Jiangsu. In September 1939, he summoned Governor Han Deqin to Chongqing, the wartime capital, and instructed him to prevent at all cost the New Fourth Army from moving into northern Jiangsu. At this time, Chen still maintained his command in the south of the Yangzi River. The force under Su Yu's Second Column had joined Chen to set up a "South of the Yangzi River Headquarters," with Su as Chen's deputy. The Chen-Su partnership proved critical in the career of both and lasted until the communist victory over Chiang Kai-shek in 1949. Su by this time had already shown his talent as a military genius, but he was not adroit in internal and external politics, an area where Chen had a long and hard experience.

In January 1940, Yanan formally rebuffed Xiang's idea of pulling more troops in southern Jiangsu back to southern Anhui. Frustrated with Xiang's unwillingness to beef up Chen Yi's efforts in his expansion in Jiangsu, Mao pointed out the fact that Xiang seemed to be backing away from the fixed strategy of expansion agreed upon between him and Zhou Enlai. But Mao did not reject Xiang's "Southern Strategy" altogether. According to Mao, whether or not the main troops of the New Fourth Army would retreat to the south (i.e., the mountains) or to the north, it would have to depend upon overall relationship between the government and the communists. If the government should decide to eliminate the communists on a national scale, Xiang's "Southern Strategy" may become sensible. But if Chiang were only to attempt at limiting the communist area of operation, then "we must seek control of the north of the Yangzi River," leaving the south to Chiang.[24] Mao's directive, though unequivocal as to the strategy of northern expansion, was rather vague concerning the validity of Xiang's "Southern Strategy," thus Xiang was given considerable room for maneuver.

Chen had his own reason to support Mao's northern expansion plan. Sensing the Party Central Committee's intention to undermine the authority exerted by the New Fourth Army leadership, Chen hoped that Xiang may be persuaded to give up southern Anhui and to move his troops and headquarters to southern Jiangsu so that their long time partnership would still count in the eyes of the Central Committee in Yanan. Together they could have enough troops to expand further into the north. Like Xiang, Chen was not keen to see the New Fourth Army leadership taken over directly by the Central Committee, as it had become obvious that Liu Shaoqi's Central Plains Bureau had already undermined Xiang's authority. Whenever he had a chance to visit Xiang at Cloud Hill, Chen would take advantage of their intimate relationship to persuade him. Xiang was known to be an excessively strict, no-nonsense type. Few people could get close to him. Chen was said to be the only person besides Xiang's wife who could sleep in one room with him. At first, Xiang got interested in Chen's plan. For example, he sent the commander of the Third Column, Tan Zhenlin, under the pseudonym "Lin Jun," to organize southern Jiangsu guerrilla units to help consolidate Chen's power base. But as soon as the information had reached him that Chiang Kai-shek was determined to shift the focus of his anti-communist activities to Jiangsu, Xiang began to hesitate.

Seeing no future in Xiang's cause, Chen began pondering the shift of his loyalty. In March 1940, after learning Xiang's final decision not to move his headquarters to southern Jiangsu, Chen formally requested direct radio communication between him and the Party Central Committee, which would give him the opportunity to report to Yanan behind Xiang's back. In April, Chen formally suggested to Yanan the advantage of moving Xiang's headquarters to Jiangsu. The split between the two friends became inevitable.

To undercut Xiang's power, the Central Committee had sent Liu Shaoqi to Anhui to organize the Central Plains Bureau. But Liu's power went beyond that of a regional bureau chief. A member of the Politburo and the soon-to-be member of its powerful secretariat---the top decision-making organ, Liu doubled his capacity as chief official representative of the Central Committee to inspect the Yangzi Valley party works, thus his appointment had taken much of the authority exerted by Xiang at Cloud Hill. Like Mao, Liu never believed in the Second United Front. The purpose of Liu's mission soon became obvious. At the first Central Plains Bureau meeting in November, 1939, Liu secretly criticized Xiang's "surrenderism." But Liu had few troop units under his control. In January 1940 he sent a wire to Xiang, asking for two elite regiments to be sent to the north of the Yangzi River. Feeling his turf directly threatened, Xiang refused point-blank. In reply, Xiang pointed out that Chen Yi's plan was more sensible, i.e., to consolidate in southern Jiangsu and to seek opportunities from there to expand into the north. He would not accept Liu's request of transferring troops directly to his command. "We cannot," Xiang stressed, "follow your instruction."[26] Knowing fully well that Liu had intended to undercut his power, Xiang made a counter-proposal to

Yanan, arguing for withdrawing his best troops in Jiangsu to strengthen the headquarters in southern Anhui. The dormant feud between Mao and Xiang quickly came to a head. A few days later, the party secretariat sent Xiang a directive. Although the language was mild, it amounted to a sever reprimand. Dated January 19, 1940, it stated, "The New Fourth Army northern strategy has already been decided by the Sixth Party Plenum, and Zhou Enlai was able to secure ... this strategy at your headquarters. Whether or not [your] southern expansion plan can be carried out will depend on circumstances." Moreover, "Our expansion will incur friction, but only if we expand our power, can we consolidate ourselves." In conclusion, it rejected Xiang's suggestion of retrenchment and the proposal to bring the best units in Jiangsu back to the headquarters at Cloud Hill. Furthermore, it explicitly demanded "Chen Yi should make efforts to expand into northern Jiangsu."[27]

The communists had by this time set up three categories of people that required different policy recipes. The "enemy" (*Di*) usually meant the Japanese with whom no compromise was possible. The "stubborn" (*Wan*) elements referred to the anti-communist elements within Chiang's government. The last category was "friends" (*You*), who ranked from the Two Lis to bandits and various other secret societies, as long as their attitude toward the communists remained friendly. Mao's major concern was the "stubborn" elements. In March 1940, Mao specified a military and political strategy in destroying this category, the principle of *"You Li, You Li, You Jie."* According to Mao, first "we must have an explainable reason to fight them." Second "we must be able to win." And the third "we must know when to stop."[28] At the same time, Mao demanded that the New Fourth Army expand without concern of the government reaction, for any violent action on Chiang's part against the communist expansion could be interpreted as being prompted by the second, the "stubborn" category within the government. In a rather bizarre instruction, Mao's fantasy went further when he told the chief political director of the New Fourth Army, Yuan Guoping, to expand the current number of troops from 10,000 to 250,000 within one year. He was confident that all this could be achieved without destroying the effort to "develop the United Front."[29]

Realizing that he could not possibly achieve that figure within a year, Mao decided to send a regular brigade under the Eighth Route Army's 115th Division to Jiangsu to beef up the New Fourth Army. With these decisions made in the first half of 1940, the communist high command began to prepare for provincial governor Han Deqin's demise in Jiangsu. The purpose was to eliminate all government influence in northern Jiangsu, until the strategic connection between the Eighth Route Army and the New Fourth Army was made. Such a bold and provocative strategy would inevitably trigger a major crisis for the United Front. Mao was well aware of the possibility that the "stubborn" elements of the government might attack Xiang Ying's headquarters in retaliation for any clash between Han Deqin and the communist forces in Jiangsu. Thus Mao instructed Xiang once again to prepare for moving his headquarters to join Chen Yi.

No longer counting on reinforcements from Xiang, Chen decided to move his own headquarters in southern Jiangsu to the north of the Yangzi River. In the meantime, an incident of "friction" between the government and the communists brought out a conflict between Chen Yi and Liu Shaoqi. Since Liu's arrival, the Communist-Government relations in the north of the Yangzi River had deteriorated rapidly as a result of Liu's aggressive policy. So far Chen had adopted a relatively moderate land policy and had refrained from setting up unauthorized local administrations in Jiangsu. Liu considered this moderation somewhat "right-leaning." He had always been keen to establish local governments in "enemy's rear" in order to collect taxes and to experiment with communist economic policies.[30] Liu was responsible for appointing a first county magistrate in eastern Anhui Province without the provincial governor's approval. The government considered such actions intolerable. The clash with the government started almost immediately. At Ban Ta, a small town on the border of Anhui and Jiangsu, the government forces under Han Deqin in mid-March 1940 surrounded a communist regiment under Liu's command. The besieged also included many leading party functionaries. Although this was Liu Shaoqi's turf, Chen agreed, under Liu's heavy pressure, to send his best troops under Ye Fei and Tao Yong to relieve Ban Ta. The mission was very successful. The government troops were repelled at a heavy loss.

Liu was more than impressed by Chen's top units, especially the Fujianese soldiers under Ye Fei. Liu summoned Ye to his study after the battle, and at once put his cards on the table. As a relatively junior officer, Ye was especially overwhelmed to receive such treatment when Liu only allowed his top deputy Deng Zihui to attend the meeting. The secret conversation lasted about two hours. According to Ye, Liu explicitly pointed out Xiang Ying's "mistakes," calling him a coward. Liu even showed Ye some top secret wires between Xiang and the Party Central Committee, assuring Ye that the party leadership would settle account with Xiang later, though not for the time being. Ye was apparently shaken by the thought that the Central Committee may have considered Chen Yi to be "right-leaning," too, since Chen was his direct superior. But Liu put him at ease by relating the differences between Xiang and Chen. More importantly, Liu told Ye that the Central Committee had decided to "solve the northern Jiangsu problem" by eliminating Han Deqin's power, and put this area under the exclusive communist control. But, Liu continued, "We could not actively attack Han, which would put us at disadvantage in front of the public opinion." The best strategy was to lure Han into attacking the New Fourth Army, so the latter could preplan a tactical pocket to wipe out Han's troops in one decisive blow. The reason he summoned Ye, Liu explained, was to ask him to carry out a secret mission: to seek an opportunity to entice Han to attack his troops. Ye hesitated, declaring that he had only two regiments, while Han had a hundred thousand best-equipped soldiers. Liu insisted that Ye need to hold on to his position for only a week, "after one week, the success or failure will not be your responsibility." Liu claimed that he would need one week to organize major shock troops to reinforce Ye's position.[31]

It is clear that the communist central authorities by this time were well prepared for a civil war in northern Jiangsu. It is also important to notice that Liu had some doubts about Chen, since he did not convey his idea directly to Chen in southern Jiangsu and there is ample evidence that Ye was instructed to keep this mission secret from both Xiang and Chen.

After the Battle of Ban Ta, Ye's troops should naturally return to Chen's command in Jiangsu. But Liu was not sure that this force would continue to obey him after its return. Ye's troops had already acquired a reputation of being among the best New Fourth Army units in terms of morale, equipment, tactics and discipline. Having had its first experience in a special warfare at Ban Ta, for this was a counter-siege mobile war that most of the New Fourth Army units had not yet been exposed to, Ye would be uniquely fitted into Liu's overall scheme to provoke Governor Han Deqin. Under the circumstances, Liu decided to rip this unit and the unit under Tao Yong away from Chen. Ye was of course placed in an embarrassing position.

Throughout April, Chen and Liu argued vehemently through telegrams over the fate of Ye and Tao. The wire skirmishes became so tense that Liu and Chen had to bring their case to the Party Central Committee in Yanan for a final judgment. Yanan at first decided to support Liu, as it had always done, but Chen's case was inadvertently saved by Xiang Ying. The government Third War Zone by now had learnt that Ye and Tao's troops in northern Jiangsu were not local guerrillas but the regular New Fourth Army units, they therefore had violated the original agreement concerning the designated areas of operation. Chiang vehemently demanded that Ye and Tao withdraw back to southern Anhui. Xiang seized this godsend opportunity to request the same, for he had long been keen to have them back since 1938. Under the circumstances, Yanan decided after long deliberations to allow Ye and Tao to return to Chen's command. It was apparently one stone killing two birds. On the one hand, it could avoid an open conflict between Liu and Xiang, since Xiang had rejected Liu's similar troop request earlier in the year. On the other, the return of the Ye-Tao units back to Chen in Jiangsu would continue undermining Xiang's "Southern Strategy."[32]

Having thus solved this dispute, Yanan issued an important directive on May 4, 1940. Known as the "Second May Fourth Directive" to distinguish it from the first one issued on May 4 of 1938.[33] This was by far the most explicit instruction criticizing Xiang's performance. Drafted by Mao himself, it pointed out that, first, "expansion means operating beyond the Kuomintang-imposed restraints;" second, "we must stress struggle instead of compromise" in dealing with the government since the "stubborn" elements were trying to "guard against, restrain and oppose" the Communist Party. Without the stress on conflict, "we may commit extremely severe mistakes," as Chen Duxiu did in 1927. Thus the New Fourth Army needed to expand in Jiangsu "all the way to the China Sea." It also accused Xiang for having "lost opportunity to expand."[34]

To reinforce the New Fourth Army's overall strategy of taking over northern Jiangsu, Yanan had ordered guerrillas under Li Xiannian to control part of Hubei Province, the communist guerrillas in Shandong to move southward, and several irregular Eighth Route Army units under Peng Xuefeng to expand into the north of the Huai River. The most important step was the decision to transfer into the area under Liu Shaoqi's control twenty thousand elite regular troops of the Eighth Route Army, formerly belonging to Lin Biao's 115th Division. Led by Huang Kecheng, this special task force was ordered to prepare for moving directly into northern Jiangsu.

Thus by the spring of 1940, a large-scale armed conflict between the government and the communists in Jiangsu seemed unavoidable. But in northern Jiangsu, there were only two communist regular units---Ye and Tao's troops. Chen could not persuade Xiang to move the bulk of the New Fourth Army forces to southern Jiangsu, so he decided in June to move his remaining troops at the south of the river to the north as well. He had married Zhang Qian in February. To cover his real intention, he sent his new bride to befriend the local government generals whose headquarters belonged to the Third War Zone. But the government commander, General Leng Xin, soon found out that Chen was preparing to move his command to the north. He immediately launched an attack in June on Chen's position at the southern bank of the river.

At the same time, the situation worsened north of the Yangzi River. In late June Ye Fei suddenly sent a urgent wire to Chen, saying that his troops were surrounded by forces commanded by the Two Lis, and who were ten times over Ye's strength. Chen was shocked, since he had worked the Two Lis for a long time, confident that they would stay neutral in case a conflict between the government and the communists should take place. The Two Lis, however, made the decision to attack Ye, not only because Ye had violated a mutual agreement by staying in an important village named Guo for an unauthorized period of time, but also because the opportunist Lis decided to seize the opportunity when Chen's headquarters south of the river was under siege and the chance for him to send reinforcements to Ye was very slim. Thus Ye's two regiments were considered easy prey. Caught between the enemy attacks on both sides, Chen ordered Ye not to engage the Two Lis under any circumstances, or at least before his arrival in person to talk to the Lis. But it was already too late.

After the Battle of Ban Ta, Ye's troops returned to Chen's command, but Chen knew neither of the conversation between Liu and Ye, nor the latter's secret task to lure Governor Han into a fight. Pressured by the Japanese and the puppet forces, Ye decided to find a safer place for an extended rest. The place he chose was Guo Village within the Two Lis' turf. The Lis initially agreed to let them stay for a short time, but Ye wanted to stay much longer. The elder Li was a cautious Kuomintang veteran, but his younger deputy was rather reckless. Prompted by subordinates who were vehemently anti-communist, they finally conspired to wipe out Ye's troops in order to prove their loyalty to the government. Seeing that Chen's troops in the south were under attack, the Lis prepared a surprise attack in the middle of the night. Chen sent three telegrams ordering Ye to give up the village, but Ye disobeyed, hoping that Governor Han Deqin might take the opportunity to join the attack so he could fulfill the task assigned by Liu Shaoqi. Militarily, Ye was confident. On the one hand, he had the support of Liu, who had promised that major reinforcements would come within a week. On the other, he was convinced that the Two Lis were not capable of fighting a prolonged battle. Their equipment was poor, training was bad and morale was generally low. Besides, unbeknownst to Chen, Ye knew that he could count on additional support from battlefield mutinies led by underground communist commanders who had been working within the Lis' forces. But some of Ye's subordinates were concerned about the decision to disobey Chen. During a meeting, Ye's chief of staff, Zhang Fan, warned Ye flatly that he should not engage in this "anti-party" activity. Ye had no choice but to disclose Liu's secret instruction. On June 29, however, Liu sent a wire to Ye, telling him that his reinforcements would not come at all. Ye had already embarked on the road of no return. In desperation, Ye demonstrated his enormous talent as a military commander during the siege battle. For days he was able to repel the Two Lis' nonstop attack wave. The Fujianese soldiers were tough and extraordinarily brave. Through active counterattack sorties and tenacious defense, Ye managed to hold on to his position until Tao Yong's troops sent by Chen arrived on the fourth day of the battle. Together they finally crushed the enemy. Chen was frustrated at Ye's apparent insubordination. He started crossing the Yangzi River with just a few bodyguards during the middle of the night of July 3. He hoped that his personal appearance would help persuade the two sides to stop the fighting. Hearing the persistent gun shots on his boat, Chen was convinced that Ye had been defeated by the overwhelming enemy force. In fact he even thought that Ye and his colleague Guan Wenwei were all dead, for he wrote down an emotional and poetic requiem titled, "In Memory of Guan and Ye."[35] While reaching the other side of the river, Chen was surprised to learn that Ye and Tao had managed to crush the enemy that was many times of their strength.

Arriving at the Guo Village, to Ye's surprise, Chen did not praise him but began reprimanding him severely and warning him never to do it again. Chen pointed out that Ye had "won the battle but lost a strategy"--- i.e., the strategy to obtain the Two Lis' neutrality in a future war with the real enemy target, Governor Han Deqin. Although Ye never agreed with this verdict, he was hard put to continue keeping his secret conversation with Liu Shaoqi from Chen. To rescue his relationship with the Lis, Chen immediately ordered Tao Yong who was keen on hot pursuit to stop at Taizhou city, the headquarters of the Lis. Ye was immediately ordered to give the village back to them.[36]

In July, Chen's deputy commander Su Yu led the remaining forces under the deactivated Southern Jiangsu Command across the Yangzi River to join Chen. Yanan in the meantime had made the decision to seek a decisive battle to eliminate Governor Han Deqin. To unify the command of all the forces under Chen and Su, the new headquarters were renamed "Northern Jiangsu Command" under the continued Chen-Su partnership. More importantly, this force was regularized for the first time, with a designated serial number for each unit. The purpose, of course, was to prepare for fighting large-scale mobile warfare. It was divided into three columns with two regiments each. A column was in fact a regularized unit equivalent to a brigade of the Eighth Route Army. Ye was appointed commander of the First Column, Tao commanded the Third, and Wang Bicheng, another seasoned soldier from Zhang Guotao's *Er-Yu-Wan* Red Army, who had performed very well in the south of the river under Su, commanded the Second. At seven thousand strong, this force was the best equipped within the New Fourth Army. Chen and Su had for the first time in their career acquired a force whose morale, cohesion and military talents of the commanding officers were unsurpassed by any of the troops they had led before. It would remain the elite troops, known as "Ye-Wang-Tao units," under their command throughout war against Japan and the subsequent civil war.

But the relationship between these commanders were not always easy. After the Battle of Guo Village against the Two Lis, someone in Ye's column had apparently reported to Chen about Ye's alleged accusation that Chen and Su were "opportunists." Worse still, it was leaked to Chen that it was also Liu Shaoqi's point of view. In one hot summer night, Chen invited Ye to his room to settle accounts. Chen was greatly angered at Liu's secret instruction over his head to the troops under his command. They stayed in bed, smoking and talking for the whole night. Fortunately, they were finally able to remove the misunderstandings and to his enormous delight, Chen learnt that Liu did not actually accuse him of pursuing right-leaning "opportunism." Liu considered that Chen and Xiang were quite different.[36]

The relationship between Ye Fei and Su Yu was even more complicated. In 1935, Su and Ye met for the first time in eastern Fujian after the disastrous defeat of Su's sacrificial troops to divert the enemy away from the escaping Party Central Committee. Ye was twenty-one, Su was twenty-eight. Su's remnants belonged to the regular "Central Red Army" in Jiangxi Soviet. Despite the humiliating defeat, Su and his colleagues showed considerable contempt for Ye's native guerrillas. The tension was immediately escalated when Su and his political commissar, Liu Ying, who was in charge of the party affairs, decided to take over Ye's command. Ye refused offhand. They broke off for a year. But one day in 1936, Ye was enticed by Su under a false pretense to a face to face meeting. Because of the mutual suspicion, they agreed to meet in a neutral place. At the dinner party, "after three rounds of drink," Su ordered Ye's arrest and tied him up with a bamboo stick inserted in his back. According to the Chinese tradition, such treatment indicated that Ye would be destined for execution. But on the way back to Su's headquarters, they encountered a government patrol unit. During the chaotic skirmish, Ye jumped off a cliff. He was only saved by a tree. This bitter experience Ye would of course never forget. The Su-Ye relationship was thus one of strange bedfellows. The mutual dislike seemed never to disappear. Although in a command-subordinate relationship, the two men were both exceptionally adroit in military strategy and tactics, and thus the competition was tense. Sometimes it would border on insubordination on Ye's part.

Tao Yong and Wang Bicheng were typical communist warriors; extraordinarily brave and sometimes even reckless. But, unlike Ye, they were far less adroit in internal politics. Ye came from an overseas Chinese family with a Filipino mother who spoke English. Tao and Wang were largely illiterate, coming from a poor peasant family background. Tao had a shepherd childhood. Wang's family could not afford to send him to obtain formal education. By comparison, Ye was well-educated, and over the years had developed elegant hobbies such as playing Go games and reading Clausewitz. Despite their differences, the troops under Chen and Su were formidable fighting forces, undoubtedly the best in the New Fourth Army. After a two-year experience of steady expansion and skillful political maneuver, Chen's newly regularized troops were thus well poised for planning the demise of Governor Han Deqin in northern Jiangsu to fulfill Mao's overall strategy of rapid expansion in this region.

Notes

1. Xiang and Chen to the Central Committee, see Ma et al, *The Chronology of Events of the New Fourth Army*, February 1938 listing.
2. This was known in the communist historiography as "The First May Fourth Directive." For details, see *WJXJ*, vol.11, p.511-512.
3. Xiang to Mao, quoted from *Biography of Chen Yi* (Official), p.188.
4. *WJXJ*, vol.514-515.
5. *Biography of Chen Yi* (Jiang), p.458-459.
6. Ibid., p.471-473.
7. *Biography of Chen Yi* (Official), p.204-206.
8. Mao, *Selected Works of Mao Zedong*, vol.2, p.215-216.
9. Jin, *Biography of Zhou Enlai*, p.424-426.
10. General Ye later recalled in a sarcastic poem, "Three years as Commander, I have tendered resignation four times." See Tong, Zhiqiang, *On Commander Ye Ting's Four Resignations*, in *Da Jiang Nan Bei Magazine*, vol.20, p.27.
11. Li, Yimang, *Mo Hu de Ying Pin---Li Yimang Hui Yi Lu* (The Fading Screens---Memoirs of Li Yimang, Beijing 1992), p.301-303.
12. Ye et al, *The Documents of the New Fourth Army*, vol.1, p.235.
13. The so-called "Er-Wu-Ba-Tuan (Twenty-five years old, eight years in the army and regimental commander level)" rule was widely implemented within the communist forces.
14. Interview with a female communist veteran's family in August 1994, Nanjing. One of her classmates was chosen to "work" for Ye Jianying. Ye was known as *Hua Shuai* (Flower Marshal), a nickname for his extraordinary sex drive.
15. For many similar stories, see *Wen Hui Yue Kan* (Literature Monthly, March 1988, Shanghai.
16. *Complete Collection of Chen Yi's Poems*, p.62.
17. *Su Yu and Chu Qing de Ai Qing Gu Shi* (The Love Story between Su Yu and Chu Qing [Mrs. Su Yu]), in *Dang Shi Wen Hui* (Literature of Party History), vol.9, Taiyuan 1994.
18. Jiang et al, *Biography of Tan Zhenlin*, p.186.

19. Chen, Yi, *Jian Chi Jiang Nan Kang Zhan de Zhu Wen Ti* (Several Issues of Maintaining the Anti-Japanese War in the South of the Yangzi River), in *Xin Si Jun Zai Maoshan* (The New Fourth Army at Maoshan, Nanjing 1982), p.8-9.
20. Chen, Yi, *Zhi Liang Tuan* (A Letter to Liang Regiment), in *Da Jiang Nan Bei Magazine*, vol.1, p.6. "Liang" was the internal name of Ye Fei's Sixth Regiment.
21. *Memoirs of Ye Fei*, p.121-122.
22. *Biography of Chen Yi* (Official), p.212.
23. *WJXJ*, vol.12, p.50-51.
24. Ibid., p.238-239.
25. Ding, Xing et al, *Xin Si Jun Ci Dian* (Encyclopedia of the New Fourth Army, Shanghai 1997)
26. *The Chronology of Events of the New Fourth Army*, the January 1940 listing.
27. *WJXJ*, vol.12, p.239.
28. Mao, *Mao Zedong Jun Shi Wen Ji* (The Military Works of Mao Zedong, Beijing 1992), vol. 2, p.521. Hereafter it will be referred to as MZDJSWJ.
29. Ibid., p.530.
30. *WJXJ*, vol.11, p.841.
31. *Memoirs of Ye Fei*, p.157-161.
32. Ibid., p.161-163. See also *Biography of Chen Yi* (Official), p.222-223.
33. See note 2.
34. For detail, see *Selected Works of Mao Zedong* (Beijing 1964), one volume edition, p.749-754.
35. *Memoirs of Ye Fei*, p.176-192. See also, Guan, Wenwei, *Guan Wenwei Hui Yi Lu* (Memoirs of Guan Wenwei, Beijing 1988), vol.2, p.50-52.
36. In his memoirs, Ye Fei still disputed with Chen's judgment on this event. See *Memoirs of Ye Fei*, p.192-200.
37. Ibid., p.212-217. See also, *Biography of Chen Yi* (Official), p.237.

Chapter Four

"Experts of Friction"

The government was preoccupied with control over the New Fourth Army activities. As early as in April 1939, the Kuomintang Central Committee issued a top secret instruction titled "Methods of Guarding Against the Alienated Political Party." According to this, the local government authorities should adopt strong measures to limit communist activities, even at the risk of "friction."[1] By March 1940, the government started active military engagement with the communists and had internally designated the New Fourth Army as "puppet troops." Chiang Kai-shek specified that the military task was to prevent the New Fourth Army from linking up with the "northern puppets"---the Eighth Route Army---and to eliminate them south of the Yangzi River.[2]

Compared with Liu Shaoqi, Chen Yi had not yet become a determined "expert of friction" (*Mo Ca Zhuan Jia*), a contemporary euphemism for those who were anxious and skillful in civil strife between the government and the communists. Chen's overall inclination was to avoid armed confrontation with the Third War Zone. But General Leng Xin, the government commander in southern Jiangsu, had forced him to make a decision through attacks on his headquarters south of the Yangzi River. Before moving to the north, Chen had not made up his mind whether or not to concentrate all his forces to seek a decisive battle with Governor Han Deqin. Still hoping to retain a base in the south of the Yangzi River, he made a last effort to entice Xiang to move his headquarters to join him in Jiangsu. In mid-May, Chen summoned Zeng Ruqing, a political officer in charge of mass mobilization at his headquarters. Chen demanded that Zeng remember his instructions by heart before embarking on a special mission to go to Cloud Hill in southern Anhui. Zeng was in a unique position to carry out this task. A former Red Army prisoner of war, Zeng was also a nephew of Zeng Shan who was one of Xiang's chief party deputies at the Southeastern Bureau. Chen trusted Zeng since, before joining Chen's command, Zeng had a rather checkered career at the New Fourth Army headquarters where he was also in charge of mass mobilization. Zeng had disobeyed Xiang's order during 1939, and violated an agreement with the Third War Zone in organizing an unauthorized guerrilla force based on local popular support. Zeng was on the wanted list by the government and scolded severely by Xiang. Chen heard the story and found a way to recruit Zeng to work for him, saying "this kind of people I need most."[3] Zeng's mission was to tell Xiang the details of Chen's plan for moving the New Fourth Army headquarters. As was expected, this last effort had no chance of succeeding. Xiang simply refused to consider Zeng's message, even though his uncle Zeng Shan may have been sympathetic to Chen's view.[4]

Squeezed by the government forces on both sides of the Yangzi River, Chen sent a wire to Yanan in June, expressing his final decision to pursue the strategy that had been suggested by Liu: to concentrate all his strength to crush Governor Han Deqin. It stated, "We are in a desperate situation, either we concentrate to crush Han in the north, or we focus on Leng in the south, I have decided to move to the north."[5] The question now became the place where Chen could seek a decisive battle with Han. After careful considerations, Chen and Su decided to move to Huangqiao, a town at the cross roads of four counties. It was easy to access and rich in food supplies and other resources. Liu Shaoqi disagreed. The main reason was that Liu did not understand the importance of securing the Two Lis' neutrality. He probably considered Chen's careful work on the Lis somewhat "right-leaning." After Ye Fei's battle against the Two Lis at the Guo Village, an operation that had Liu's personal blessing, Liu had practically written the Lis off. He preferred to provoke the Lis by deliberately entering their turf so as to urge them to combine forces with Governor Han. The communist troops could then wipe out the two troops together in one strike. Liu was also impatient with Chen's cautious approach aimed at winning local public opinion. In a directive to party organizations in northern Jiangsu dated in May, Liu ordered the expansion of troops to 10,000 within three months. This proved to be totally unrealistic.[6]

Chen's deputy commander Su Yu especially objected to Liu's idea on military grounds, since, unlike Huangqiao, the Lis' turf was too close to the Japanese. A confrontation with Governor Han and the Two Lis simultaneously might tempt the Japanese to take the opportunity to engage the communists in their rear. After considerable bickering between Liu and Chen in late July, Chen received a wire from Yanan, which confirmed the correctness of Liu's strategy to destroy Han. But it also agreed with Chen's idea of seeking battle at Huangqiao instead of the area preferred by Liu. More important, Chen was explicitly authorized to secure the Two Lis' neutrality before the battle against Han.[7] Hence Chen quickly made a secret deal with the Lis at the expenses of the Governor.

Chen's three columns began to move to Huangqiao immediately. As was prearranged, the Lis ordered their troops to open fire in the sky, pretending to engage the communists, and "chased" them all the way in the Huangqiao direction. It took just one night of battle for Chen to take over the town after crushing a small irregular government force stationed there. Chen's objective was to provoke Governor Han's attack, but Han must be made to appear in the wrong in front of public opinion. For this purpose, Chen took several clever steps. The first step was to engage the Japanese. In southern Jiangsu, Chen's force had already acquired a reputation of being able to challenge the Japanese in frequent skirmishes throughout the past two years. Although small in scale, these battles were designed to belittle the image of the government troops who, after a spectacular effort against the Japanese in 1937, had not done much to fight the enemy in this area. As soon as Chen arrived at Huangqiao, he reported to Yanan that he intended to demonstrate to the local population that his move to Huangqiao was purely for fighting the Japanese. He then quickly organized successful attacks on two Japanese strongholds.

Chen's second step was to publicly isolate Governor Han and to utilize all his talent as a consummate orator and deal-maker to mobilize the local gentry class behind him. The two most important local luminaries fell for his charm. One was a venerable former provincial governor, the other was an ex-military commander who had worked directly under Dr. Sun Yat-sen. Here Chen was at his best. His favorite activities included the exchange of classic poems with the local gentry class and engagement in Chinese chess or Go games. Chen's social skills worked so well that many gentry leaders volunteered to become buffers between Chen and Governor Han. Chen's highly publicized plea for peace usually found sympathetic echoes everywhere. Governor Han, as a result, was put on defensive and greatly outshone by Chen's dynamic personality.

Thirdly, Chen began to set up a local administration. His trusted former guerrilla colleague Chen Pixian and the Jiangsu native Guan Wenwei were put in charge of local administrative affairs. Within weeks, numerous local governments and associations were established. To postpone land reform, the communists started with a moderate reduction of rents, a policy that immediately became very popular. Mechanism to collect local taxes was also set up. Knowing all these activities were considered intolerable from Governor Han's point of view, Chen began to prepare for war quietly.

Han did not at first have a clear idea what kind of the communist troops he had to deal with. By numbers the Governor had at his disposal forces ten times that of Chen's. But he was handicapped by at least two factors: the absence of a unified command and the lack of a reliable intelligence source. In August 1940, Han secretly started transferring his troops to the area near Huangqiao, but his activities were quickly made known to Chen through undercover communists who worked for Han. One of them was Ji Fang, a senior government advisor working at Han's headquarters. Ji was a former lecturer at the Whampoa Academy and had known Han and most of his senior commanders as students. Through intimate conversations, Ji had detected that a mood to engage the communists was prevalent within Han's elite units.[8] It soon became clear to Chen that the actual number of troops which Governor Han had absolute control over were only some thirty thousand. The other semi-independent troops, those of the Two Lis', for example, had secretly decided either to maintain neutral or to sit on the fence to see how the coming battle would go before making a decision. Nevertheless, Governor Han still had an overwhelming numerical advantage over Chen's seven thousand forces.

At first, Chen had banked on the reinforcements from the Eighth Route Army from the north, as was originally promised by Mao. But in September when Han was adequately provoked and the communist troops under Chen were fully ready for the showdown, Mao suddenly sent a urgent wire, telling Chen the bad news that the Eighth Route Army could not arrive in time if Han should decide to launch attack in a few weeks. Furthermore, it stated, "The Eighth Route Army at this moment could only cooperate with the New Fourth Army strategically, not tactically [in actual battles]," therefore Chen had better "maintain a defensive strategy" to "repel" Han's attacks. Chen and Su were greatly disgruntled, since "repelling" would be meaningless for them. A defensive war of attrition against Han would be more costly in the long run, because of the numerical inferiority on Chen's side. Besides, troop morale was so high that they feared that a further delay might lose the momentum for war. After long and hard considerations, Chen and Su reported to Mao that they were determined to single-handedly carry out their original plan to wipe out Han's power in one decisive battle. They knew that the risks were high but the benefits could be high, too. Mao was not sure about the wisdom of this decision. In a telegram dated September 5, Mao urged again that Chen must maintain a defensive posture in order to "facilitate our public statements." Chen and Su replied that Han was determined to launch an attack within a week. They argued that Han "was afraid of the Eighth Route Army" in the north, but "looked down upon the New Fourth Army" in the south. Under the circumstances, Han "must be tempted to crack his southern front before turning northward."[9]

The key factor that gave Chen and Su confidence in defeating Governor Han was their success in securing the Two Lis' neutrality. In early September, Han imposed a grain blockade against Chen's troops at Huangqiao. In response, Chen ordered attack on Jiang Yan, a key government stronghold controlling the routes of grain transportation.[10] Since it was an active attack, it did not go well with public opinion. Han took the opportunity to demand that Chen give back Jiang Yan as a precondition for any peaceful negotiations. It was a clever strategy. Since the communists now depended on grain supply from Jiang Yan, Han calculated that Chen would never give it up, therefore he would be put in a righteous position to launch the long-planned attack on Huangqiao. After careful consideration, Chen decided to give Jiang Yan to the Two Lis. This counter-move proved to be one stone killing two birds. On the one hand, the Lis were nominally government forces who had legitimate rights to take it over and they had coveted the rich Jiang Yan for a long time. Their acquisition of Jiang Yan would therefore further guarantee their neutrality. On the other, Chen could publicize widely his painful concession made to the government and if Han should launch attack, Chen's well-designed active defense operation would be fully justified. To further promote the conflict between the Lis and Governor Han, Chen, during the process of transferring the possession of Jiang Yan, even suggested that the Lis extract a large sum of cash reward from Governor Han for the efforts of "taking back" this important stronghold.

In late September, Han made up his mind and amassed over thirty thousand troops for the attack. But he did not realize that the details of his attack plan had already been leaked by the Lis to Chen and Su. Han intended to attack Huangqiao with three advancing columns: the left, the right and the center. The Lis were supposed to cover Han on the right wing, another semi-independent, hence unreliable, local government force was to protect Han on the left. Han's main attack was at the center, which was to be launched by shock troops consisted of all the elite units under his personal control.

This was by far the largest civil strife since the founding of the Second United Front in 1937. Chen and Su designed a bold battle plan: firstly, they decided to use a small force, Tao Yong's column at less than two thousand in strength, to hold on to the town of Huangqiao; secondly, and most daringly, the bulk of the forces, i.e., the two columns under Ye Fei and Wang Bicheng, were to be deployed outside of the town to form a tactical pocket. This bold move was aimed at wiping out Han's central column without concerning about his left and the right wings, whose actions were expected to be lukewarm and ineffective. Such a strategy had derived above all from their confidence in the Two Lis' neutrality. As a result, Chen's numerical disadvantage would turn into an advantage in mobile warfare. Its surprise quality was totally unexpected from Han's point of view.

The Communist Central Committee in Yanan was by no means as confident as Chen and Su were. In a last minute effort to prevent what had been considered to be a premature clash, Yanan ordered Huang Kecheng's twenty thousand Eighth Route Army men to move southward as quickly as possible, and at the same time, it tried to avoid the showdown by telling Chiang's government "If Han does not attack Chen, Huang will not attack Han. If Han attacks, Huang will engage Han."[11] Chiang knew that this was just a wishful thinking since Huang Kecheng's troops could not possibly arrive in time to relieve Chen, as Han's battle plan would be in operation within a few days.

On October 3, Han's central column closed in at Huangqiao. After surrounding the town with one of his elite units, the 89th Army, Han ordered the immediate attack with the support of strong artillery fire. Although the New Fourth Army was not familiar with the infantry-artillery synchronized attack, Tao Yong's defense column was able to repel two major attack waves and he held his position until the next afternoon, when another of Han's shock troop units, the 6th Brigade arrived. This was Han's favorite unit known for its shining weapons, equipment and well-cut uniforms. Underestimating the communist capacity to fight, its commander, General Weng Da made a fatal mistake in forming a single column on the march. Ye Fei's First Column was hiding near Huangqiao and waited patiently for them to fall into its pocket. Ye had three thousand troops, equivalent to that of Han's 6th Brigade. The surprise attack was launched and was so swift that the snake-shaped marching troops were cut off in several pieces and wiped out in just a few hours. The 6th Brigade's flamboyant commander committed suicide.

The government shock troops surrounding Huangqiao, the 89th Army, quickly realized that the main communist forces were outside of the town. Its commander, General Li Shouwei, made a wise decision to launch fierce and nonstop attacks on Tao's defense, hoping to overcome it before the regrouping of Chen's columns to encircle them. This strategy was bold, since if they could take Huangqiao, Chen's three columns would be cut off from each other and the table would be quickly turned. More dangerous for Chen was the indication that the Lis might change their attitude, should Huangqiao fall. The Lis' neutrality was guaranteed only on the premise that Chen would win in the battleground. If not, they were in fact prepared for entering the war to share the glory of victory with Governor Han at any moment.

The government 89th Army fought a courageous battle, and at one point broke into the downtown of Huangqiao. Tao's defense was tough

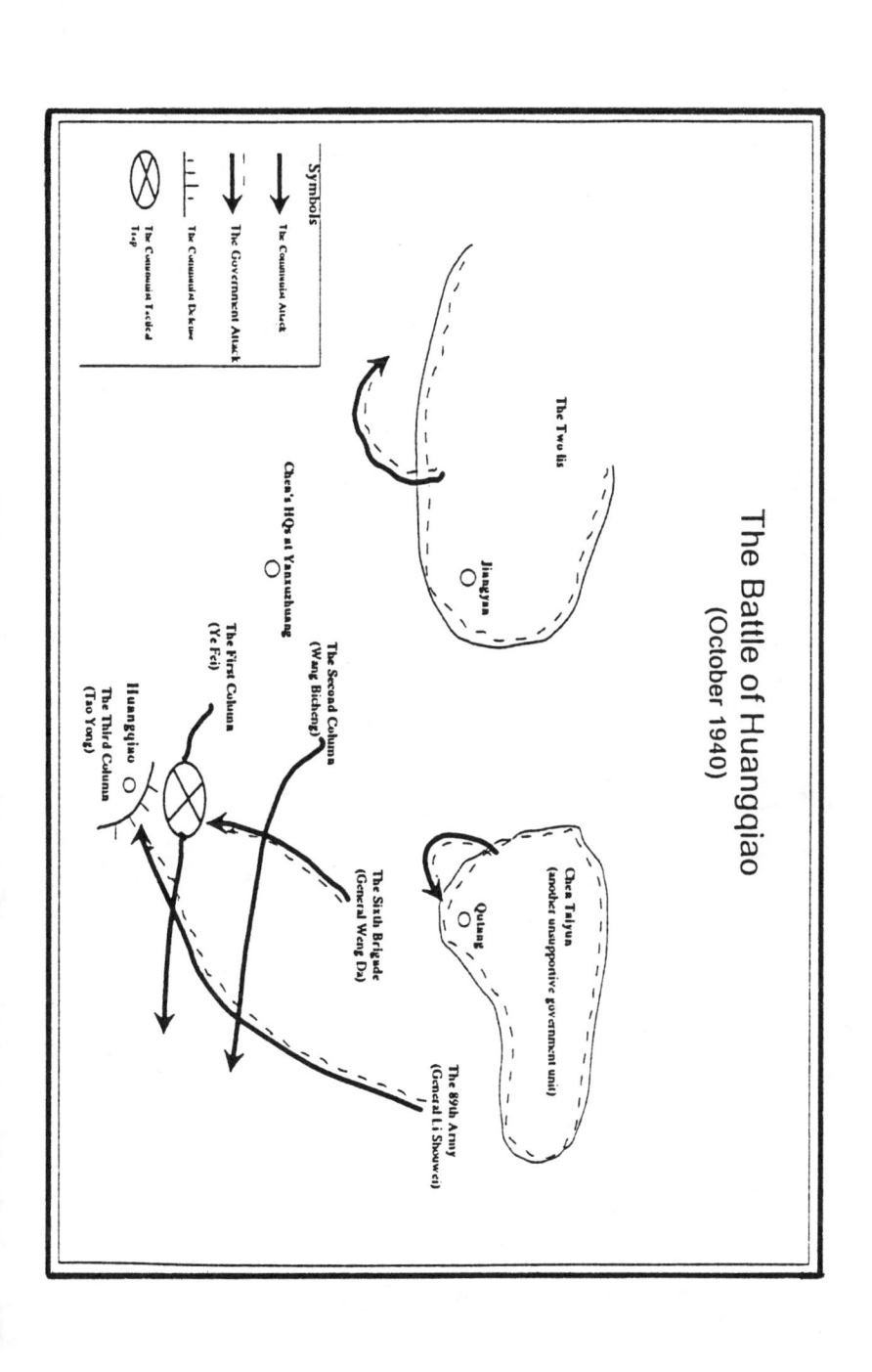

The Battle of Huangqiao
(October 1940)

but greatly weakened. At the critical juncture, Su Yu, who was at Tao's command post, heard the news that one communist battalion may have crossed the Yangzi River to reinforce them, so he quickly spread the news, Although this would turn out to be a rumor, the defense troops' morale was regained. Tao's bravery certainly boosted the troop confidence. At a critical moment, Tao and his chief of staff stripped off their clothes, and waved swords at the front position to reorganize their defense and repelled once again the final attack wave by the 89th Army.

Meanwhile, Ye and Wang's columns had gained time for redeployment to surround the 89th Army from its rear. By accident, Ye's original regimental home, the First Regiment, located the enemy headquarters, and decided to launch immediate attack. Although ferocious in resistance, the enemy's command system collapsed. The government 89th Army was destroyed within the next day. Its commander General Li was drowned while trying to ride across a ditch. By October 6, Han's elite troops suffered casualties of over ten thousand. The governor himself fled to Xinghua to prepare for a last-ditch defense. At the same time, Huang Kecheng's Eighth Route Army troops had finally arrived in Jiangsu on October 10, though too late to join the battle. Governor Han decided to accept the humiliation of defeat and to seek a truce. Ironically, however, Han's peace initiative was made through the mediation of the Two Lis. For the first time the strategical link between the communist Eighth Route Army in northern China and the New Fourth Army in the south was firmly established.

The Battle of Huangqiao was the largest civil conflict since 1937. The government lost not only a battle but also public opinion. Chen's political isolation campaign proved very effective. Su's military talent began to make impressive marks on communist military history. But it would be unfair to attribute the cause of this battle to the government alone, since the New Fourth Army had long planned Han's demise. It was not purely a defensive battle to begin with.[12] As Su Yu made it clear when summarizing the battle in late October 1940, its significance lay in the fact that, "Firstly, it has solved a biggest problem: the link-up of the Eighth Route and the New Fourth Armies ...... Secondly, it has created our leadership position in northern Jiangsu." According to Su, "Before [the battle of Huangqiao], the Japanese were ... number one [in the region], Han Deqin number two. the Two Lis number three, we were only number four. After the battle of Guo Village [with the defeat of the Lis], we had risen to number three. After the Battle of Huangqiao, we have become number two." "Thirdly, our victory over forces three times larger than ours depended on the Lis' neutrality. It has worked very well. Fourth, Han no longer has the capability to fight us ... and fifth, we have acquired a base area."[13] It seems hard to deny the fact that the communist priority in northern Jiangsu was to compete with the government rather than to fight the Japanese. In fact, Chen Yi did admit the connection between the Battle of Huangqiao and the subsequent demise of the Second United Front that led to widespread civil war. In his summary of the battle years later, Chen accepted the fact that "the drowning of Li Shouwei [the commander of Han's 89th Army] is a bad thing. It could have been better to let him go home alive. The result of the incident was the ... beginning of the second round of the anti-communist campaign [on the government side]," culminating with the "Southern Anhui Incident" that eliminated Xiang's headquarters.[14]

Meanwhile, another potential large-scale civil war was brewing quickly. Having lost northern Jiangsu, Chiang Kai-shek began to seek revenge elsewhere. The obvious target was the New Fourth Army headquarters and its nine thousand troops in the mountains of southern Anhui. For a long time, the "Southern Anhui Incident" which ended up with the demise of Xiang's headquarters at Cloud Hill has been attributed to two factors, according to official communist history. First, it was due to Chiang's scheme to eliminate the New Fourth Army. Second, it was due to a major mistake committed by the communist top man in charge---political commissar Xiang Ying. In reality, neither argument seems to hold water. To be sure, Chiang's government did have a penchant for limiting the communist activities. But the incident occurred against the backdrop that it was the first time a legitimate provincial governor had suffered the humiliation and crushing military defeat at the hands of the communist partners within the United Front. Chiang felt his anti-communism vindicated.

It is worth noticing that Chen's victory at Huangqiao could not be attributed in any way to Xiang Ying, the New Fourth Army headquarters and the party's Southeastern Bureau in southern Anhui. Chen's activities in northern Jiangsu were now controlled by Liu Shaoqi's Central Plains Bureau and the Party Central Committee through direct wire service between Chen and Yanan. In effect, Chen had been weaned away from his direct superior in Anhui. Liu Shaoqi further undercut Xiang's power after the Battle of Huangqiao, suggesting to Mao that Chen command all military forces, including Huang Kecheng's Eighth Route Army unit, in northern Jiangsu. Chen had thus been put on a *de facto* equal footing with Xiang.

Throughout 1940, Xiang resisted vehemently the suggestion by the Politburo of the Central Committee to move his headquarters to Jiangsu. From the outset, Xiang had never been Mao's favorite. Xiang's political attitude was considered in the same league as that of Wang Ming's and the Muscovites in general. In 1930, Xiang as head of the party in the Jiangxi

Soviet had righted Mao's excesses in weeding out the imagined AB Clique, and protected Red Army officers during the Futian Mutiny when the disgruntled Red Army officers openly declared "Down with Mao." On the issue of land reform, Xiang also considered Mao's penchant for absolute equality in distributing land a wrong-headed policy. He supported local party organizations who preferred distribution of land based on labor force per household in order to raise productivity. This dispute between Mao and the local party organizations had triggered Mao's ruthless drive for political conformity through mass murders, a method Xiang greatly resented.

Moreover, the dislike between Xiang and Mao was deepened by the fact that Xiang was, to a certain extent, a Moscow favorite, while Mao was not. Xiang was among the very few top communist leaders coming from a true working class background. He had built an impeccable career through trade union activities. He considered himself to have nothing in common with descendants of landlords such as Mao. At the time when Stalin was doubting the loyalty of the the new Chinese communist leadership emerging from the Long March, a person's family background did count very much with the Communist International in Moscow. While in Moscow, Xiang had worked for years as Chinese representative to the "Red Trade Union International," a branch under the Comintern Executive. On one rare occasion, he alone was received by Stalin in person. The Russian-fluent Wang Ming was his interpreter and the two immediately struck a good rapport. Stalin praised Xiang as the only "real Bolshevik" in China with impeccable working-class roots. Such praise carried enormous weight with the leadership of the Chinese Communist Party. Throughout later years, Xiang would never fail to carry two personal mementos, an ivory-handled Browning pistol and a fountain pen, both personal gifts from Stalin.

The New Fourth Army period for Xiang, to be sure, was a low point in his life. He was losing importance at the Party Central Committee and worse still, he had to obey a former subordinate of his, Mao Zedong. He realized full well that Mao's ascendance to the top derived from a power base built through controlling military forces, and it seemed to him that the preservation of his New Fourth Army troops could only be guaranteed in mountainous terrain, as Mao had done long time ago in the Jinggang Mountains. Thus to him, the move of his main troops to Jiangsu was tantamount to a suicide mission.

In May 1940, Mao and the Central Committee sent the first clear signal of political disapproval to Xiang, accusing the New Fourth Army headquarters of having abandoned the political principle of maintaining independence within the United Front. It further pointed out that it was wrong to print and distribute speeches made by the Kuomintang leaders. It stated pointedly, "The political principle developed during the Red Army period is still applicable today. The regulations you have designed [to accommodate the government] are not proper .... The [Third] War Zone's political instructions should be rejected absolutely, because the Kuomintang political regulations are completely for anti-communist espionage purposes."[15] In internal communist language, this was a severe charge. Xiang and his chief deputy, Red Army veteran and political director Yuan Guoping, bore the brunt of this attack. Xiang was angered by the method of this attack, and immediately offered his resignation. In three telegrams throughout May, Xiang suggested that he be fired "in order not to repeat the mistake of 1927 [i.e, Chen Duxiu's blind reliance on the United Front]," and "I will not make a personal statement for the interest of the party." Referring to the style of the directive, Xiang argued that it was made to sound like an open "declaration," not a secret directive, so that "I have lost authority [in front of the rank and file] and therefore cannot continue the leadership." Besides, Xiang maintained, the Central Committee directive had "shown no specific evidence while making this accusation," which began to affect "not just our day to day work performance here, but the whole [political] line and strategy." Finally, Xiang expressed great resentment at Mao's attitude, complaining that, "I believe [the Central Committee] should not treat a responsible leader (or just to say an old comrade) this way. You should point out my mistakes directly, and should not use indirect and vague innuendoes .... I must openly declare that I have lost confidence in continued leadership role."[16]

Mao and the Central Committee were apparently taken aback by Xiang's vigorous reaction and the defense of himself. They quickly sent a conciliatory telegram confirming that Xiang and the Southeastern Bureau "have carried out the United Front policy .... A few mistakes committed by you are not affecting general line, but just isolated mistakes." The telegram insisted that Xiang maintain his leadership. Xiang was of course not convinced.[17]

But the major dispute continued, centering on Xiang's "Southern Strategy" and his unwillingness to move to the north. As early as in April, the Central Committee directed Xiang to "move the headquarters to southern Jiangsu," but again, without dismissing his "Southern Strategy" altogether. It would be wrong to argue that, as Chinese official historians still do, Xiang's "Southern Strategy" had no support from either the Central Committee or the New Fourth Army rank and file. In fact, even Chen Yi, the dedicated expansionist, believed that the possibility to carry out the "Southern Strategy" existed after a base was secured and consolidated in Jiangsu. Following the Central Committee directive in April, Chen also assured Xiang that his "Southern Strategy" was still valid but the two New Fourth Army troops should converge and consolidate in a safer base area like Jiangsu. In a telegram to Yanan, Chen pointed out explicitly that, after "we combine forces at southern Jiangsu, we may advance southward toward the Tianmu Mountain and westward toward the Yellow Mountain."[18] Both mountains were top choices on Xiang's list for base building. As the wind of war was gathering in northern Jiangsu in September, Mao sent another telegram to Xiang, stating that, "Your headquarters should move to Jiangsu before we resolve the problem with Han Deqin."[19] Xiang again stressed numerous difficulties. After the Battle of Huangqiao, the Central Committee sent a telegram dated October 8, which for the first time explicitly began to reject Xiang's "Southern Strategy" by pointing out that "[the idea of] moving into the Yellow Mountain is least to our advantage on both political and military grounds."[20] A few days later, Mao stated in another directive, "Chiang may join the Anglo-American allies ... the whole southern China might become a dark world. But Chiang is still [at this moment] fighting the Japanese, we cannot carry out guerrilla activities in southern Kuomintang area. Therefore, your headquarters should move to the north at once."[21]

Chen's surprising victory at Huangqiao was both good and bad news for Xiang. On the one hand, he could continue to insist on the difficult environment caused by the escalated conflict in the north. On the other, his isolated troops in Anhui would become an obvious target for government retaliation. On October 19, Chiang's Chief of staff, General He Yingqin, and his deputy, General Bai Chongxi, sent a telegram to the communist leaders, accusing them of, "1. Disobeying the government war zone orders; 2. unauthorized expansion of troops; 3. destroying local administrative system and 4. not fighting the Japanese but only devouring friendly armies."[22] In conclusion, the telegram demanded that all the Eighth Route and the New Fourth Armies move to northern China within one month. The political impact of this *de facto* ultimatum was strong. Although General He was Chiang's protege, General Bai represented Chiang's chief rival---the Guangxi Clique. Bai was also known to be somewhat pro-communist and a personal friend of Zhou Enlai. The telegram thus indicated a general consensus within the government, a rare occurrence, over the issue of the communist expansionist policy.

The communist high command in Yanan responded by further consolidating their position in central China. Through establishing local governments and active policies of rent reform, i.e., to reduce rent owed by the peasants, the communists continued to work hard to attract local popular support. Militarily, through unifying command in central China, Mao hoped to concentrate enough forces, especially those under Xiang and Chen, to repel the expected attack by the government troops. Mao believed that there was no room for accommodation with the government on the issue of unrestrained communist expansion. Thus from Yanan's point of view, Xiang's move to the north had become all the more urgent. But Xiang continued to drag his feet. The most important factor that had prompted Xiang to stay in Anhui was his personal struggle with Mao and Liu, as was becoming apparent day after day. Realizing Xiang's reluctance to follow orders, Yanan finally decided in early November to put its cards on the table. At the urging of Liu Shaoqi, Mao requested General Ye Ting, the figure-head commander of the New Fourth Army, instead of Xiang, the actual decision-maker, to be transferred to the north immediately. Ye was designated to take over a new command called "the Central China Eighth Route and New Fourth Armies Joint Command." Chen Yi would be his deputy and Liu would be the political commissar. The purpose of this appointment was two-fold. On the one hand, Ye as a government appointee was still useful politically for the communists. On the other, Ye's authorities were deliberately expanded at Xiang's expense. Xiang and his key colleagues at Cloud Hill were not even on the list.[23] Understandably the feeling that the Central Committee had written them off was strong. Xiang and his chief deputies had to ponder what advantages, if any, they would have after two troops had joined. The future was clear, they would lose all their power.

General Ye was, of course, highly motivated by this appointment, after years of inactivity at the New Fourth Army headquarters. But he was decent enough not to abandon his troops in Anhui. He went to negotiate with his former classmate at the military academy, government general and commander of the Third War Zone, Gu Zhutong, who apparently agreed to allow Ye's troops to move unhindered to southern Jiangsu, as the first step further towards the north.[24]

Mao quickly seized the opportunity to declare his willingness to make concessions to the government. The pawn on his chess board was Xiang's headquarters. Instead of accepting the government deadline to move all communist troops to northern China, Mao agreed only to move the troops under Xiang's control to the north, through which he hoped to extract some favorable responses in public opinion as well as to force Xiang's hand. At the same time, the Party Central Committee further started depriving Xiang's authority by merging Xiang's most important power base, the party's Southeastern Bureau, with Liu's Central Plains Bureau to form a Central China Bureau under Liu's overall direction. Xiang was thus cornered into an extremely difficult position. On the one hand, moving to the north without any authority over his troops would mean the end of his career and, knowing Mao's character so well, he realized that the beginning of a purge would be expected to follow. On the other, if he disobeyed both Mao and Chiang Kai-shek, it would mean the end of his troops which could be wiped out by the government on legitimate grounds. Under the circumstances, Xiang had no choice but to follow Mao's orders.

The issue now became the choice of route for the troop to move. The main concern was, of course, the security on march for this large troop movement. In mid-October, Mao stated in a directive that he intended to alleviate tension in northern Jiangsu, apparently for the purpose of reducing government incentive to attack Xiang's troops, should they decide to move to the north.[25] Although General Ye Ting had earlier secured General Gu Zhutong's approval to move to southern Jiangsu, the Communist Central Committee suddenly contradicted its earlier intention of guaranteeing Xiang's safety by not creating another conflict with the government. By November 19, however, Mao approved a plan to seek another battle with Governor Han Deqin at Cao Dian, in an effort to foil Han's recent attempt to link up with a major government unit in northern Anhui.[26] Prompted mainly by Liu Shaoqi, this plan was made at the time when the government had not yet objected to Xiang's move to Jiangsu.

This proved to be a disastrous decision both for military strategy and for Xiang's troop movement. Although most Chinese communist veterans and historians prefer ignoring this critical event that helped bring about Xiang's demise, General Huang Kecheng refused to keep silent. In his memoirs, Huang recalled bitterly that he was opposed to this battle from the outset, but was severely reprimanded by Chen Yi and Liu Shaoqi. After the Battle of Huangqiao, Governor Han Deqin retreated to Cao Dian with twenty thousand remnant troops at his disposal for a last-ditch defense. Politically, such an attack plan would make it an active offensive and provocation, not self-defense. It could hardly be justified in front of public opinion. Militarily, Huang pointed out to Liu and Chen that the old communist strategy of human-wave attacks would not work this time and the communist troops lacked equipment and experience in taking this type of stronghold. Cao Dian was very different from Huangqiao because of its unique terrain conditions. It was surrounded by a large grid of rivers and swamps in addition to a well-fortified defense structure. It was much easier to hold than to take. Huang preferred a protracted siege battle to wear the enemy down. But none of his views was accepted by Liu and Chen. The Battle of Cao Dian soon ended in disaster, not only the communists failed to crack the enemy defense, but also lost over two thousand casualties within a few days. Finally, Liu and Chen decided to pull the troops out after eighteen days of bitter fighting. Huang as part of the attacking command was accused of lacking enthusiasm and removed from his position. Nevertheless, Chen admitted two years later in an internal speech that, "In the Battle of Cao Dian, we attacked the other side without any reason."[27]

It is undeniable that the Battle of Cao Dian had a direct link with the government decision to change its mind as far as Xiang's route of withdrawal was concerned and it certainly provided an excuse for Chiang to plan to finish Xiang's headquarters with one blow. Having thus been provoked in northern Jiangsu, it became hard for Chiang to approve the original idea of allowing Xiang's troops to move to southern Jiangsu. From there the newly-arrived troops could then be in a convenient position to reinforce Chen's forces in the north of the Yangzi River. By December, Chiang ordered Xiang to move by the end of the year to a different area in northern Anhui and along a different route. They were further ordered to move to the north of the Yellow River by January 30, 1941. In the meantime, Chiang issued a secret order to mobilize troops to prepare to wipe out Xiang's men, "if Chen's bandits should further attack Han Deqin or the deadline arrives before Xiang's movement."[28] Mao hurriedly ordered a cease-fire in northern Jiangsu in late November, but the events quickly began to spin out control.

Mao's approval of the disastrous Battle of Cao Dian was based on his underestimation of the serious nature of Chiang's ultimatum made a month earlier. This misjudgment on the part of Yanan as to Chiang's real intention undoubtedly contributed to the lack of preparation and the ultimate demise of Xiang's headquarters. To be sure, Mao's chief motive for Xiang to move was to take over the latter's troops. The fear of attack was only a secondary factor, as was indicated by the absence of serious preparation for war at the communist high command in Yanan. Mao and the party secretariat apparently dismissed Chiang's determination to start a major civil war in Anhui. As late as November 21, Mao instructed Xiang to delay for "one to two months (in order to demand more money from the government [to cover departure expenses] and cessation of hostility in the north)." Thus the lack of urgency on military grounds prompted Xiang to further legitimize his delay in action. As the Battle of Cao Dian was eminent, Xiang suggested that they had better stay where they were, since a major war was again coming in Jiangsu. Mao felt that Xiang was becoming elusive again and began to regret his earlier instruction authorizing Xiang to delay. He immediately ordered Xiang to "move within twenty days and General Ye should depart earlier."[29]

Sensing Xiang's fear of the impact of the Battle of Cao Dian in the north, Mao continued to alleviate that fear by dismissing the thought that Chiang's open threat was serious this time. On November 30, Mao misleadingly stated in a top secret directive, "The current anti-communist campaign [launched by Chiang] will be smaller than that of the last time." But, Mao added, "This point should not be told to the troops, for they might loosen up vigilance." Even as late as mid-December, Mao still thought "large-scale attack is not possible."[30] Meanwhile, Mao continued to be frustrated by the inaction on Xiang's part. By the end of the year,

Mao's patience finally ran out. In a harshly worded telegram dated December 26 criticizing Xiang's delay tactics, Mao severely reprimanded him, "The Central Committee had given you direction one year ago, you have created excuses not to follow it ... nowhere in the whole country like your place where there is a lack of decisiveness and ways to overcome difficulties.... We do not understand what instruction you want from us, and what you yourself want?" In conclusion, Mao warned, "You will suffer a great deal in the future."[31]

The language and contents of Mao's telegram were devastating to Xiang and his colleagues. At a top military conference at Cloud Hill on December 28, Xiang apparently gained support from his chief deputies who also considered Mao's sudden flare-up to be unfair to the New Fourth Army leadership, since the difficult conditions for them to move troops were not all caused by their delay in action. The impact of the battles of Huangqiao and Cao Dian, for example, were totally beyond their control and certainly to their detriment. Without any choice, they finally decided to move.

But it was still very difficult for them to decide on a retreat route. The government had recently made it clear that moving to southern Jiangsu was now forbidden. Chiang only specified northern Anhui as the route he would not block by force. At this critical juncture, Zhou Enlai, the communist representative at Chongqing did another disservice to Xiang's cause by relating an intelligence report, which was perhaps not quite reliable, that Chiang had fully prepared for wiping the troops out in northern Anhui---the designated area by the government. Besides, Zhou added, Japanese steamboats were usually patrolling in high frequency the section of the Yangzi River designated by Chiang for the troop crossing. Thus, Zhou suggested avoiding this route at all costs. Under the circumstances, the party secretariat decided on a direct route to southern Jiangsu without detour, knowing full well that it would violate government orders.[32] At this point, Yanan apparently still maintained the view that Chiang would not go as far as to launch a full-scale attack on Xiang's troops. In a telegram to Zhou Enlai on November 21, Mao called all the threats by Chiang "bluffing," including the ultimatum, because "if he could not compromise with Japan, it will be impossible for him to attack the communists on a large scale." Thus Mao suggested active use of bluff to counter Chiang's threat to the communist side.[33] This persistent miscalculation proved to be a disaster for Xiang.

After weighing all the factors, Xiang and his colleagues chose a strange yet fatal route, neither directly northeastward to southern Jiangsu, nor northwestward to northern Anhui, but to the south. The idea was ostensibly to divert government attention away from the real route toward southern Jiangsu by moving troops through the southern mountainous area and, if unopposed, they could turn around toward Jiangsu. The key to this strategy was to keep the troops following the natural shape of the high mountain ranges. Despite the fact that Mao and the Central Committee had been assuring Xiang that no large-scale attack was forthcoming, by choosing this route, Xiang perhaps hoped to provoke some limited clash, knowing very well that the southern direction was blocked by the government. So the intention of this decision seemed clear: if the government should attack (presumably on a small scale, as was believed in Yanan), they could easily legitimize their quick retreat into the mountains, since their troops would then be marching along the edge of the mountain range in the first place. This was Xiang's last straw to salvage his original dream of the "Southern Strategy."

From a military point of view, this decision would lead to a voluntary fall into the enemy's waiting trap. It simply made it too easy for Chiang to devour the prey. Xiang's mistake was fatal not only from military, but also from political perspectives. Since this decision in effect bordered on insubordination to Chongqing as well as Yanan. Xiang gambled on the fact that Chiang would not launch an all-out attack, for such an attack would leave Xiang and the New Fourth Army high command in a no-win situation against both Chiang and Yanan.

In order to avoid further hindrance to his decision by Yanan, Xiang deliberately sent a vaguely worded telegram to Mao, which simply confirmed the final decision to move to southern Jiangsu without providing any further detail. Xiang also delayed the transmission of this predated telegram to Mao for as long as four days. Since the date of departure was set at January 4, 1941, Xiang's decision made on December 28 did not reach Yanan on January 2. Mao could not possibly have time to smell trouble about the details. Thus, the route chosen by Xiang would have become a *fait accompli* before Mao could intervene. The fact that Yanan was deceived on this issue was indicated by a very short telegram sent by Mao on January 3, the day before Xiang's departure, which simply stated with enormous delight that Xiang had finally decided to follow orders.[34]

The next day, Xiang led nine thousand troops, divided into three marching columns in combat formation, to embark on a tearful departure towards the south. Chiang had made it clear that the only route allowed was to the northwest across the Yangzi River towards northern Anhui, and he was known to have deployed main forces blocking the south and the northeast.

But Xiang's intention to provoke a small incident became all the more obvious on the next day, when, seeing that no skirmish had occurred, he ordered a full day rest at Maolin, a small town not too far in the south from Cloud Hill. This was a typical mountain town surrounded by a

The Southern Anhui Incident
(January 1941)

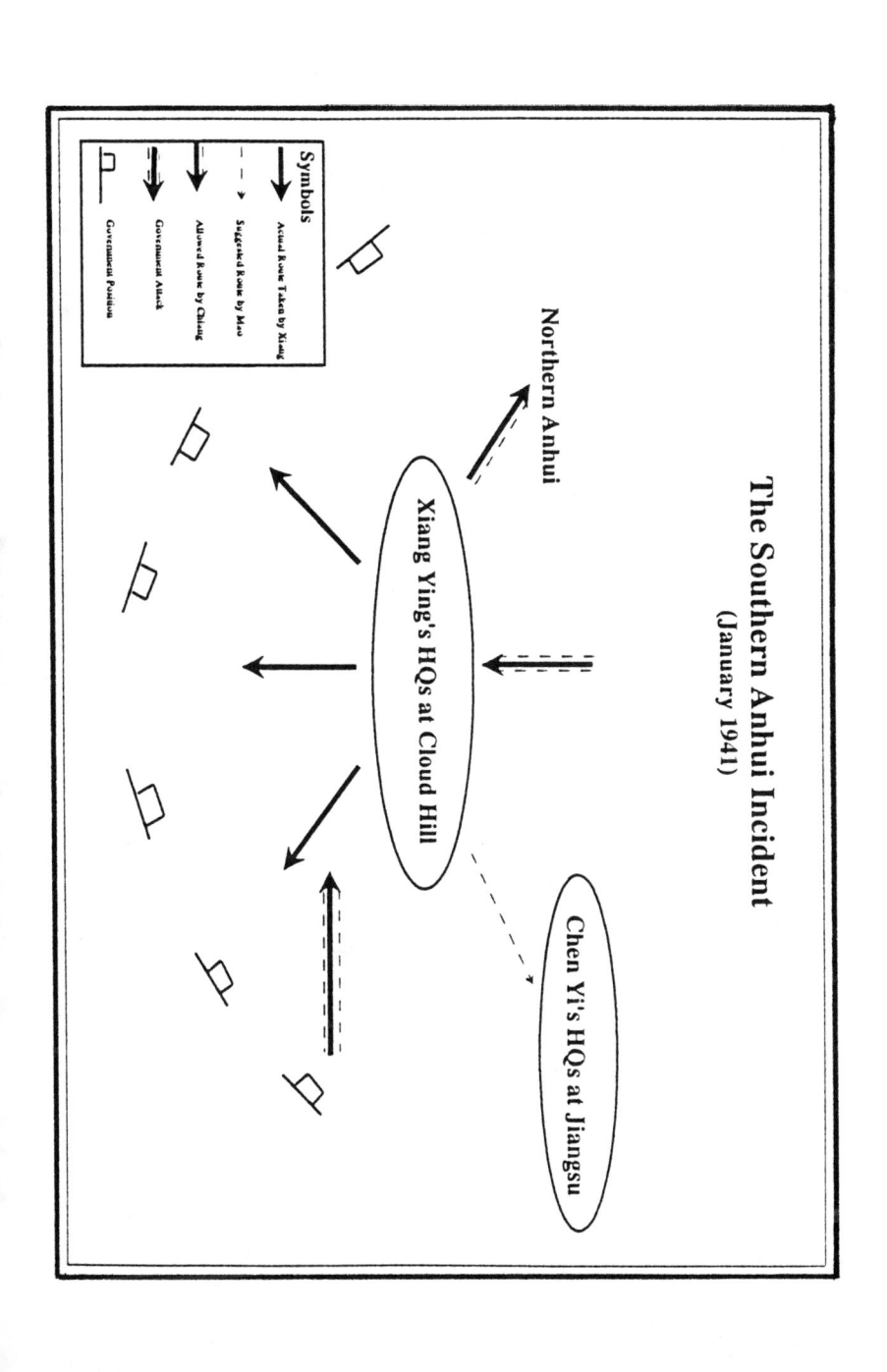

Symbols
- Actual Route Taken by Xiang
- Allowed Route by Chiang
- Suggested Route by Mao
- Government Attack
- Government Position

Northern Anhui

Xiang Ying's HQs at Cloud Hill

Chen Yi's HQs at Jiangsu

terrain that was ideal for a major ambush. This was exactly where the government had decided to launch such an attack. The Party Central Committee discovered that it was too late to order Xiang to change direction, but it managed to send him an extremely urgent message, "You should not stay in Maolin for long ... you must quickly move east and break through the encirclement." As soon as a large-scale government ambush became apparent, Commander Ye Ting suggested an active strategy of offensive defense, but Xiang had by this time reached a stage of nervous breakdown. The turn of events seemed totally beyond his careful calculation and expectation. After seven hours hesitation, panting with remorse and guilt, he missed the chance of breaking through the enemy encirclement. In a narrow mountainous pocket, the nine thousand New Fourth Army troops fought a heroic but hopeless battle. In desperation, Xiang finally decided to turn around back to Cloud Hill, but his command system that was previously based on the three-column marching formation quickly became chaotic and dysfunctional.

In the early morning of January 9, Xiang and his chief deputies deserted the troops and simply disappeared. General Ye was now in full charge, ironically for the first as well as the last time. But it was too late to organize any meaningful breakthrough. In a telegram to Mao, Ye expressed his decision to fight to a man. He was so angered at Xiang's irresponsible action that he vented his spleen in a personal telegram to the Communist Central Committee, frankly attributing the defeat to Mao's favorite "political commissar system."After Xiang's desertion, his chief political rival Liu Shaoqi blatantly suggested to Mao that Xiang be fired right away, "one day earlier the better." Liu also recommended that his protege, a party functionary at the Southeastern Bureau named Rao Shushi take over Xiang's position. Mao replied that such announcement was premature and should be delayed for the moment.

But on the next day Xiang and his entourage suddenly returned to the command, apparently unable to sneak through the encirclement line. In a last telegram explaining his desertion, Xiang admitted that he was "shaken under pressure," and did not tell General Ye before the departure, which "left a very bad influence [with the rank and file]." He continued, "I am waiting for punishment from the Central Committee. I have decided to die or live with the troops."[35] The New Fourth Army soldiers held on to their position for eight days before their ultimate demise. This was the bloodiest civil strife since 1937. It formally ended the Second United Front and was quickly dubbed as the "Southern Anhui Incident." It cost the New Fourth Army seven thousand soldiers. Only two regiments had narrowly escaped. General Ye at the last minute decided to negotiate with the government. He was taken prisoner for the next four years. Xiang and his chief deputies also made the escape and disappeared with several hundred men into the mountains. His political director Yuan Guoping, however, was killed during the escape. Hiding in a cave for months, Xiang did not seem keen to cross the Yangzi River to return to communist bases in the north. His subordinates were becoming increasingly restless. After a revolt from the remnant rank and file, Xiang and his personal entourage became completely isolated and began to stay in a separate cave from the other soldiers. Fate decreed that Xiang did not have to go back to Yanan to face the music. He and his deputy chief of staff, Zhou Zikun, were shot to death in one stormy night by his most trusted aide-de-camp named Liu Houzong. Liu had served him since the guerrilla years in the 1930s, loyal as a dog and brave as a tiger. Aside from total disappointment with Xiang's political future, Liu's action was motivated less by any political purpose. The murder was more prompted by greed, for the peasant-born Liu had been coveting a large amount of gold and cash carried by his beloved "commissar" for some time.

Yanan's initial reaction to this crushing defeat was to respond with large-scale military action. In a telegram to Zhou Enlai in Chongqing dated January 15, 1941, an extremely agitated Mao stated, "whatever Chiang says is nonsense, you should never believe him. The Central Committee has decided to launch political as well as military campaigns." But Liu Shaoqi had different ideas. Having written off Xiang Ying's career for a long time, Liu felt no need for sacrificing what remained of the New Fourth Army troops under his control to retaliate for a lost cause. He sent a very well crafted letter on the same day to Mao, opposing any military action. According to Liu, first of all, "the Kuomintang has not surrendered to the Japanese, and dared not risking a split with communist party .... Besides, Chiang had also tried to stop the fight, indicating that he does not want to escalate the conflict. At this time, we should not use the 'Southern Anhui Incident' to depart with the government." Secondly, "we do not have enough troops to consolidate our position in central China ... it would be better for us to stop large-scale military confrontation with the government for a half or one whole year .... Thirdly, "Han Deqin still has a strong defense .... We cannot even solve this problem yet." Therefore, Liu suggested using only political means to put Chiang to the bar of the national and international public opinion.[36]

To Liu, the incident was a godsend, which resulted in his complete control of New Fourth Army affairs, a position he had been wrestling with Xiang for since 1939. Two days after the incident, Chiang announced the New Fourth Army to be a "rebellious army" and should be disbanded. The government also put General Ye Ting on court martial. Yanan immediately countered the government announcement through re-establishing a New Fourth Army headquarters in northern Jiangsu. It appointed Chen Yi the "acting commander" and Liu the political

commissar. The Second United Front was in effect at its end.
Free from all the constraints imposed by the Third War Zone, the reestablished New Fourth Army began expanding at a breathtaking speed. By the end of January, 1941, seven divisions at ninety thousand strong were formed, which included Chen's elite troops as well as all the Eighth Route Army units and other communist guerrillas active in this area. Confident that the New Fourth Army would follow orders in the future, Yanan assigned it to fulfill the strategic task of maintaining a base area in central China. The First Division commanded by Su Yu was formed by the original elite "Ye-Wang-Tao" troops." Huang Kecheng's Eighth Route Army unit became the Third Division. Both were the strongest and best equipped divisions. Their joint task was to hold on to northern Jiangsu. The Second and the Fourth divisions stationed in northern Anhui, both derived from Gao Jingting's (who was executed for insubordination in 1939) units combined with local guerrillas. The Fifth Division under Li Xiannian remained in Henan. The Sixth Division was based on Tan Zhenlin's guerrilla in southern Jiangsu and the Seventh division was commanded by Zeng Xisheng in southern Anhui which included the remnants who escaped from the "Southern Anhui Incident." Neither of the last two divisions was fully manned, at just one brigade each. These divisions were given the designated areas for the New Fourth Army to operate. They were to become major targets for Japanese "mopping-up" (*Sao Dang*) campaigns from 1941 to 1945. Su Yu's First Division in central Jiangsu, in particular, was directly under the Japanese nose. But it is remarkable that the New Fourth Army was able to hold on to these areas until the end of the war against Japan and this strategic situation would become critical for the communists at the beginning of the civil war.

One important result of the New Fourth Army's reorganization was that it deliberately eliminated guerrilla character of the troops, which was widespread before the Southern Anhui Incident. Of the ninety thousand troops, only a fraction, mainly the First Division, were original "bandit remnants" from the Red Army period. By replacing "column" with "division," it enhanced professional military orientation. This was, to be sure, a somewhat different army. Even within Chen's original elite First Division, a gradual transformation of character had taken place. Regionalism was undermined by bold recruitment of Jiangsu natives who were important for attracting local support and who were typically better educated than the Red Army veterans, mostly from the poverty-ridden Jiangxi and Anhui area. According to a 1942 report by Zhong Qiguang, political director of the division, among 2,411 officers in the division, over 1/4 had high school diploma, 983 with elementary school education and 504 with private schooling. The illiterates were merely 103.

Moreover, by mid-1941, most of the commanders and political officers of the First Division were "outsiders." Zhong reported that there were only 532 original guerrilla members of the First Division's officer corps among 2,411 officers mentioned above.[37]

Ye Fei continued to command his troops which were now re-designated as the First Brigade of the First Division. Even his beloved regimental home was now commanded by outsiders like Liao Zhengguo, an ex-officer of Zhang Guotao's and Zeng Ruqing, Chen's last special envoy to southern Anhui in May 1940 and an ex-POW from the Jiangxi Soviet. But Ye's brigade enjoyed troop cohesion that remained strongest within the New Fourth Army, for the "outsiders" skillfully maintained soldiers' pride about the regimental history that could be traced back to eastern Fujian guerrilla years.[38] The regional diversity and the dilution of factional loyalty also occurred in Wang Bicheng's Second and Tao Yong's Third Brigades.

After years of wrestling with Xiang Ying, Mao now had complete control of the New Fourth Army. Ironically, the elimination of communist troops in southern Anhui made Xiang's "Southern Strategy" all the more appealing to Mao. In February, Mao sent a telegram to Liu and Chen, urging them to organize guerrilla forces in the mountain area where Xiang had hoped to retreat to. Mao stated, "Xiang Ying's wrongful 'Southern Strategy' will be a rightful one for the future." "Your task [in central China] is to eliminate all anti-communist forces within one year, and expand to the west and the south .... You should then prepare to go to Hubei-Henan-Shaanxi and Fujian-Zhejiang-Jiangxi border areas." This odd directive exactly echoed Xiang's "Southern Strategy."[39]

But Mao's fantasy was soon to prove unrealistic, for the Japanese now decided to cleanse Henan and Anhui. General Hideki Tojo openly declared in Tokyo that it was a good opportunity to wipe out the Chinese government forces in that area, since "we cannot count on the the Chinese civil war to solve the China problem." Chiang had thought that the Japanese would not engage government troops that were eliminating the communists in civil strife, but he was wrong. Since Chiang's objective, as indicated by the Southern Anhui Incident, was to drive the communist forces to northern China, which was the strategic center for Japan in the China theater, General Tojo declared that this was unacceptable. As a result, the Japanese swept through Henan and Anhui, forcing a major government retreat. It was no longer possible for the New Fourth Army to move in that direction. Mao admitted in a telegram to Zhou Enlai, this Japanese attitude towards the Chinese civil war "has not been expected by us."[40]

In April, Mao changed his mind completely. No longer interested in a southern strategy, he decided that the New Fourth Army should stay where it was to fight the Japanese. As he stated in a telegram to Peng Dehuai, deputy commander of the Eighth Route Army, "The Kuomintang is in a panic, we predict that under the Japanese pressure, they have to court us, [our] relationship [with them] will change, our party will gradually take over the leadership position in the anti-Japanese war. We must [now] cooperate with the government in fighting the Japanese invaders."[41]

Having eliminated government influence in northern Jiangsu, the New Fourth Army decided to shift attention to the Japanese, for its ultimate credibility and popular support derived above all from the promises to engage the Japanese. In January, the troops under the Two Lis were lured by the Japanese and Wang Jingwei to join the puppet regime based in Nanjing, the prewar capital city of China. Chen and Su decided to seize the opportunity to eliminate further all the other forces beyond communist control. They openly announced a "Crusade Against the Traitors." The First Division (The Ye-Wang-Tao brigades) led by Su and Ye attacked the Lis on February 18, and defeated them in just two days, wiping out five thousand badly-equipped troops. The Japanese were greatly provoked. But they did not have a sizable force in northern Jiangsu to carry out a major retaliatory operation.

As early as at the end of 1939, the Japanese already began to concern themselves about the serious situation in their occupied areas. General Nishio Juzo, commander of the Central China Expedition Army, reported the filling by the communists of the power vacuum in northern Jiangsu. Japanese intelligence analysts believed that the communists, more than the Kuomintang, were able to arouse a hostile attitude among the population towards the Japanese occupation troops.[42] As a result, the Japanese adopted a two-fold policy: establishing a puppet regime under Wang Jingwei to rival Chongqing in order to compete for popular loyalty; and eliminating communist bases through ruthless "rural pacification"(*Qing Xiang*) drives. But the Japanese still hoped to use puppet forces to maintain order and carry out local pacification duties, since they did not have enough troops in this area. The Japanese main forces were concentrated in northern China. This was due to the far more active engagement of the Japanese by the communist Eighth Route Army in the north. One of the most notable examples was the so-called "Hundred Regiments Offensive" launched in August 1940. With four hundred thousand troops consisting of one hundred fifteen regiments, the communists simultaneously attacked the Japanese forces in five provinces in northern China. The battle lasted for three months. Casualties on both sides were heavy.

In Jiangsu, the situation was different. Throughout the civil war in Jiangsu, the Japanese simply sat back and enjoyed the show. Although frequently ambushed by the communists in the past few years, the

Japanese headquarters in China did not take it very seriously. With the elimination of the Lis, the Japanese were faced with a severe situation. Either they had to give up northern Jiangsu, or to increase forces. The communists, unlike the government forces, were able to mobilize masses through calculated policies. Contemporary Japanese intelligence reported that, at the beginning, "the peasants did not necessarily give the New Fourth Army a warm welcome or trust it. Since the peasants did not receive honest government from the KMT or Nanking [puppet] regimes, they did not expect the New Fourth Army to be different." But the peasants were impressed by well-disciplined communist soldiers who "did not requisition coolies and showed kindness to the masses."[43]

Under the circumstances, the Japanese Central China Expedition Army decided to concentrate troops aimed at striking directly at the New Fourth Army headquarters now relocated at Yancheng. By early 1941, they began to move a regular brigade to northern Jiangsu, an area they had previously ignored. The Japanese quickly occupied Huangqiao and other strategic towns and points of communication. The Communist Party Central Committee had by now unified the command of the New Fourth Army through combining two regional party bureaus---the Central Plains under Liu and the Southeastern---under Xiang into one: the Central China Bureau. Liu became the party boss, Chen was put in charge of military affairs. Liu and Chen's first decision was to divide the area under the New Fourth Army control into four small "administrative zones;" the South of Huai River (Huainan), the North of the Huai River (Huaibei), the Northern Jiangsu (Subei) and the Central Jiangsu (Suzhong) zones. The latter two included all the northern area of the Yangzi River in Jiangsu, which was previously designated simply as "northern Jiangsu."

Secondly, the new leadership decided to deploy their best troops: the First Division (the original Ye-Wang-Tao troops) and the Third Division (troops under Huang Kecheng) in Jiangsu's two administrative zones. This proved to be a very costly decision. But Liu and Chen's willingness to challenge the Japanese with elite forces in this sensitive region derived from the overwhelming concern about winning local popular support. Throughout early 1941, the New Fourth Army began to adopt a string of moderate policies that could never have been imaginable during the Red Army years. They were reflected in two fundamental deviations from the original communist dogma. On the one hand, they began to set up local administration based on a so-called "Three-Three" (*San San Zhi*) system, i.e., the communist administrators would not exceed 33% of the administrative positions while other parties and nonpartisan members would fill the rest. On the other, the old agricultural revolution policy was to be abandoned altogether. In a private letter to a New Fourth Army economist named Song Liang (alias Sun Yefang), Liu made it clear that the lack of flexibility in land policy had contributed to the failure of the Red Army period. Therefore, Liu proposed a "25% Rent Reduction"(*Er Wu Jian Zu*) policy, which had already been practiced by Chen Yi earlier at Huangqiao, to be rigorously implemented. The question of the land ownership would not be touched at all.[44]

But moderate local policy was not enough to win popular respect. The key issue in competition with the government was after all the attitude toward the Japanese. During the civil war in Jiangsu, the New Fourth Army excelled themselves in utilizing brilliant tactics of mobile warfare to defeat government forces whose morale and strategy were poor. They had not engaged the Japanese in large-scale war and the rank and file were far less confident in fighting the Japanese. In March, Liu and Chen wrote a letter to Su Yu and the other leaders in Central Jiangsu, pointing out the political danger if the troops were afraid of fighting the Japanese. It stressed that they had only three choices: one, fight the Japanese; two, surrender; three, escape. "We think the first choice is the best."[45]

From a military point of view, Chen realized that the method in the civil strife could hardly be applied to the war with the Japanese whose troop cohesion, spirit and strategy were unsurpassed in Asia. According to a contemporary report made by Lai Chuanzhu, the Chief of Staff of the New Fourth Army, the Japanese solders were far superior in tactical cooperation, troop organization and training. The only thing they were lacking was the will to fight a prolonged war.[46] Under the circumstances, Chen decided that he had to return to guerrilla warfare. In the same month, Chen instructed Su to prepare for shifting bases to the countryside, and to forgo the preoccupation with taking cities. Amongst the troops, the return to guerrilla warfare was hardly popular. According to a handwritten note outlining a speech made by Su in April, the "wrong attitude" toward the issue of engaging the Japanese among the rank and file was prevalent. This included avoiding battles with the Japanese in order to preserve troops; hoping to move into to the enemy's rear; hoping to move to Shanghai; waiting for international crisis and a Pacific war, etc.[47]

Befitting a renewed guerrilla strategy, Chen and Su decided to break the troops into smaller units. More innovative was a plan, shortly before the Japanese launched massive attack in July, to "localize" the regular army through combining regular forces with local communist militia. Since local militia was especially useful in disrupting enemy's movement and engaging the puppet forces, the Eighth Route Army in northern China had nurtured its rapid development. In Jiangsu, the New Fourth Army had so far received lukewarm support from the local population in organizing militia. Thus, as Su admitted in June, the communist regular armies were faced with a dilemma. Before the enemy's massive attack, there was a lack of forces to hold on to many strategic points. But if the enemy succeeded in breaking the communist defense, the forces became too big to play hide-and-seek guerrilla tactics. The key to its solution was therefore the expansion of local militia and to reduce the size of regular units. But ordinary citizens were not interested in joining the militia, because central Jiangsu was a prosperous and culturally developed area where people tended to look down upon a military career. A dominant theme among the population was still the ancient adage, "a good man will not be a soldier, and good iron will not be made into nails." As a result, local militia organizations were more often than not manned by hooligans, gangsters, and professional mercenaries.[48]

But Chen and Su did not have time to carry out this "localization" plan when the Japanese launched the attack in July. Spearheaded from four directions, the Japanese intended to carry out a *blitzkrieg* to knock out the New Fourth Army headquarters once and for all. Chen and Liu decided to abandon Yancheng and ordered Huang Kecheng's Third Division to cover the headquarters' retreat. The First Division under Su Yu was supposed to strike in the enemy's rear. The retreat was chaotic, and coordination between the two divisions was poor. It took only two days for the Japanese to occupy Yancheng. With a large group of staff members, political and cultural officers, the headquarters were so top-heavy that their whereabouts became hard to conceal. The seek-and-hide game with the Japanese became dangerous day by day. At one point, a group of top communist propaganda officers including some of the best writers from Shanghai were killed. Huang's Third Division was not able to fulfill its task to cover the retreat, since it had to move away from Chen and Liu, due to the fact that the government troops also entered the fight on the Japanese side. Huang was unwilling to fight enemies on both sides. Under the critical conditions, Liu and Chen decided to split. Liu who knew nothing about guerrilla war led a company of guards to escape while the former guerrilla expert Chen continued to stay put in the enemy zone.

The desperate situation was only saved by the First Division whose active attacks in the enemy's rear diverted Japanese attention. But internal coordination was also poor under Su's command. At one point, Ye Fei decided on his own to attack an enemy stronghold, but Su refused to endorse his plan. Bordering on insubordination, Ye carried out his attack anyway and it was very successful. While still in desperation, Chen was delighted to hear the good news that over a dozen enemy-occupied towns were knocked out by Su's troops. Although the Japanese commander refused to be diverted by these attacks in his rear and continued to seek Chen's headquarters, he hesitated when Taizhou, his own headquarters, was surrounded by Ye's First Brigade. In early August, the Japanese decided to withdraw with casualties of two thousand, most of which were in the puppet troops. The communist losses were also heavy at about one thousand. The Japanese attempt was not successful, but the bloody lessons for Chen and Liu were more than obvious. On the one hand, the concentration of troops after they were regularized in current forms did not seem to have worked well in campaigns against the Japanese. On the other, the remnant government forces in this area remained a thorn in the side for the New Fourth Army, as Huang Kecheng was painfully aware. In August, Liu and Chen reported to the Party Central Committee that it was no longer possible to establish a base area in Jiangsu where the New Fourth Army headquarters would be safe. The headquarters should be moved to northeastern Anhui. Yanan consented that, should the Japanese launch another major attack at the headquarters, this could be done.

But in northeastern Anhui, the government forces were still active. In the aftermath of the Japanese attack, Liu suggested that Chen go to the border area between northern Anhui and Jiangsu to organize campaigns against his old rival, Governor Han Deqin. In September, Chen led a small staff to Peng Xuefeng's Fourth Division headquarters which was assigned the task of control over the north of the Huai River zone. Peng's Fourth Division, like Huang's Third Division, derived from the units of the Eighth Route Army, which had never been subject to Chen's command before. Many Eighth Route Army officers were proud of their background of being the descendants of the "Central Red Army" in Jiangxi Soviet, and they were never comfortable with the New Fourth Army leadership. Chen as commander of the re-established New Fourth Army had not been able to exercise direct control over divisions other than his own---the First Division. In 1940, for example, Chen had fallen out with Huang Kecheng over the Battle of Cao Dian, and accused the latter of insubordination. Now he found Peng Xuefeng no more receptive to his direction.

During the Japanese attack against Chen's headquarters in July, Governor Han Deqin's remnant troops took the opportunity to occupy an important town called Chengdaokou, a place that allowed him to control both banks of the Grand Canal. The idea was to open a route for the main government forces under General Tang Enbo to advance into this area. Due to a misjudgment, Peng's Fourth Division which had been active in this area had suffered four thousand casualties when fighting with General Tang in spring 1941. Based on this victory, the government troops intended to regain superiority in northern Jiangsu. Chen's plan was to take Chengdaokou at whatever price, Peng's officers hesitated. According to Xiao Wangdong, Peng's political director who accompanied Chen to northeastern Anhui, Chengdaokou had a strong defense network, "even the Japanese could not overcome it by using armored vehicles." Chen was upset at the low morale prevalent among Peng's rank and file. Upon arrival, Chen severely scolded Peng and other commanders, and sent Liu a telegram, harshly criticizing the work done by the Fourth Division. According to Chen, Peng's base area had shrunk due to incompetence. Military and political strategies were poorly coordinated, and there was a lack of will and sound local policy. Liu, like Mao, never fully trusted Chen's judgment. But he decided to back up Chen's position this time, since he was very keen to control Jiangsu and to give Governor Han a final blow. Liu went so far as to grant Chen the "signatory right" of political commissar, a personal privilege he alone enjoyed. Under the circumstances, Chen was able to persuade Peng to carry out his attack plan. This was siege warfare against a well-equipped and fully fortified enemy. It took five days hard battle to overwhelm the government defenders.[49] Governor Han finally became impotent militarily. The New Fourth Army's chief rival in Jiangsu thus all but disappeared.

Chen did not return to headquarters until January 1942, when the war against Japan had taken a new turn. On December 7, 1941, the Japanese fleet under Admiral Yamamoto Isoroku attacked Pearl Harbor. The United States officially entered the Pacific War. China suddenly became a formal member of the anti-fascist alliance. For both the government and the communists, continued civil war became a political liability in front of the domestic as well as international public opinion. To Mao and the Party Central Committee in Yanan, the attack on Pearl Harbor was a godsend for power consolidation. Throughout 1941, the communist base areas in northern and central China had suffered heavy losses incurred by the Japanese. In northern China, the Japanese were determined to exterminate the communists and their local support through "Sanko-Seisaku" (the three-all policy: burn all, kill all and loot all). In central China, though less severe towards civilians, the devastation was also extensive. The communist commitment of elite troops to engaging the Japanese resulted in strong reprisals from Tokyo. All the communist troops badly needed a prolonged respite.

Shortly before Pearl Harbor, the Party Central Committee had already decided in a directive drafted by Mao to give up mobile warfare because "there is no possibility of concentrating troops to wipe out [the Japanese] enemy." It also suggested reduction of unnecessary personnel, and to pursue a "lean troop" policy, because of the continued shrinkage of base areas. The directive also pointedly stated, "in the past, Xiang Ying had pursued a 'lean troop policy,' but at that stage, it was wrong [because of his unwillingness to expand troop numbers]. We should, however, pursue this policy now."[50] After the attack on Pearl Harbor, the party secretariat made its position even more clear in an instruction titled, "The Central Task for 1942." Dated December 28, it stated, "In 1941, our base areas have suffered heavily, we should take the opportunity of the Japanese preoccupation with the Pacific War to recover.... We should not take any large-scale military attack, which will ... incur 'mopping-up' reprisals [from the Japanese]."[51]

But Mao also had other more urgent issues in his mind. Having established *de facto* control over the party since 1935, Mao's position had not yet been legitimized by the position of the party chairmanship. More important was the party's lack of ideological conformity with his thinking. As a seasoned fighter in intra-party power struggle, Mao believed that even the institutionalization of his grip over the party organization was not sufficient for him to exercise absolute decision-making power. There must be political conformity at all levels. Thus the idea of the "Yanan Rectification Campaign" was born. As soon as military activities waned, the internal political battle waxed. The first signal came in January 1942, merely a month after Pearl Harbor, when Mao ordered the printing of thousands copies of "The Resolution of the Ninth Congress of the Red Fourth Army" and distributed them to the garrison troops at Yanan. Mao demanded "officers at all levels should read it over many times."[52] This was the resolution in which Mao settled accounts with Zhu De and Chen Yi in 1929 over the issue of "the party versus the gun," after Mao's command having been twice released and replaced by Chen.

Ominous as it was, Chen at this time was very much immune from the campaign which began to gain momentum only after the spring. In the first few months, the campaign was largely localized at Yanan. Chen was too far away to be concerned. But Chen's life was not made easy when, in January, Mao's major political ally Liu Shaoqi was recalled to Yanan. Instead of appointing Chen to the number one position, i.e., the party secretary at the New Fourth Army, Liu left his job, apparently with Yanan's full approval, to Chen's subordinate Rao Shushi. For a long time Rao had been a leader in party's underground urban work. This was the secret territory of party operation long dominated by Liu. Rao was also Xiang's successor at the Red Trade Union Executive in Moscow under the Comintern after 1935. Like Liu, Rao had no military background but excelled himself in intra-party politics. Upon return from Moscow, Rao took over a deputy party secretary position at Xiang's Southeastern Bureau. During the Southern Anhui Incident, Xiang deserted the troops for a day. At Liu's recommendation, Rao was put in charge of the party work, acting on Xiang's behalf.[53] After the demise of Xiang's headquarters, Rao managed to flee to Hong Kong and returned to the newly-established New Fourth Army headquarters a few months later. He was immediately appointed by Liu deputy secretary at Central Plains Bureau in charge of party propaganda. Now as party secretary of the

Central China Bureau, Rao would assume concurrently political commissar's duty, thus becoming the *de facto* number one in the command chain.

By 1942, Chen's record had remained impeccable, and the communist success in Jiangsu was largely done by his elite troops, the "Ye-Wang-Tao columns" which had formed the First Division of the New Fourth Army. Chen's contribution was duly acknowledged by Liu before his departure for Yanan, as he told the audience at the last Central China Bureau's conference under his auspices, that the "First Division has for the last few years achieved the most successes. It has fought most of battles and contributed most in wars of friction [i.e., the civil war]."[54] Such a favorable verdict was important for Chen's continued leadership, despite his being only the second in command. There is little doubt that Chen's prestige was much higher than that of Rao. He commanded enormous respect, which Rao could only dream of having, from the rank and file. Therefore he was in a position to effectively control the New Fourth Army affairs despite Rao's promotion.

The newly promoted Rao was very cautious at the beginning. He refrained from expressing his true feelings about Chen. But the character and style of the two were too far apart. Chen was a known extrovert while Rao was always an introvert. Because Chen was involved in the early Red Army history, many anecdotes coming from his mouth could easily be interpreted as offensive to Mao. Rao patiently bought his time and sought opportunities to destroy Chen's prestige. The conflict between the two did not erupt until a year later at the peak of the Yanan Rectification Campaign, which was in effect, a brutal political purge that would force all communist leaders to choose between absolute conformity to Mao and self-destruction.

Notes

1. Ye et al, *Reference Materials of the New Fourth Army*, vol.2, p.227-230.
2. Ibid., p.273-275.
3. Zeng, Ruqing, *Hui Yi Zhang Xiaochun He Ta de Tong Lin Sha Zhou You Ji Da Dui* (In Memory of Zhang Xiaochun and His Guerrilla of Tong Lin Sha Zhou), in *Jue Huo Bu Xi* (Fire Never Extinguishes---Essays in Memory of General Zeng Ruqing, Taizhou 1992), p.30-31.
4. Ibid., p.38-39.
5. *Biography of Chen Yi* (Official), p.227.
6. *Selected Works of Liu Shaoqi*, vol.1, p.168-169.
7. Ma et al, *The Chronology of Events Related to the New Fourth Army*,

July 1940 listing.

8. Ji, Fang, *Wo Liang Ci Ru Dang de Qian Qian Hou Hou* (Before and After My Two Admissions to the Party), in *Su Zhong Kang Ri Geng Ju Di* (Central Jiangsu Anti-Japanese Base Area, Beijing 1990), p.549.

9. *Biography of Chen Yi* (Jiang), p.500.

10. Known as "Jin Jiang Yan (Gold Jiang Yan)," it was the richest town in northern Jiangsu.

11. *Biography of Chen Yi* (Official), p.251.

12. The communist histories never agree with this judgment.

13. Su, Yu, *Huangqiao Zhan Yi Zong Jie* (The Summary of the Battle of Huangqiao), in Sun, Keji et al, *Su Yu Jun Shi Wen Ji* (The Military Works of Su Yu, Beijing 1989), p.56-57.

14. Chen, Yi, *Huangqiao Zhan Yi Zong Jie* (The Summary of the Battle of Huangqiao), in *Xin Si Jun He Huang Zhong Kang Ri Geng Ju Di Shi Liao Xuan* (Selected Historical Documents of the New Fourth Army and the Central China Anti-Japanese Base Area, Shanghai 1984), p.283.

15. *WJXJ*, vol.12, p.389-390.

16. For these three telegrams, see *Wan Nan Shi Bian* (The Southern Anhui Incident, Beijing 1982), p.66-69.

17. Ibid., p.65-66.

18. Ibid., p.56-57.

19. Ibid., p.62.

20. Ibid., p.63.

21. *WJXJ*, vol.12, p.504-505.

22. *The Southern Anhui Incident*, p.85-87.

23. *Biography of Chen Yi* (Official), p.259-260.

24. *The Chronology of Events Related to the New Fourth Army*, November 1940 listing.

25. *MZDJSWJ*, vol.2, p.560.

26. Ibid., p.583.

27. *Memoirs of Huang Kecheng*, vol.1, p.309-311.

28. *The Chronology of Events Related to the New Fourth Army*, December 1940 listing.

29. *MZDJSWJ*, vol.2, p.585.

30. Ibid., p.591.

31. Ibid., p.600-601.

32. In fact Zhou had said to Chiang Kai-shek that the northern Anhui route was "unreliable." See *Zhou-Chiang Tan Hua* (Zhou-Chiang Conversation Record), in *The Southern Anhui Incident*, p.121-122. For the telegram to Xiang dated December 30, suggesting a direct route to Jiangsu, see *MZDJSWJ*, vol.2, p.602.

33. *The Southern Anhui Incident*, p.103-104.

34. Ibid., p.103.

35. For frequent wire exchanges during the battle, see, Ibid., p.128-147.
36. Ibid., p.147-p.150.
37. *Hao Zhu Ren Zhong Qiguang* (Good Director Zhong Qiguang---Essays in Memory of General Zhong Qiguang, Beijing 1993), p.517-518.
38. For this unique regiment's history, see *Fire Never Extinguishes*, op. ct., *Tian Jun Xiao Jiang* (The Best General of the Iron Army---Essays in Memory of General Liao Zhengguo, Jiangsu 1992) and *Ru Jiang Feng Fan* (Model Scholar General---Essays in Memory of General Zhu Qixiang, Jiangsu 1995).
39. *MZDJSWJ*, vol.2, p.622-623.
40. Ibid., p.633-634. Tojo's speech was quoted by Mao in the telegram.
41. Ibid., p.641.
42. Johnson, Chalmers, *Peasant Nationalism and Communist Power* (Stanford 1962), p.41.
43. Ibid., p.143.
44. Liu to Xue, April 1941, in *Materials of Party History*, vol.4, p.1-5.
45. *Central Jiangsu Anti-Japanese Base Area*, p.49.
46. *Xin Si Jun Chong Jian Jun Bu Yi Hou* (The New Fourth Army After the Reestablishment of Its Headquarters, Nanjing 1983), p.47-48.
47. Ibid., p.70-71.
48. Ibid., p.103-105.
49. *Biography of Chen Yi* (Official), p.271-277.
50. *WJXJ*, vol.13, p.213.
51. Ibid., p.272.
52. *MZDJSWJ*, vol.2, p.675.
53. *The Southern Anhui Incident*, p.129.
54. Liu's report was quoted in Sun, Keji ed., *Su Yu Lun Su Zhong Kang Zhan* (Su Yu on Central Jiangsu's War Against the Japanese, Nanjing 1993), p.140, note 1.

The Chen Brothers in 1929

Marshal Chen Yi in 1955

The "Bandit" leaders in 1938.
Front row from left: Zhang
Yunyi, Ye Fei, Chen Yi,
Xiang Ying, Huang Dao.

The wedding, 1940

Zhou Enlai's trip to Cloud Hill in 1939.
From left: Chen Yi, Su Yu, Fu Qiutao,
Zhou Enlai, Zhu Kejing, Ye Ting.

The Mayor of Shanghai

Chapter Five

Politics of Conformity

To a large extent, 1942 was the most difficult year for the New Fourth Army, especially for Chen's elite troops, the First Division under Su Yu's command in central Jiangsu. After the Battle of Huangqiao of 1940, the New Fourth Army became the second strongest power in this area. According to a contemporary report, the three brigades under Su (the Ye-Wang-Tao units) were at a strength of 13,700. The Japanese had 5,600 soldiers in the same area, plus puppet forces at over 30,000. Within central Jiangsu, the Japanese had occupied some 500 square kilometers of territory, where the Japanese had established 17 strongholds under their exclusive control, 74 under joint Japanese and puppet control and 77 under the puppets alone.[1] Because of its approximate position to Shanghai and Nanjing, this area commanded relatively important strategic value. Moreover, the communists were determined to hold on to this area, not so much for the purpose of fighting Japan, as for the power competition with the government at the end of the war.

In mid-1942, Mao had already begun thinking about the post-war strategic chess board. Somehow convinced that the Japanese would be defeated by the allies by the end of 1943, Mao decided that two strategic areas were of the most important long-term value. The first was Central Jiangsu. On the one hand, the communist army in this area would be the first to take Shanghai and Nanjing at the time when the Japanese were forced to surrender, thus increasing stakes in bargaining with the government. On the other, if the allies should decide to carry out an amphibious landing in China, as was widely speculated about the time, Shanghai and the nearby coastal area would be the natural landing point. Therefore, the communists would be the first to receive and to deal with the allies. The second most important strategic area was Shandong, a province situated between Jiangsu and Manchuria. Mao believed that at the end of the war, the government would be in the weakest position in northern China and Manchuria, where Chiang Kai-shek had practically withdrawn all his troops. In a top secret personal telegram to Liu Shaoqi dated July 9, 1942, Mao called Shandong a "pivot for strategic transformation" for the post-war period. According to Mao, the Yangzi Valley was Chiang's power base; it would be the key area the government must take control under any circumstances. Thus the communist forces may at the end of the war have to retreat to northern China and Manchuria. If Chiang should control Shandong, the strategic connection between the Eighth Route and the New Fourth Armies would be cut off. Chiang must try to stop the latter from moving to the north. Therefore Shandong must be put under communist control at all costs. Mao added, "This point should not be told to anyone."[2]

Long-term strategic planning aside, Mao was still more preoccupied with his "Rectification Campaign." In February 1942, Mao announced a campaign against "subjectivism, factionalism and the stereotyped style of writing." The campaign appeared harmless at first. But it was quickly turned into a major political purge, which was surpassed only by Mao's Anti-AB Clique campaign of the early 1930s. This time, it was called "rescue operation (*Qiang Jou Yun Dong*)."

Throughout the first half of 1942, the "Rectification Campaign" was still limited to verbal abuse. Mao's objective was to undermine the "Muscovites" by attacking their dogmatism. Since the Southern Anhui Incident, the "Muscovites" had lost all the power at central as well as local levels. Xiang Ying was considered a chief villain associated with the leading Muscovite, Wang Ming. Beating them up one more time proved to be a much easier task. But to impose political conformity upon the rank and file was not as easy as Mao had thought. Most base areas away from Yanan responded to the "Rectification Campaign" with a lukewarm attitude. Military commanders in particular tended to view the political commissar's work with considerable suspicion. Developed during the Red Army years, the political commissar, a title invented in Soviet Russia, was the chief political officer of an army unit. He therefore held the final say on all decisions concerning political as well as military affairs. More often than not a political commissar was totally unfamiliar with military strategy and tactics. A conflict between him and the commander naturally arose. It had been Mao's firm conviction since the Jinggang Mountains days that the party (represented by the political commissar) must control the gun (represented by the commander). The Rectification Campaign, to a large extent, was to reaffirm this principle, which made many field commanders uncomfortable.

In the spring of 1942, the widespread "rescue operation" finally began to take shape. In Yanan, intellectuals from urban and metropolitan areas bore the brunt of the attack. Although Mao halfheartedly instructed the party's central purge machine not to execute suspects or to force confessions, his loyal servant Kang Sheng, a Politburo member in charge of the purge, understood Mao's intention and pursued his objective with zeal and passion.

By September, Mao found the result unsatisfactory. In an important directive dated September 1, Mao called for "unifying leadership under the party." Stressing once again his favorite political commissar system, Mao demanded the dissolution of the dual responsibility system under which commander and commissar shared equal leadership roles.[3] Chen was immune from implementing this policy because the constant skirmishes with the Japanese had put military work always at the top of the priority list. According to Zhong Qiguang, a key political officer under Chen, the New Fourth Army simply did not have enough time and a safe place to carry out the purge campaign.[4]

In Yanan, the campaign continued to escalate. In a telegram to Peng Dehuai, Deputy Commander of the Eighth Route Army, Mao complained that the Yanan Rectification Campaign is very successful .... But in base areas it has not been deepened yet." Mao told Peng that his intention was not just to urge studies and self-criticism, but also to "reexamine cadres' history." According to Mao, his main targets were "high level officials, at one to two hundred in each base area. Next will be the middle level officials, at several hundred to several thousand each." This would be a "serious struggle."[5]

To jump-start the purge, Mao and Kang jointly signed a sensational order in August, claiming the wide existence of spies within the party. It made a shocking statement at the outset, "So many spies exist, we should not be taken by surprise." One member of the purge machine at Yanan, General Li Yiming, recalled many years later that, "in the fall of 1943, the caves of Yanan were lighted twenty-four hours a day. Kang Sheng and his colleagues set up a command center to 'rescue' thousands of suspects." Participating in one of the typical interrogations together with Wang Dongxing, Mao's security chief, Li recalled that the suspect, a young man named Zhang Keqin, vehemently denied being a spy sent by the government. So they focused on his father, a famous doctor practicing Chinese traditional medicine, who had obviously treated several high-level government officials. After forty-eight hours non-stop harassment, the young man could not take it any more and "confessed" that he was introduced to join the Kuomintang by one of his father's patients. At one point, even the communication department at the communist headquarters was paralyzed because over one thousand officers in charge of decoding and telegraphy were being "rescued." The head of the department, Wang Zeng, had to bring his staff to line up outside Mao's cave, where the latter decided to acquit them on the spot.[6]

By all accounts, Chen seemed less than enthusiastic about the campaign, having known Mao's excesses all too well in the past. In Chen Yi's territory, the campaign process was characterized throughout 1942 as "mild wind and drizzle" (*He Feng Xi Yu*). Although many new recruits from urban areas were subject to abuse and accused of being spies, there was relatively little personal struggle within the party organizations. Chen preferred to concentrate on local administrative issues. In May 1942, Chen had a son. He was excited by his first child at the age of forty-one. Throughout the year of 1942, Chen was busy with political work, since Mao had instructed him to avoid active engagement with the Japanese. In January, the Central Committee directed all communist base areas to begin implementing a rent and interest reduction policy. To avoid conflict with landowners, the directive suggested at the same time that peasants should be made to pay the reduced rent and interest on time.[7] In Chen's area of control, the reduction was modest, only twenty-five percent, because the peasant population had fared much better than those in most other places in communist-controlled territories. Even so, many peasants were not sure that this was a good idea. In Ye Fei's jurisdiction, many peasants worried that their landlords may not be willing to rent them land at a reduction. Some of them even returned the remaining part of the rent to the landlord in the middle of the night after having ostensibly paid seventy-five percent during the day to satisfy the communists.[8]

More important, Chen and Su were finally able to pursue their plan, which was delayed by the Japanese "mopping-up" campaign, to localize part of the regular army in order to control and expand the communist militia. Consistent with Mao's "lean troop" instruction, Chen boldly decided to send one-third of the regular troops under his command to reach this end. Most of the localized troops were very successful in expanding the communist influence. Not only were they able to train and discipline local militia, but they could also expand a large base for future recruitment, a factor that would prove to be of decisive importance at the end of the war against Japan. According to Chen Yi, this policy was one stone killing two birds. On the one hand, the regular units became much smaller, more mobile and effective. On the other, local militias were to be regularized. Ye Fei sent his trusted commander Zeng Ruqing to regularize militia forces in Taizhou. Zeng at first discovered that many militia members were opium addicts and local bullies. But within a year, Zeng was able to expand the battalion he had brought to Taizhou into a regular regiment. By 1943, the new regiment had already acquired the ability to "independently engage the Japanese."[9]

But the party work proved to be rather difficult. In Su Yu's Central Jiangsu Military Region, the jurisdiction assigned to the First Division, the communists found it hard to recruit new membership. As late as November 1942, Su reported only ten thousand party members among the over five million population under his control. Moreover, most of the party members were within the regular army, therefore, there was a constant shortage of party members to fill local administrative positions. The communists established four levels of administration in 1942: prefect, county, district and township. According to one contemporary report, only leaders at the prefect and county levels were communists in Central Jiangsu. In ninety-five districts, merely forty-five directors were members of the party. Further down to the township level, there were 136 party members in charge, while the rest at over one thousand were in the hands of non-party members.[10]

Tax collection proved to be an easier task. Through coercion as well as rent and interest reduction, the peasants and landlords were made to pay taxes on time. During 1942, the Japanese established a "Northern Jiangsu Material Control Commission" headed by the local commander of the Japanese brigade. Its purpose was two-fold: to collect taxes on the puppet regime's behalf, and to impose an economic embargo against the communists. But the communists were still able to increase grain collection as part of the taxes. In the summer harvest season of 1942 alone, such collection exceeded that in the whole year of 1941. The peasants and the landlords would rather pay taxes to the communists than to the puppet regime. Even the puppet troops themselves were not enthusiastic about carrying out the Japanese orders. During the process of requisition of coolies to build roads for the Japanese troops in northern Jiangsu, many puppet soldiers told the reluctant villagers who were afraid of reprisal from the communists, "You may send your oldest son to build the road during the day, and send your second son to destroy it during the night, nobody will bother you any more."[11] It is clear that in the prosperous Jiangsu, the communists could not, but for the Japanese invasion, build up a strong popular base. Therefore, as Chalmers Johnson has pointed out, peasant nationalism, instead of communist ideology, was crucial to the success of the communists in this area.[12]

At the end of 1942, the New Fourth Army headquarters finally moved to eastern Anhui. Chen no longer had any excuses for not deepening the Rectification Campaign as Mao had wanted. Chen's preference for a "mild wind and drizzle" approach did not bode well with Yanan. By the spring of 1943, the "rescue campaign" began to affect the rank and file of the New Fourth Army. Ye Fei's First Brigade, for example, claimed to have ferreted out a secret society clique from Shanghai. Many intellectual recruits were executed. It turned out that, before joining the New Fourth

Army, these recruits who were brutally purged were members of a left-leaning book club named "One Heart Reading Club" in Shanghai. For the first time in the history of the New Fourth Army, the sense of terror replaced a usually open atmosphere. The fear was deepened by the fact that the majority of the rank and file was now from Jiangsu, Zhejiang and Shanghai areas. Few had any knowledge about the dreadful Anti-AB Clique campaigns of the Jiangxi Soviet years to realize that this was by no means the worst of its kind.

Indeed, for those who had endured Mao's excesses before, the terror appeared relatively modest. One survivor of Mao's purge in the Red Army years, Huang Kecheng, was able to tone down the campaign in his Third Division in order not to repeat the dreadful Anti-AB Clique experience of the 1930s. In one incidence, Huang found that his colleague, commander of the Seventh Division, Zeng Xisheng, was terribly worried when his wife was accused by her best girl friend of being a government spy. Huang personally interrogated the accuser, only to find out that she was coerced by her superiors to make this false charge. In the Second Division, the campaign was carried out with enormous enthusiasm. Its political commissar, Tan Zhenlin, a Jinggang Mountains veteran and long time Mao crony, proudly declared that each of his regiments had "rescued" several hundred soldiers. According to his memoirs, Huang then made a suggestion to Rao Shushi, the party chief of the New Fourth Army, to stop this nonsense, and Rao apparently agreed.[13]

But Rao had other ideas in mind. His main concern was about Chen Yi. Rao knew that the high-level officers were Mao's chief targets. Throughout 1942, Rao was criticized severely by the rank and file during a mild campaign within the New Fourth Army leadership. Suspecting Chen's hand behind it all, he began to seek an opportunity for revenge. Rao knew Chen's history of having replaced Mao twice during the Jinggang Mountains period. When the "rescue campaign" was authorized by Mao in August, Rao immediately took action. In one clever move, Rao deliberately left the headquarters to inspect various troop units and let Chen take charge of the campaign. With Rao's absence, high level officers became daring enough to challenge Rao's work style and authority during a meeting that lasted for two days. But Rao returned abruptly and began to hold private conversations with numerous high-level commanders, indicating to them that Chen had opposed Mao many times in history. He pointedly suggested that Chen had long been hostile to Mao's favorite "political commissar system." The commanders were terrified. Many began to fear that Rao may have had secret instructions from Mao to launch a campaign to purge Chen. Expediency alone dictated that they had no choice but to distance themselves from Chen.

Chen was quickly isolated. For a month, as Chen would recall years later, "not even a devil dared to knock at my door."[14] In mid-October, Rao decided that it was the time to stop beating around the bushes and to put his cards on the table. According to a somewhat dramatized account, Rao listed ten charges against Chen. Among them the most serious were: opposing Mao during the Red Army years; opposition to the political commissar system; putting too much trust in intellectuals; favoritism towards his own elite troops such as the First Division; and showmanship at public functions. Rao had apparently been somehow supported by commanders who had held grudges against Chen, such as Peng Xuefeng and Zhang Yunyi. But Rao's scheme went further. He aimed to remove Chen from his command position.[15] In a personal telegram to Mao and Liu Shaoqi, Rao stated that Chen had organized meetings to attack him because he disliked the idea of a political commissar controlling the New Fourth Army affairs in general. Mao was, of course, greatly agitated by this report. Moreover, Rao was able to urge or coerce other top commanders to send similar telegrams to Yanan confirming his point. The strategy worked. Although most Chinese communist historians have tried to extricate Mao from this incident, because Rao was allegedly to rebel against Mao in 1954 and was purged together with Gao Gang, it is clear that Mao strongly endorsed Rao's position. After Chen had made an apology to Mao about his "careless remarks" on Red Army history, Mao suggested that Chen temporarily leave his command and come to Yanan for at least "half a year."[16]

Chen was shocked by Mao's decision. He had reached a high point in his career with his hard work at the New Fourth Army. It appeared that he might, as in 1930, quickly sink to the bottom again. But, unlike 1929, Chen did not really "oppose Mao" this time. Furthermore, Mao's method indicated something ominous. As every Chinese communist insider had known by that time, a mere accusation of "opposing Mao" was tantamount to a death warrant. Chen had never been to Yanan, and was happy to be away from the center of the intra-party power intrigues. He did not know what kind of music he would face there. In an unusually melancholy poem written shortly before his departure in November, Chen stated, "Those who truly know me are but a few. Let's don't talk about the road ahead." In another poem to his wife who just had a second son, and was not allowed to accompany him to Yanan, Chen deplored, "I will go to the north, but you have to stay in the south. We are both lonely, taking care of ourselves."[17]

Chen's humiliation suffered at Rao's hands sent a shock wave through the rank and file of the New Fourth Army. In the Central Jiangsu Military Region commanded Su Yu, the impact was somehow cushioned by Su's decision not to spread the details down to the rank and file. According to Guan Wenwei, who was present at the meetings organized by Rao to attack Chen, most of Chen's proteges were so panic-stricken that none of them dared to mention a word about the meeting to each other. The stakes were of course high for those who had followed Chen for the past few years. As a rule, if Chen should officially become an anti-Mao element, his subordinates could hardly escape the purge that would be sure to follow. Only Su Yu calmly pointed out that there was no official document supporting Rao's attack on Chen, therefore the detailed information about Chen's temporary dismissal could be concealed from the troops. Huang Kecheng, despite his personal problems with Chen in the past, also decided on his own not to tell the story to his subordinates.[18]

Chen was worried sick about his future. But he did not know that Mao had something else in store for him. Since Chen was one of the original founders of the Jinggang Mountains base area, Mao needed Chen's support to finalize his victory within the party to become the Chinese Stalin. Chen's trip took more than three months while crossing enemy zones on horseback and sometimes on foot in the deadly northern Chinese winter. At one point, Mao instructed him to stay for a while at Deng Xiaoping's 129th Division headquarters in the Taihang Mountain base area to "read some documents." Deng was Mao's confidant, but he was also Chen's fellow student in France. Thanks to him, Chen was able to read many sensitive internal documents that Rao had been keeping from him in the past.

Ten days later, Mao finally decided to summon Chen to Yanan. The two men had not seen each other for eight years now. Chen was too naive to think that Mao understood his problems with Rao. During their first meeting, he began to vent his spleen and to complain about his mistreatment by Rao in central China. But Mao immediately gave him a cold shower. As Chen would recall years later, Mao said, "If you want to talk about guerrilla war in Jiangxi, or anti-Japanese war in central China, I will organize a special meeting, allowing you to talk for three days and three nights. But, about Xiao Yao [Rao's nickname], I think you'd better mention nothing at all." Mao added, "Rao has sent me a telegram [concerning Chen], if you want to read it, I will consent, but I think you would better not read it for the moment." Chen reluctantly agreed.[19]

Mao was testing Chen's loyalty. A few days later, Mao told Chen that, "After thinking for more than a week, I have concluded that your basic attitude is good. You should now send a telegram to Rao, making some self-criticism in order to settle this issue." Chen followed Mao's order. In an accompanying telegram, Mao told Rao that, "The Chen-Rao conflict is just over the working relationship .... Chen should not be placed in the same league as Xiang Ying." Rao was not, however, willing to stop there. In a private telegram to Mao, Rao insisted that, "The conflict between Chen and me is neither over main political line, nor just over the working relationship. It is because Comrade Chen is incorrect in his thinking and conception about our organization." More pointedly, Rao stated, "Chen ... is right-leaning on the United Front, on the attitude towards intellectuals and on the principle of our party institution. Chen holds many grudges against certain historical issues, and sometimes adopts a very bad working style." Rao's innuendo about the Chen-Mao conflict in history was devastating. Chen wrote a letter to Mao, asking for his final judgment. Mao did not reply for a few weeks. To Chen, this boded ominously. The suspense ended when suddenly a letter from Mao came, "You should have more patience, think more about your mistakes ... and tolerate others." The language was surprisingly mild and friendly. Realizing that Mao had no intention of purging him, Chen was greatly relieved.[20]

In May 1943, Mao decided that Chen had passed an initial loyalty test and began to assign him to work. It turned out that Mao intended him to fulfill a task of enormous importance: to draft the military report on behalf of the Central Committee for the long-planned Seventh Party Congress, which was designed to establish Mao's indisputable status as the Chinese Stalin. Chen was flattered. Such a job was usually reserved for Politburo members, but Chen was not even a member of the Central Committee. Within the Central Committee, most top leaders had already been converted into Mao's supporters. The power now lay with the so-called "Big Five Secretaries" (*Wu Da Shu Ji*)---the powerful secretariat, which included Mao, Zhou Enlai, Zhu De, Ren Bishi and Liu Shaoqi. Zhou as the official communist representative was based in Chongqing, the wartime capital. He had supported Mao since 1935. Liu was a committed Mao crony. Ren, though a "Muscovite," had turned against his old friends Wang Ming and Bo Gu in recent years. Chen's old colleague Zhu De had no political ambition and was commander in chief in all but name. The key purpose of the Seventh Party Congress was to establish the myth that Mao had always been correct when the others were wrong. Like all party congresses in history, the Seventh Congress would focus on three aspects: political, military and party history. Having been given the military report job, Chen's status was greatly enhanced.

The choice of Chen was apparently a calculated move on Mao's part. On the one hand, Chen was a living witness to the Red Army's history. Having replaced Mao twice and been subject to Mao's excesses, Chen's conversion would be extremely convincing in proving Mao's infallibility. On the other, Chen was considered to be a practitioner of Mao's correct line. As a top commander in a major strategic base area, Chen's enormous success with the New Fourth Army could be attributed to Mao's brilliant leadership. Moreover, Chen's contribution could also put an official end to the Mao-Xiang dispute in central China, and further destroy the credibility of the Muscovites who were alleged to have associated with the failure of the initial period of the New Fourth Army history. But the ever suspicious Mao was unwilling to fully trust Chen until the latter had completely converted through admitting his own mistakes. At the end of 1943, after a long period of painful meditation, Chen wrote a letter to Mao, stating that he had realized the absolute need for party unity. More importantly, Chen began to adopt the Yanan method of self-criticism, stating that, "Thinking back about the last few years in central China, I have suppressed opposition from at least over a dozen top commanders .... Last winter I was angry ... now I realize I was wrong in many aspects." This was what Mao had been patiently waiting for. Mao was delighted and wrote back, "Once you have thought it through, everything will be fine .... You should be prepared to persist with truth, but to right mistakes all the time. Nothing will go wrong with that attitude."[21]

Throughout the 1944, aside from drafting the military report, Chen was idle and largely jobless. Mao did not assign any official position to him. But Chen was invited to whatever official functions in Yanan. By August 1944, Mao asked him to participate in decisions concerning foreign relations. This was an experience that would turn out to be very helpful after being appointed the Minister of Foreign Affairs years later. Earlier in June 1943, General Joseph Stilwell's political advisor, John Service, suggested the establishment a military mission at Yanan. Chiang had resisted this idea until June 1944 when American Vice President Henry Wallace persuaded him to allow a US military observing group to visit Yanan. Led by Colonel David Barret, the group, dubbed the Dixie Mission, arrived on July 22. John Service, who had accompanied the group, found Chen Yi a very interesting figure. Service was born in the China Inland Mission at Chengdu, Sichuan province, where Chen had also spent his childhood. Service took enormous interest in Chen's background and interviewed Chen a few days later. According to Chen's record of conversation, which he sent to Mao, Service raised the question: if the government troops should move into the area controlled by the New Fourth Army, what would he do. Chen answered that, the New Fourth Army alone could deal with government attacks. It is interesting to note that Service was more convinced than Chen that Chiang would launch an overall attack against the communists at the end of the war.[22]

Meanwhile, Chen continued to work on the important military report. In May 1944, the Central Committee decided at a meeting to set up a preparation committee which would take over day to day affairs of the party until the opening of the planned Seventh Congress. The old Politburo was thus deactivated. It was Liu Shaoqi who suggested at the meeting that Mao should be given the interim title of "Chairman of the

Central Committee," a title that had never been used in the party's history. Due to apparent internal conflict, the preparation committee chaired by Mao had to work for eleven months before they felt secure enough to convene the congress in April 1945. Chen was converted during the process into a Mao fan. But he carried his political conformity a bit too far, when he produced a military report with fifty-seven-thousand words. In this report he extolled Mao to a position even Mao himself at the time felt embarrassed by. According to Chen, "In the last sixty years, the Chinese did not have a national military science.... It is due to Mao's genius and creativity we now have a military science that represents national character." Chen was the first to coin the word, "Mao Zedong military school," which was later changed into "Mao's military thought." Chen made a major mistake to utilize many controversial historical facts of the communist party and the Red Army to prove his point. But the report did not go well with the other members of the preparation committee. Many felt hurt, others booed at Chen's report during a preliminary discussion in March 1945, one month before the congress. Sensing the obvious opposition, Mao decided hurriedly to kill Chen's report on the spot and arranged for Zhu De to draft a new and more succinct military report. Chen was greatly embarrassed by this debacle. But his loyalty to Mao was rewarded with membership in the new Central Committee established in May 1945.[23] Nevertheless, Chen was allowed to make a major speech at the congress, in which he reiterated a few paragraphs about "Mao's military thought." And, to Mao's delight, he admitted once again his own "mistakes" during the Red Army years.[24]

Meanwhile, Chen's elite troops under Su Yu had been holding on to the Central Jiangsu base area since Chen's sad departure. Su was not keen to preoccupy himself with the "Rectification Campaign." Living under the Japanese nose in central Jiangsu, Su had adequate excuses to limit the campaign to occasional study sessions. The Japanese continuously staged bloody "mopping-up" campaigns in 1943, but with little success. At first, the Japanese refrained from adopting the "*Sanko Seisako* (Three-all)" policy in communist-controlled area. Their preferred policy was called "30% military, 70% political," which meant using propaganda and other non-military means to destroy the New Fourth Army's reputation. Increasingly frustrated with failures, they began to escalate the level of brutality. According to a contemporary report, in a nine-month long "mopping-up" campaign in Tao Yong's Third Brigade territory, 62,000 local people were killed, 1,855 women raped and tens of thousands of houses were burnt. The Japanese and the puppets also lost over 4,000 soldiers.[25]

Mao became less enthusiastic about the strategic importance of Jiangsu at the beginning of 1943. Encouraged by the Soviet victory at the Stalingrad, Mao began to ponder the possibility of withdrawing all the communist troops back in order to control the north of the Yellow River. The idea was to divide the country into northern and southern spheres of influence. In a telegram to Rao Shushi dated January 5, 1943, Mao stated that "We are negotiating with the Kuomintang to merge the Eighth Route and the New Fourth Armies .... Our general post-war policy is to move to the north of the Yellow River."[26] Since the New Fourth Army was declared by the government to be illegal and a "rebellious army," Mao endeavored to obtain its legal status by sending Lin Biao to Chongqing for the negotiations. By July, the negotiation did not yield any substantial result. The Central Committee had to give up this idea. Liu Shaoqi sent Rao a telegram dated July 23, warning the New Fourth Amy leadership not to harbor "any illusions about the Kuomintang."[27]

By 1944 the Japanese no longer had the capacity to exterminate the communists, as the table of the Pacific War began to turn in the allies' favor. After Chen's departure from central China, Su's forces had been anxiously waiting for Yanan's verdict on Chen's fate and they were relieved to learn that Chen was not the target for purge after all. Chen was admitted into the Central Committee and Su was awarded an alternate membership. The New Fourth Army was now, however, under the firm control of Chen's rival Rao Shushi. But Rao's headquarters was in Anhui. Su and his commanders enjoyed relative independence during Chen's absence. In the spring of 1944, Su Yu and Ye Fei---who had been promoted to the deputy commander of the First Division since 1941---decided to launch a major attack on the Japanese. The target was a stronghold at Cheqiao which was located between two Japanese garrisons in Jiangsu. The enemy's tactical coordination was very weak. As an apparent defiance to Political Commissar Rao, Su and Ye did not report to him before the battle was over. The plan was to take Cheqiao by surprise and at the same time, to induce enemy reinforcements into a tactical pocket that was deployed outside of Cheqiao. The plan worked exceedingly well. Ye's regimental home, the First Regiment, bore the brunt of the attack from the Japanese reinforcements. The battle ended up with eight hundred Japanese casualties. More spectacularly, the communists captured forty-two Japanese soldiers and officers. Since the Japanese were known to be able to fight to a man, the capture of so many of them alive was considered a miracle. A contemporary official Chinese communist account pointed out that this was the battle that had captured the most Japanese prisoners of the war since the beginning of the Sino-Japanese conflict in 1937.[28]

Rao was, of course, outraged by this act of defiance. Suspecting once again a hand of Chen Yi behind the scenes, he reprimanded Su and Ye severely. But Yanan found this unauthorized battle very useful for propaganda purposes. The Party Central Committee through its official newspaper *Liberation Daily* immediately publicized a major victory at Cheqiao against the Japanese. Rao was quickly silenced.[29] During 1944, Mao was mistakenly convinced that the allied forces may land in the coast somewhere near Shanghai. Therefore, the New Fourth Army's strategic task was specified as, "breaking the enemy and taking the capital city [Nanjing] (*Po Di Shou Jing*)"so as to increase the bargaining position with the government at the end of the war. Xiang Ying's much-criticized "Southern Strategy" once again became attractive. In September 1944, Chen Yi was authorized to draft a telegram on behalf of the Central Committee to Su Yu, urging the First Division to move to the south and set up a base in Tianmu Mountain in Zhejiang Province, for the purpose of controlling the coast line.[30] Su immediately started preparations. For Su, this mission was an emotional rendezvous. The Tianmu Mountain area was his old guerrilla base after the devastating defeat of his troops that had covered the Party Central Committee's retreat in 1934. As early as 1942, the New Fourth Army had sent Tan Qilong and He Kexi to establish a new guerrilla base there, but their position remained very precarious, because of the lack of strong local support. Moreover, the government forces had been ordered to prevent the communists from entering this area. To make such a move to the Tianmu Mountain area, it would trigger once again a clash with the government Third War Zone after a three-year lapse since the Southern Anhui Incident. For months, Su trained his troops for fighting in mountain terrain. The communists smuggled many seamless steel tubes from Shanghai to manufacture numerous portable 52 mm mountain guns. By December 1944, the assembled troops, now called the First Echelon, were set to go. Su personally led them across the Yangzi River. The First Echelon consisted of Tao Yong and Wang Bicheng's brigades. Ye Fei and his First Brigade remained in central Jiangsu to take over Su's responsibility. As was expected, the First Echelon under Su immediately encountered government attack. This was the beginning of a new round of the civil war which had been absent since 1941.

In February 1945, the first major battle occurred at the mountain town, Xiaofeng. The result was inconclusive, but the communists were able to hold on to the town. In March, the Third War Zone launched the second attack at Xiaofeng with a larger troop formation consisting of twelve regiments. Again they were beaten back. Su, however, was frustrated by the numerical advantage on the government side. He sent a telegram to Ye Fei, asking for his reinforcement. Ye was put into a difficult position. The departure of Ye's brigade would mean the absence of any regular army in the Central Jiangsu Base Area. The local party functionaries were vehemently against this decision. But Ye was more sympathetic with Su's view, since he also had a penchant, sometimes even more intense than Su had, for taking part in large-scale mobile warfare. He would not let another opportunity slip through his fingers. Understanding Su's dilemma better than the party functionaries, Ye's military instinct prevailed. In April, Ye led his First Brigade across the Yangzi to join Su in the mountains. At this time, the Third War Zone decided to concentrate an even larger force to seek a decisive battle with the communists in the Tianmu Mountain area. Led by General Shangguan Yunxiang, who had acquired enormous reputation for having wiped out Xiang Ying's headquarters in 1941, the government amassed fourteen divisions to attack the town of Xiaofeng for the third time. In the face of numerical inferiority, the communists decided to utilize the same strategy used during the Battle of Huangqiao of 1940. After leaving a small force to hold on to Xiaofeng city, the main troops hid outside the city to ambush the government troops. In June, General Shangguan's elite unit, the 52nd Division, made a major mistake of advancing directly at Xiaofeng without cover on its left and right wings. Once again, the Ye-Wang-Tao troops coordinated remarkably well to crush the 52nd Division. Although the battle raged for six days, the government lost three full regiments. The communists also suffered heavy casualties, but the government attack was foiled. According to a government report, the communist troops were a far cry from the troops under Xiang Ying's command in 1941. The 52nd Division had participated in both battles, but it underestimated "the quality, equipment, morale and tactics of the communists this time."[31] This was the largest civil strife on the eve of the Japanese surrender.

After the battle of Xiaofeng, Su and Ye realized that the Party Central Committee's strategic objective of establishing a base in the Tianmu Mountain was totally unrealistic. First of all, the troops were exhausted by a month-long mobile war in mountainous terrain. The casualties were mounting. Secondly, they realized that local support was not strong enough to provide food and other supplies for a major regular force with three fully-manned brigades. In fact, throughout the month-long struggle, food had to be transported from southern Jiangsu. Such logistical arrangements apparently could not last very long. Thirdly, it would be difficult for the communists to mobilize the peasants if they started chasing grain supplies in the mountains, since there was already a constant shortage of rice production in this area even without war.

Based on these realistic calculations, Su and Ye decided to abandon altogether Mao's fantasy of setting up a base to wait for the allied amphibious landing. The troops were split in July to avoid any large-scale battle with the government forces.[32] By this time, the table of the Pacific War was suddenly turned. The Chinese civil strife was replaced by the more urgent race to take the cities. In August 1945, the Americans dropped two atomic bombs in Hiroshima and Nagasaki. The Soviet Red Army, in accordance with the Yalta secret agreement by the Big Three, launched a major attack in Manchuria with a million Red Army soldiers. Both Chiang and Mao were caught by surprise by the turn of events. On August 9, Mao hurriedly declared a "Last Battle against Japan," demanding all communist troops to attack the Japanese and the puppets wherever possible. Chiang immediately issued three counter-orders: first, all communist troops should stay where they were, no unauthorized attacks. second, only government forces could advance into the cities. third, all Japanese and puppet troops should guard their own territories and to surrender only to the government.

Yanan refused to accept these orders and continued to advance towards big metropolitan areas. But Mao was too carried away with his original fantasy plan of "Breaking the Enemy and Taking over the Capital." He over-estimated the strength of the New Fourth Army in southeastern China and began unilaterally announcing the appointments of governors and mayors. Thus Huang Kecheng was supposed to be governor of Jiangsu, Ye Fei, the governor of Zhejiang and Su Yu the mayor of Nanjing. Su's main troops were still in the mountains of Zhejiang. They were ordered to take major cities immediately . The fantasy was quickly running to the ground when the initial plan of taking over Shanghai turned out to be based on false information. According to Ye Fei, who was appointed commander for the Shanghai operation, the Party Central Committee had first thought that the underground communists in Shanghai had organized tens of thousands workers armed for uprising. But in fact there were only three hundred workers who were barely armed. Yanan even appointed Liu Changsheng, the underground party boss in Shanghai, to be the new mayor. Realizing the fact that such plan would have no chance of succeeding, Yanan promptly put a stop to this nonsense.[33]

A few days later on August 22, the Central Committee, prompted by Moscow, suddenly changed its mind. It urged the communist troops to drastically alter strategy. No longer aiming to take big cities, a directive stated that "the Soviet Union is, as it is constrained by the Sino-Soviet Treaty, not able to help us. Chiang is in a legal position to accept the Japanese surrender .... We should therefore change our policy ... to focus on small towns and the countryside."[34] The direct pressure from Stalin was apparent. Mao had no knowledge about the Yalta secret agreement which had awarded Stalin with territorial gains in Manchuria in exchange for, among other things, the Big Three consensus in recognizing Chiang Kai-shek to be the only legitimate national leader of China. Nevertheless, Mao decided to implement his plan to compete with the government in power vacuums such as Shandong and Manchuria. In September, General Patrick J. Hurley, the flamboyant American Ambassador, urged Mao to come to Chongqing for negotiations with Chiang Kai-shek. Mao accepted the invitation. As part of the concession made to Chiang, Mao announced withdrawal of the New Fourth Army troops from areas that were threatening Nanjing and Shanghai. But "since the issue of Manchuria was not on the negotiation table," Mao pointed out in an internal directive after the Chongqing negotiations, "the plans of our party [to expand in Manchuria] should be carried out accordingly."[35]

Mao's strategic plan was, as we have pointed out earlier, to secure the Shandong corridor so as to rapidly dispatch the best troops into Manchuria. This task was assigned to Chen Yi. At first, Chen was given two choices, either to go to Manchuria or to go back to central China. Chen preferred not to go back to the New Fourth Army, because of the strained relationship between him and Rao Shushi. But Mao decided to send him back in his old capacity as the military commander of the New Fourth Army. Nonetheless, Chen was excited by the prospect of being able to see his family back in central China, which he had not seen for over twenty months. But the Central Committee suddenly changed his assignment while he was already on his way back. In late September, Chen was asked to go to Shandong immediately to take over Luo Ronghuan's position. Luo was Lin Biao's political commissar who was in charge of the Eighth Route Army's 115th Division after its commander Lin Biao left for an extended stay in the Soviet Union in 1939. Luo was seriously ill at this time. The Central Committee had by this time decided on a new strategy of "expanding in the north and defending in the south." Lin Biao's 115th Division of the Eighth Route Army which had been active in Shandong for the past few years was to be transferred to Manchuria. South of the Yangzi River, Mao preferred to maintain a defensive posture. Chen was greatly disappointed with the new assignment. His wife Zhang Qian was even more depressed by the news that her husband had to stop at Shandong. She sent him a emotional poem saying that, "I was hurt like a lonely cicada."[36]

Chen's new task was formidable. He was ordered to stop the rapid movement of government troops to the north before the communist troops could consolidate themselves in Manchuria. But he had only a small force at his disposal. Upon arrival at Shandong, the main communist troops were at sixty thousand in strength, but the bulk of this force had already been destined for moving into Manchuria. Chen was left with all but two regular divisions and some local forces to block the overwhelming number of government troops. The communists started by sabotaging the main railway line connecting Tianjin and Nanjing---the Jinpu Railway, but the government troops were able to continue advancing at a fast speed. In October, Chen decided to engage directly the government forces along the Jinpu Railway. The strategy was to control one section of the railway while at the same time launch attacks on several important cities along the rail line. Mao instructed Chen to concentrate forces to build a strong field army at the strength of some forty thousand.[37] But it was beyond the realities in Shandong. In the first place, the Shandong troops had never been subject to Chen's command. Secondly, many troops were recently regularized communist militias, the discipline and training were poor. Chen did not know most of the commanders in Shandong, nor did he understand well the style and tactics of Lin Biao's Eighth Route Army unit, which was typically known for ambush and siege battles, but weak in mobile warfare. The regionally based local communist forces were even worse in coordinated large-scale operations. Many simply refused to fight outside their home bases. As a result, Chen could only organize a battle along the rail line with scattered forces to launch uncoordinated attacks simultaneously. Nonetheless, the sabotage battle was successful. By early November, Chen was able to control over 100 miles of rail road and effectively slowed the government movements into northern China and Manchuria.

Having thus temporarily secured the Shandong corridor, the communists were able to transfer troops continuously via the sea. The race to Manchuria quickly paid off. On November 1, Mao stated clearly that "our party's task now is to seize Manchuria, consolidate in northern and central China. The focus of war will shift to Manchuria after November."[38] To reinforce troops in Manchuria, Mao decided to send in the best units under the New Fourth Army command as well. The Party Central Committee had earlier in September instructed the New Fourth Army to withdraw from the south of the Yangzi River. The withdrawal to northern Jiangsu was carried out with deliberately staged public fanfare. But the real purpose was carefully concealed: to move them further north into Manchuria. This was to be a highly secretive operation. Huang Kecheng's Third Division at thirty thousand strong departed first in October. The communists now had a combined forces of over eighty thousand in Manchuria by November. Furthermore, the Central Committee set up two strategic military regions: the Shandong Region under Chen Yi and the Central China Region under Su Yu.

In November, Yanan instructed the newly formed Central China Military Region to send yet another elite unit led by Ye Fei to Manchuria. Reorganized as the New Fourth Army First Column at over twenty thousand strong, this force had the three brigades at Ye's disposal. Su Yu, as commander of what had remained of the Central China Military Region, was of course not happy with Ye's departure. He ordered Ye to leave all the weapons since it was widely believed at the time that the Soviet Red Army would provide them with better weapons and equipment in Manchuria. According to Ye, there was a widely circulated rumor that the Soviet soldiers were heavy drinkers. Once they were satisfied with booze, they would readily allow the Chinese communists to take whatever they wanted from their captured Japanese arsenals. Ye was skeptical and disobeyed Su's order by carrying all he had with him, including heavy weapons. It soon turned out that the rumor about the Soviets was not accurate, since the Red Army was constrained by the Yalta Agreement. After initially giving some weapons to the communists, the Soviet Red Army authorities stopped this practice immediately when the Chinese government protested. Ye felt that he had been lucky to retain his weapons.[39]

At the end of 1945, civil war in China already seemed inevitable. The United States' China policy, however, entered a new and twisted phase. Prompted mainly by domestic considerations, President Harry S. Truman appointed General George C. Marshall to be his personal representative to China. The sudden appointment was designed to "steal thunder away" from Ambassador Patrick Hurley who had made public his reasons for resignation by revealing the internal division over China policy within the administration.[40] To everyone's surprise, Marshall in a matter of days was able to secure a general cease-fire agreement between the government and the communists. But the cease-fire on paper could not be translated into reality. Both sides seemed half-hearted and skeptical about it.

Chen Yi was least of all influenced by the cease-fire agreement. In fact, even during the short period of truce, he instructed his subordinates to prepare for war at all times. The military situation in Shandong changed at the end of 1945. The government began to concentrate troops along the Jinpu Railway. By adding six armies to the existing seven, the government seemed to start shifting its strategic focus to Shandong and Jiangsu. When Ye Fei's First Column was waiting for transportation in Shandong to Manchuria, Mao suddenly changed his mind and ordered Ye to join his old boss Chen Yi's command.[41] Chen was of course delighted, for he had not seen his elite troops for two years now. He knew this unit so well that he could easily command respect from the rank and file. Ye was having a hard time because his soldiers found it hard to adapt into the shockingly impoverished conditions in Shandong. Almost one hundred percent southerners, Ye's soldiers were considered eccentric by the Shandong peasants who had traditionally been very conservative. This was the province that, after all, produced the ancient sage Confucius. The locals did not understand a word when the southern soldiers talked. Compared with the more Spartan Eighth Route Army soldiers, the southerners appeared slick, fair-skinned and well-attired. Most locals were appalled to see them wearing well-combed long hair and silk shirts. The peasants considered them to be "spoiled." Worse of all, these southerners had to endure the harsh daily diet of millet and sorghum---the stuff considered in prosperous southern China to be only fit for feeding animals. Many angry soldiers alienated the locals by throwing millet out of the window. It took quite some time for the troops to gain respect from the local population.[42]

Chen Yi participated in General Marshall's mediation efforts in Shandong. On March 1, 1946, Chen boarded an American airplane heading for Jinan, the capital of Shandong province. Since Chen represented the Shandong communists, he decided to take Ye Fei along as his negotiation deputy. While Chen was busy with public functions, he instructed Ye to do some "sightseeing," which in effect was aimed at examining the government defense structure in the capital city.[43] After a short stay in Jinan, Chen flew to Xuzhou to negotiate directly with Marshall and Gu Zhutong, the government commander of the former Third War Zone. Su Yu and his deputy Tan Zhenlin were also flown in to present facts accusing the government of violating the cease-fire agreement in central Jiangsu. In his encounter with Marshall, Chen defended vehemently Su Yu's action in Jiangsu against the government forces and resented an improper dinner protocol when the communists were assigned less prestigious seating. To his surprise, Marshall agreed to attend to both matters promptly.

Chen utilized the brief cease-fire period to train his troops. In February, he organized a "One Hundred Day Training" program that lasted until May. The government meanwhile also began to secretly transfer troops to central China. According to a contemporary account, from January to June, the government increased troops from seventeen to twenty-three armies, at over a half million total.[44]

On the communist side, the main problem was the difficulty to concentrate troops for major mobile warfare. Chen now had some fifty thousand in Shandong, while Su commanded thirty thousand in Jiangsu. But these two troops were officially under two jurisdictions and theaters of war. Su's troops were battle-hardened elite forces, fully manned and well equipped. More importantly, they had long experience in battle coordination, especially between Tao Yong and Wang Bicheng's units, despite the departure of Ye Fei. In Shandong, the troop quality was a far cry from that in Jiangsu. Most regiments were not fully manned and the coordination experience was non-existent. Troop strength was also shrinking. Ye Fei's First Column, for example, had to reduce its regiments from nine to seven, due to the lack of new recruits.[45]

In front of the overwhelming concentration of government forces, the communists had to avoid the brunt of the enemy attack and to amass forces at chosen point to knock out the exposed enemy wing in one swift blow. But the concentration of troops encountered enormous difficulties. On June 24, Yanan suggested the quick convergence of two forces in Shandong and Jiangsu. Chen's Shandong troops should move southwards, while Su's units move northwards to meet at the Xuzhou area to seek a decisive campaign with the government. Moreover, Mao ordered the former 129th Division of the Eighth Route Army commanded by Liu Bocheng and Deng Xiaoping to coordinate with Chen through taking control of the Longhai Railway that connected coastal Jiangsu with the hinterland.[46] Su Yu objected to this directive. In several telegrams, Su pointed out that it was still too early to coordinate battle operations between two strategic theaters. He stressed the need to maintain his position in central Jiangsu and to seek battles with the government in the enemy's interior line. Besides, Su emphasized that many of his soldiers were local Jiangsu recruits, it would be disappointing to the local population if they simply abandoned the base and moved to Shandong.

While Chen naturally preferred the option suggested by Yanan, Su's argument carried weight with Mao when intelligence reports indicated that Chiang intended to strike in all directions instead of focusing on one particular area. On July 4, Yanan finally abandoned the idea for a Xuzhou campaign and approved Su's plan. A directive pointed out that, since Chiang would attack in several directions simultaneously, it would be "politically to our advantage to seek battle inside the enemy line with a defensive posture," even though Yanan was not at all sure about Su's military advantage in this strategy. Su therefore was under enormous pressure, for he carried personal risk if he could not win in Jiangsu. His troops had to face government forces four times greater than his own.

But Su had one enormous advantage over the Shandong troops under Chen: troop quality and impeccable coordination. In mid-July, Chiang launched major attacks in Jiangsu and Shandong. The cease-fire forged by General Marshall was put to a *de facto* end. Within a month, Su Yu emerged as a brilliant tactician in organizing seven successful battles based on swift maneuver and surprise attack. With only fifteen regiments, Su was at his best in being bold and innovative. He preempted the enemy with active attack first, then engaged in swift feint attack and siege warfare in order to lure enemy reinforcements into various tactical pockets. The decisions were made swiftly on the spot and each battle being connected to another. It ended up wiping out over 50,000 government forces.[47] The result was a pleasant surprise to Yanan. In a directive dated August 28, Mao highly praised Su's tactics of concentrating troops with absolute superiority at chosen weak point of the enemy, therefore Su "is invincible." Mao suggested that all military commanders learn from Su's experience.[48]

Meanwhile in Shandong, Chen's troops did not fare nearly as well. The badly coordinated forces were engaging the enemy in several directions. This was by no means effective, the tactics was poor and morale was low. Some blamed Su for his unwillingness to bring his force to join Chen's command. Others blamed Chen Yi for his lack of patience and sound military judgment. On several occasions, as Ye Fei recalled in his memoirs, his First Column failed repeatedly to cooperate with the best unit of the original Shandong troops, the Eighth Division. They disagreed on almost everything. Ye's troops were famous for mobile battles in open field, while the Shandong Eighth Division was known for success in siege warfare. But bad coordination and misunderstanding prevented both troops from fully utilizing their best qualities. Most battles in Shandong were war of attrition. Chen's bad judgment also contributed to the frustration among the rank and file. In the siege battle of Sixian, Chen and his chief of staff ignored warnings that the heavy rain would render a successful attack on the heavily fortified Sixian city impossible. But the impatient Chen insisted on carrying out his plan, which prompted Yanan to advise him to be cautious, stating, "an impatient attitude is inappropriate." The attack turned out to be a disaster. Not only did Chen fail to overcome the enemy defenses, but also suffered over 2,000 casualties while wiping out only 3,000 enemy forces in return. The elite Shandong Eighth Division was humiliated by this failure. To comfort the troops, Chen had to write a letter of apology to the Eighth Division and to indicate his willingness to take all the responsibilities.[49]

Chen's ineffectiveness in the north affected Su's position in the south. Chiang took advantage of his success in the north to move his main force back to the south to focus on Su's units. In September 1946, the government troops succeeded in occupying Huaiyin city where Su's headquarters were stationed. In desperation, Su was forced to withdraw from central Jiangsu and joined Chen's command. On September 23, Yanan formally announced the merger of command of the two forces under Chen and Su. For the second time, the direct partnership between the two men was established.[50]

Before Chen and Su could combine their forces together, the battlefield situation changed again. Chiang was greatly encouraged by the further success in taking over Su's headquarters in Jiangsu. He immediately decided to finish off all communist troops in Jiangsu by the end of the year. Amassing twenty-eight brigades in early December, Chiang was all geared up for a showdown. His strategy was to advance in four columns to cut off the connection between Shandong and Jiangsu, then to converge all troops in the area for eliminating the communist forces in one decisive strike. After careful planning, Chen and Su decided to seek an opportunity to knock out one of the columns advancing in the Suqian direction. This was the first time since the Battle of Huangqiao in 1940 that Chen and Su planned and carried out a major battle together. Knowing Su's military brilliance and patience, Yanan specifically recommended Su to take charge of all technical aspects during the course of the battle.[51] But Su was much less confident. Years later, Su admitted that he was extremely nervous for two reasons. On the one hand, this was the first coordinated campaign between Shandong and Jiangsu troops. Yanan was concerned with their new relationship and demanded "absolute victory for their first combined battle."[52] A failure would further strain the already precarious relationship and both would suffer in the future. On the other hand, the attack troops Su was supposed to command during the coming battle were not his own. His troops, Tao Yong and Wang Bicheng's columns, for example, were ordered to stay in Jiangsu to perform defense functions to lure the enemy into a pocket. The main surprise attack would be carried out by the Shandong Eighth Division and Ye Fei's First Column. Su was, of course, familiar with the units under Ye, but the two men did not get along very well.[53]

With only a small staff, Su took over command in mid-December. The battle plan was bold but highly risky. Ye's column was supposed to utilize its best tactical character to cut off the connection between the enemy units and to isolate the chosen target, which was at over 20,000 strong. The Shandong Eighth Division was to carry out the plan of taking over Feng Hill, the highest strategic point in the battleground so as to control the overall situation and then to complete the encirclement. During the course of the battle, something went terribly wrong. The Eighth Division tried but failed several times to take over Feng Hill. With Su's approval, they decided to withdraw. At the same time, Ye's advancing column had already cut deeply into the enemy line and isolated the target. If the Eighth Division should withdraw at this point, Ye's column would be surrounded by overwhelming enemy troops. Ye argued vehemently with Su over the telephone. At one point, Ye hanged up on his commander in great anger. Cornered into a desperate position, Ye decided to risk all he had to launch surprise attack on the target alone. The enemy was totally unprepared for this bold move, and their morale was quickly shaken. Encouraged by Ye's success, the Eighth Division tried one more time to take over Feng Hill and succeeded. As a result, the battle plan was fulfilled largely due to Ye's decisiveness and the fighting spirit of his troops. Over 20,000 elite government forces were wiped out in three days. After the battle, Ye demanded that Su be reprimanded, but Chen simply ignored his request.[54]

The Battle of Suqian was a major turning point during the civil war in central China. It proved the wisdom of concentrating troops to seek mobile battles. In Chen's report to Mao, it was pointed out that, in the past, he was preoccupied with defending and taking cities. Now he had realized the need to release troops from cities and to concentrate them in order to focus only on enemy's troops. More importantly, Chen reported that the tension between the two troops were alleviated by the success in the battleground. "The Shandong troops were uneasy about moving southward and the Jiangsu troops were unwilling to move into Shandong, now the battle results have smoothed things over."[55]

The better coordination between the two troops quickly led to another major victory. At the same time the Battle of Suqian was raging, another government division advanced alone into southern Shandong. Supported by an American-trained motorized unit, the government division did not pay attention to communist troop movements until it was too late. Chen and Su amassed twenty-seven regiments and launched a surprise attack on January 2, 1947. Ironically, the government commander was not even at his post. He was celebrating the new year elsewhere, drinking and watching traditional opera. Within two days, 30,000 troops were eliminated. If this battle was won by luck, it did show the swiftness and decisiveness on the battleground under Chen and Su's leadership. More importantly, the communists for the first time captured numerous US-made tanks, trucks, and heavy artillery, which provided incentive for Chen and Su to form a "Special Column (*Te Zong*)," which was a specialized artillery and armored unit. This was an indication that the communist forces had come of age and began to enter the period of modern warfare. At the end of the month, Yanan decided to formally unify the command in central China through establishing an "East China Field Army" under Chen Yi. The field army concept signaled the beginning of the communist regularization of forces fit for large-scale warfare. The confusion of troop names was also eliminated. Chen now had nine infantry columns plus one special artillery column under his disposal. Adding local forces into his command, Chen's overall strength was at over 300,000. Such a formidable force situated in the Shandong corridor would soon prove to be critical in the overall communist strategy to break Chiang's backbone in the next two years.

Notes

1. *Su Yu On Central Jiangsu's War Against the Japanese*, p.134.
2. *MZDJSWJ*, vol.2, p.681-682.
3. *WJXJ*, vol.13, p.426-429.
4. Zhong, Qiguang et al, *Xin Si Jun Zheng Feng Yun Dong* (The Rectification Campaign in the New Fourth Army), in *Da Jiang Nan Bei Magazine*, vol.37, p.23-26.

5. *WJXJ*, vol.14, p.14-16.
6. Li, Yiming, *Li Yiming Hui Yi Lu* (Memoirs of Li Yiming, Changsha 1986), p.112-119.
7. *The Chronology of the Events Related to the New Fourth Army*, p.224.
8. *Memoirs of Ye Fei*, p.286-288.
9. Zeng, Ruqing, *Zhu Li Di Fang Hua de Dao Lu* (The Road to Regular Army Localization), in *Fire Never Extinguishes*, p.83.
10. *Memoirs of Guan Wenwei*, vol.2, p.238.
11. Su, Yu, *Nankan Hui Yi Zong Jie* (Summary at the Nankan Conference) (November 1942), in *Central Jiangsu Anti-Japanese Base Area*, p.173-176.
12. Johnson, *Peasant Nationalism and Communist Power*, preface.
13. *Memoirs of Huang Kecheng*, vol.1, p.298-301.
14. *Biography of Chen Yi* (Official), p.286-287.
15. Hu, Zhaocai, *Huang Hua Tang Chen Yi Meng Yuan* (The Framing of Chen Yi at Huanghuatang), in *Da Jiang Nan Bei Magazine*, vol.26, p.4-8.
16. *Biography of Chen Yi* (Official), p.288.
17. *Complete Collection of Chen Yi's Poems*, p.115-117.
18. *Memoirs of Guan Wenwei*, vol.2, p.251-252.
19. *Biography of Chen Yi* (Official), p.295.
20. Ibid., p.295-298.
21. Ibid., p.298-300.
22. Ibid., 304-306.
23. Ibid., 321-324.
24. Chen's speech first appeared in *Da Jiang Nan Bei Magazine*, vol.34-35.
25. *Memoirs of Guan Wenwei*, vol.2, p.222-223.
26. *WJXJ*, vol.14, p.5.
27. Ibid., p.80-81.
28. *Memoirs of Ye Fei*, p.319-324.
29. Wu, Jinyu, *Cheqiao Zhan Yi Shi Mo* (The Origins and Result of the Battle of Cheqiao), in *Da Jiang Nan Bei Magazine*, vol.40, p.24-30.
30. *Biography of Chen Yi* (Official), p.316.
31. Quoted from *Memoirs of Ye Fei*, p.340-341.
32. Ibid., p.340.
33. Ibid., p.345-346.
34. *WJXJ*, vol.15, p.243.
35. *MZDJSWJ*, vol.3, p.55.
36. *Complete Collection of Chen Yi's Poems*, p.165.
37. *MZDJSWJ*, vol.3, p.67.
38. Ibid., p.107-108.
39. *Memoirs of Ye Fei*, p.357-358.
40. For detail, see Xiang, Lanxin, *Recasting the Imperial Far East---Britain and America in China* (Sharpe: New York 1995), p.53.

Politics of Conformity 133

41. *WJXJ*, vol.15, p.463-464.
42. *Memoirs of Ye Fei*, p.358-360.
43. Ibid., p.368.
44. *Biography of Chen Yi* (Official), p.335-336.
45. *Memoirs of Ye Fei*, p.376.
46. *WJXJ*, vol.16, p.214.
47. For detail, see Su, Yu, *Su Zhong Zhan Yi Zong Jie* (Summary of the Battles of Central Jiangsu), *Military Works of Su Yu*, p.257-275.
48. *MZDJSWJ*, vol.3, p.438.
49. *Biography of Chen Yi* (Official), p.340-342.
50. Ibid., p.346.
51. *WJXJ*, vol.16, p.311.
52. *MZDJSWJ*, vol.3, p.500.
53. Su, Yu, *War Memoirs*, p.411-419.
54. For detail, see *Memoirs of Ye Fei*, p.392-396. In his memoirs, Su shied away from explaining the fact why he was shaken under pressure.
55. *Biography of Chen Yi* (Official), p.349-350.

Chapter 6

The Struggle for Mastery in Shandong

It is important to point out at the outset that, Chen Yi's success in Shandong played the pivotal role in breaking the government's backbone. Lin Biao's victory in Manchuria would not have been possible if Chen's East China Field Army had not firmly tied down Chiang's elite forces in the Shandong corridor. Without the control of Shandong, the government could not spare reinforcements for Manchuria. Numerically speaking, although Lin Biao was able to devour large chunk of government troops in one decisive campaign, it was Chen Yi and Su Yu who were the most innovative and successful in military tactics. The struggle for mastery in Shandong throughout 1947 and 1948 was decisive also because it directly threatened the Yangzi Valley, the center of the government power. Chiang could afford to write off Manchuria, but not Shandong.

This was a most creative and decisive phase in Chen and Su's careers. In the summer of 1946, Chen's wife Zhang Qian gave birth to another son in Shandong, Chen named him appropriately "Xiaolu" (Little Shandong). Having suffered two major defeats at the hands of Chen and Su, Chiang in January 1947 sent General Chen Cheng, his chief of staff, to Xuzhou to take over personal command. Chen Cheng had learnt from the lessons of the previous battles, and decided to adopt a new strategy. He concentrated sixty regiments at Xuzhou to advance from the south towards Linyi in southern Shandong where Chen Yi's headquarters and main forces were resting. While at the same time, the government forces stationed in the north, belonging to General Wang Yaowu's Jinan Pacification Headquarters were ordered to move southward to cut off the communist rear in order to prevent their escape. It was in effect aimed at squeezing the communist troops into a narrow corridor between the hammer and the anvil, forcing them to engage in a major campaign. General Chen was very cautious. Knowing fully well the communist habit of seeking weak and exposed wing for surprise strike, he ordered his main attack troops from the south to advance at synchronized speed, never allowing a march at more than four miles a day, thus no weak wing was allowed to expose itself. Chiang considered this campaign decisive for the government to survive.

Initially Mao preferred the old strategy of "You Di Shen Ru (luring enemy into the deep)." But the change of strategy on the government side compelled him to provide Chen and Su with a lot more room to innovate tactically. Mao further suggested on January 31 that Chen and Su should allow the enemy from the southern direction to advance as close to Linyi as possible, and if necessary, they should be prepared to give up Linyi. This instruction proved to be critical, for although Chen and Su were not prepared to abandon Linyi, they were given space and time to make decisions that would take into consideration of losing Linyi.[1]

Chen and Su initially prepared three plans for defeating the enemy, all based on defending Linyi and seeking a weak wing during rapid maneuver: first, to deploy the main force outside Linyi while focusing on the enemy right wing that was the weakest; second, if the left wing should advance faster than the center and the right, they could redeploy troops to wipe it out; third, if none of the wings was willing to expose itself, they could strike at the center, which consisted one of the best government units, the American trained and equipped 74th Division. Chen and Su naturally preferred the first plan. In preparation, they assigned strong units to the task of resisting the enemy in a widely deployed frontal defense line, the objective was to blunt the movement of the enemy center column and to force two wings to jut out. But General Chen Cheng refused to take the bait this time. As a result, despite enormous pressure at the center, the government forces maintained their synchronized movement to avoid any exposure of troops.

It seemed certain that the old communist strategy would not work this time. Mao changed his mind and instructed Chen and Su on February 3 that they should alternate troop uses to limit their appetite to three enemy brigades in each battle, and be prepared to engage seven or eight small battles like this in two months.[2] In other words, Mao had decided to give up the idea of one large-scale battle. Chen and Su were not impressed. To them this was tantamount to a war of attrition. Given their numerical inferiority, such a tactic would only benefit the enemy side. Since Mao had acquiesced in January that in emergency they could give up Linyi, Chen hit upon a brilliant idea of abandoning the southern front, while at the same time swiftly moving main forces to the north where three government armies led by General Li Xianzhou from Jinan began to move southward to form a hammer and anvil posture for the purpose of a coordinated attack at the communist rear to support Chen Cheng's main attack on Linyi at the southern front. Chen's plan was bold and innovative. In the southern front, the government had sixty regiments at over 300,000 in strength. They were comparable to the communist strength. But in the northern front, the government had moved out only 70,000 troops. Chen's plan to shift to the north would create a temporary numerical superiority over this force, offering an opportunity for a *coup de main*. But Chen's gamble was extremely risky. The sudden shift of battle target required precision of timing in troop transfer and it had to rely on absolute secrecy concerning large troop movement. Despite the organizational efficiency of the communist troops and popular local support, it was still not possible to conceal such a big movement of troops for more than a few days. In other words, Chen had to move his troops and finish off the enemy in the north within a very short period of time. Since they would operate in the enemy's interior line while facing attacks on both sides, any substantial delay in crushing the northern front, either because of troop movement or because of bad deployment would mean the end of their forces that might be caught in a narrow pocket. The chance of escape would be very slim. More importantly, Chen must succeed in deceiving enemy troops on both sides, since he could put his troops in serious danger if, either the government main forces in the south should find out Chen's plan, or the northern enemy troops should sense something and refuse to move further south. The deception must be perfect.

By February 10, Chen and Su organized a brilliant deception plan in communist military history. He left only two columns commanding six divisions to build a defense structure that was so wide that the enemy was made to think that Chen's main forces were still bent on defending Linyi. At the same time, Chen ordered communist local militia to ostensibly build bridges on the Yellow River, leaving the impression that his main forces were prepared to withdraw to the west bank of the river if the defense of Linyi was not successful. Chen even personally wrote a poem titled "Song of Decisive Victory" and had a composer make music out of it to teach the small defense force at Linyi to sing ostensibly so as to let the enemy know of Chen's determination to seek a showdown with the government forces at Linyi. In the pitch darkness at midnight of February 10, however, Chen's main troops began to move swiftly and quietly to the north.

General Chen Cheng took the bait this time. Five days later, the government attack troops in the south finally took Linyi after a cautious and prolonged battle. In his report to Chiang, Chen Cheng exaggerated his victory at Linyi, claiming to have wiped out sixteen communist brigades.

Chiang made a secret speech a few days later to his top generals, stating that, "Among the five communist bandit groups, I consider Chen Yi's troops are the toughest, the best trained, the best in tactics. Since we took over Linyi, Chen Yi has lost his nest and thus become dysfunctional."[3] Chiang was, of course, too complacent. At the time he was making the speech on February 19, Chen and Su had already completed the half encirclement of General Li Xianzhou's two armies near Laiwu city in the north. But the conditions for a *coup de main* were still premature. General Wang Yaowu, Li's superior at Jinan Pacification Headquarters began to sense the communist movement of troops toward him and ordered Li to retrench back to the north. But General Chen Cheng was convinced of his victory at Linyi and ordered Li to continue advancing to the south. Su Yu immediately organized a tactical encirclement aimed at cutting off Li's retreat route and isolating his two armies from Jinan. The plan was to disconnect the two armies from each other and to wipe them out in two separate battles.

But at this moment, Su's plan went wrong, when the troops assigned to disconnect Li's two armies did not succeed, a failure that allowed over 40,000 government troops to be able to concentrate at Laiwu city. Under the circumstances, Su's tactical pocket became too thin since only one column, the First Column commanded by Ye Fei, at half of Li's strength, was able to arrive at Laiwu in time before Li could organize counterattacks for a breakthrough. Furthermore, even if General Li should decide to hold on to Laiwu with his two fully-manned armies, government reinforcements were also within the reach in both directions, once the communist plan became clear. Ye's original task was to join four other columns to clear of the enemy outside Laiwu city and to prepare for a joint attack on one isolated army in Laiwu from several directions. But the other columns had not arrived yet. Thus the burden of preventing Li's two armies from withdrawing from Laiwu before Su's redeployment of forces to launch attack fell on Ye's column alone. Despite enormous grudges against Su's misjudgment, Ye ordered preparation of trench warfare around Laiwu. At the critical juncture, General Li panicked. With no careful plan, he made the fatal mistake of abandoning Laiwu city and tried to break through Ye's thin encirclement line towards the north. Ye's troops fought a heroic battle. The casualties were exceedingly heavy, but Ye was able to hold on to his position until the communist reinforcements arrived. Li's troops were now in a chaotic situation, the 40,000 crowd mixed together with numerous trucks, horses and other heavy equipment were confined to a narrow corridor of two square miles. The general attack was launched by Su at the noon of February 23. The government troops were finished off in only five hours. General Li himself also fell into communist hands.[4] The communists lost only six

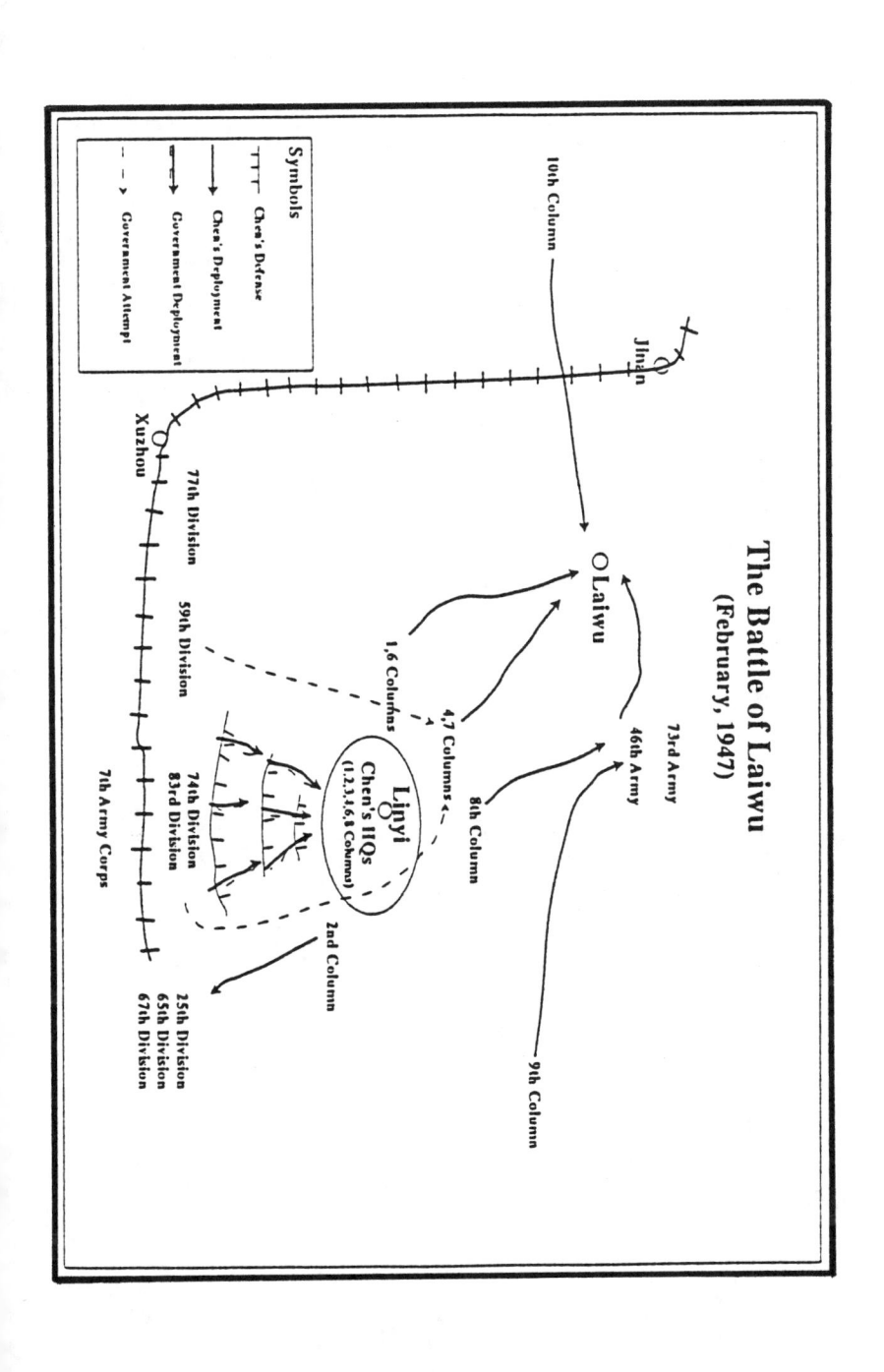

The Battle of Laiwu
(February, 1947)

thousand casualties, many from Ye's column. The battle of Laiwu established Su's indisputable position as one of the most brilliant battle planners in the communist military establishment. As Chen Yi told news reporters in March "Su is invincible .... The more battles he conducts, the more surprises and successes."[5] Su was more modest. In his report on the battle, he attributed the success to the close coordination among the columns, especially among his old troops, the Ye-Wang-Tao columns. Ye Fei's First Column was mentioned to have made the greatest contribution by holding the bulk of the enemy back for a few days.[6] As usual, Ye was more critical of Su's judgment, but he was delighted by the fact that Su referred to his column as "number one" factor for victory during the battle.[7]

This was the first time the communists invented the strategy of "counterapproach march (*Dui Jing*)"---or march from opposite direction towards the enemy, without being detected within a very close physical distance. The security on the march and the reliable intelligence were the key factors for Su's success in his superb employment of interior line. Government analysts would admit years later that the lack of support from the local population rendered their intelligence totally ineffective, and the government lost the battle, because security on march was "virtually nonexistent."[8] The internal conflict and rampant factionalism were, of course, instrumental in paralyzing the coordination among the government troops. The communist forces under Chen and Su, however, enjoyed enormous popularity with the locals. According to Ye Fei, over a half million local population participated in supporting the troops during the battle. Ye claimed to have seen peasants dismantling their own mud houses in order to provide hay for the troops.[9]

In the wake of the surprising success of the Battle of Laiwu, Mao and the Party Central Committee in Yanan were carried away, and became hot-headed. They sent a directive to Chen on March 6, demanding the East China Field Army to "wipe out four to five enemy brigades each month for the next ten months." Inspired by Su's "counterapproach march" strategy, Mao also began to consider the possibility of employing Liu Bocheng and Deng Xiaoping's troops at Taihang Mountain area to the south of the Yellow River. Mao demanded that Liu and Deng lead the troops all the way towards the Dabie Mountains in the Hubei-Henan-Anhui border area. To make this strategic movement a fast and direct one, Mao intended for them to counterapproach the enemy through forceful marches to connect with Chen's East China Field Army.[10] In the meantime, Mao's headquarters in Yanan were under heavy pressure from the overwhelming government forces led by General Hu Zongnan. In a bold move, Mao and his colleagues decided to abandon Yanan and to engage the enemy in hide-and-seek games. Mao's own troops would therefore operate on exterior lines. But Chen's troops in Shandong were allowed to continue operating on interior lines.

Throughout April 1947 Mao's rather rigid demand for eliminating four to five brigades each month forced Chen and Su to move the troops around in rapid speed in order to seek whatever opportunities to fulfill the unrealistic quota. The government was panic-stricken by the Laiwu debacle. In March, Yanan fell to government hands, Chiang's spirit was up again. The government office of military operation presented three possibilities for Chiang to choose from: first, shifting the strategic focus to Shandong; second, seeking destruction of Liu Bocheng and Deng Xiaoping's forces in Northern Henan; and third, continuing the mopping-up campaign in Northern Shaanxi against Mao's Central Committee. Chiang chose Shandong.[11] In March Chiang began to mobilize a much larger force to concentrate on Shandong. He appointed General Gu Zhutong, the old enemy of the New Fourth Army as well as a *bete noire* of General Chen Cheng, to be the new commander in charge of the whole operation in the Shandong corridor.

At close to half a million strong, General Gu had at his disposal some of the best government troops such as General Zhang Lingfu's 74th Division. Fully manned at 20,000 strong, this army-sized division had been Chiang's elite garrison guard in the capital city of Nanjing. The 74th Division was considered by the communists to be one of the five best units (*Wu Da Zhu Li*). It had also been a formidable enemy to Su Yu, since, in 1946, it was responsible for spearheading the attack at Huaiyin, Su's headquarters in Jiangsu. One of Su's best commanders, Wang Bicheng, had suffered a major humiliating defeat during the battle of Siqian when Zhang crushed Wang's defense at the critical Lianshui city. Chen and Su decided that it was the time to seek the 74th Division's total destruction. Having set the target, they moved the main forces southward, leaving a small unit performing diversionary operations to attack the Jinpu Railway. The bulk of the forces hid near Linyi and Mengying to ambush the government reinforcements, hoping Zhang Lingfu's 74th Division could be lured to the southern direction. Unfortunately, Chen's trick was immediately detected by the government. It turned out that a new communist recruit was a government spy who reported the communist troop movement and helped to locate Chen's headquarters for a government air raid.

In a great hurry, Chen and Su had to change battle plans while the government had already begun to launch major attack in mid-April. The communists succeeded in separate operations against Taian city, but the overall objective to eliminate Zhang Lingfu's 74th Division failed. Chen's troops were totally exhausted during April when they had to move back and forth some three hundred miles in twenty days. The rank and file were disgruntled, complaining that "Commander Chen's wires da, da, da, our feet ta, ta, ta," meaning that they had to be constantly on the run without much success in engaging the enemy.[12] In May, the Party Central Committee realized that its earlier directive had confined Chen's operation to ineffective use of forces. Mao advised Chen "not to be impatient, never split troops and lure the enemy deeper in order to seek opportunities."[13] By giving up his originally fixed quota of destroying four to five brigades each month, Mao thus provided Chen and Su with enormous space and time to make different and more effective battle plans. The government troops had so far been extremely cautious, always closing ranks if any wing was attacked by the communists. But on May 10, government General Tang Enbo, General Zhang Lingfu's immediate superior, began to advance with his main force, which included some of the best troops, toward Chen's headquarters at Tanbu. Spearheaded by the elite 74th and 25th divisions, the government objective was to directly seek destruction of Chen's headquarters. This enemy troop movement was a godsend for Chen and Su. By luck, the communists were able to decipher General Tang's attack schedule and basic strategy. It appeared that Tang intended to break through the center of Chen's defense with his best units. The objective was to knock out Chen's command center and if Chen refused to engage them, the government forces would drive them all the way across the Yellow River. General Tang was convinced that the communists would only strike at the weaker wings but dare not challenge his strongest unit at the center. Based on the deciphered information, Su Yu designed a much bolder but also highly risky plan: to surprise the enemy through forceful isolation of the 74th Division alone and to concentrate all the troops he could amass to finish it off at a very fast speed. This was a strategy of head-on collision at the center, which was rarely used by the communists and certainly anathema to Mao. Chen immediately approved this plan, and called it "a hungry tiger ripping the heart off the enemy's chest." The battle plan was made in great hurry. Chen's elite troops, the Ye-Wang-Tao columns and the other columns consisting of the best units in Shandong formerly belonged to Lin Biao were assigned the task of ripping the 74th Division away from the main government troop formation and then wiping it out with absolute numerical superiority. The troops of lesser quality would perform the function of blunting the government reinforcements from all the directions. For this battle, Chen and Su gambled with all of their nine columns at 220,000 strong.

Fortunately, the Communist Central Committee sent two directives to authorize Chen and Su to determine on the spot which wing they were going to attack. Chen sent a reply on May 13 to Mao, reporting his decision to strike exclusively at the 74th Division. According to the battle plan, Su Yu permitted General Zhang Lingfu's 74th Division to reach a point where it could be ripped away from another parallel marching unit close by, the elite 25th Division at a close distance. Thus the most difficult task was to swiftly cut these two divisions off without being detected. Once again, Chen decided to use Ye Fei's hard-boiled First Column which was considered the best unit in performing deep penetration into enemy positions. Originally, Ye was ordered to rest his troops for this battle, because of the exhaustion and heavy casualties incurred during the Battle of Laiwu. Ye was far from thrilled when the order came. By May 13, the 74th Division finally arrived at Menglianggu, a mountainous area designated by Su for the *coup de main*. At the same time, Ye's First Column was marching towards the same direction. The two troops were so close at one point during the night that the government officers mistook Ye's soldiers for those from the government 25th Division. No skirmishes occurred. After blunting the government advances with a small force at the center, Su began to execute a brilliant maneuver in the history of military strategy through bold infiltration into enemy's front-line position, cutting the 74th Division off from the other government units and closing a tight encirclement within a much larger government encirclement against the communist troops by the overwhelming number of forces.

There was another ace up Su's sleeves. This was Wang Bicheng's Sixth Column which was operating in southern Shandong for the purpose of diverting government attention. Wang had suffered heavy casualties at General Zhang Lingfu's hand a couple of times before. So he was more than keen to seek revenge this time. His troop morale was high when the order came for Wang to cut off Zhang's retreat route as soon as Zhang's position had jutted out.[14] The rapid march by Wang overnight from southern Shandong to Zhang's rear proved to be a major surprise for the government. By the next morning General Zhang Lingfu found his rear was completely severed by Wang Bicheng's column. He quickly decided to retreat into the Menglianggu Mountain to wait for reinforcements that were stationed nearby from all directions.

Chiang Kai-shek in fact was not initially discouraged by General Zhang's plight. Knowing this division so well that Chiang personally directed the 74th Division to hold on to the position long enough to allow the government to complete a tight encirclement of all the best units under Chen Yi for the final kill. The timing thus became critical. As soon as Wang's column arrived at the scene, Chen and Su immediately decided to launch general attack on Menglianggu the next day, May 15. General Zhang's hard-driven, American-trained professionals were enormously difficult to overcome. The communist attack troops were now put under Ye Fei's overall command. Chen told Ye over telephone that no

The Battle of Menglianggu
(May 1947)

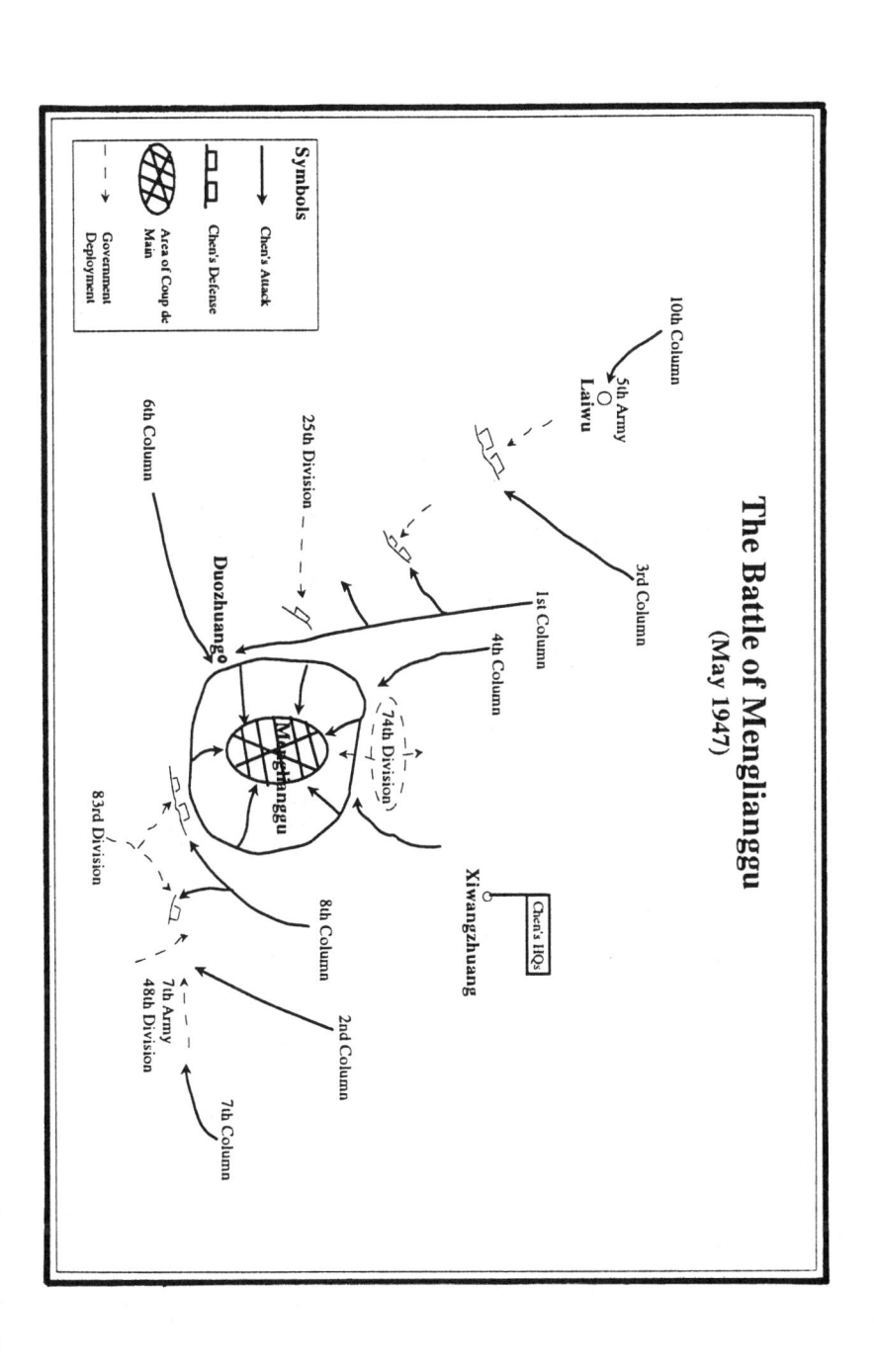

matter how much it would cost, even at two whole columns, he must finish the 74th Division off within 24 hours, because Chen's troops were already surrounded by ten government divisions at this time. The attack and the counterattack were ferocious. It was perhaps the first time during the civil war that a besieged government force decided to fight to a man.[15] The general attack was launched in the morning of May 16. Throughout the day, General Zhang vigorously defended his position to the last minute. But the terrain was to his disadvantage. This was a rocky mountain with sparsely distributed trees and bushes. The troops had few places to hide. Also Zhang's American weapons did not work well, since most of his heavy machine guns required water-cooling while the barren mountain did not have many spring water resources. His headquarters were finally taken in the afternoon. Zhang was captured alive but was shot to death by an angry communist officer under Wang Bicheng's command, who considered his column's previous defeats at Zhang's hand major insults to the unit's reputation.[16]

The Battle of Menglianggu was one of the most stressful experiences for Chen. The casualties on the communist side were heavy, for the 74th Division fought to a bitter end by leaving 15,000 dead and only some 5,000 captured.[17] The communists lost some 12,000.[18] Upon hearing General Zhang Lingfu's death, Chen sighed heavily to his staff members, "What stressful three days and nights. I will never allow my son to be a military commander when he grows up."[19] Mao was delighted by this victory. On May 22, the Party Central Committee sent Chen a telegram, stating that, "the elimination of the 74th Division is extremely significant, though at enormous cost. It proves that patience and concentration of troops in your present area have paid off." More importantly, it instructed Chen to continue the same strategy but they should aim at eliminating all government troops in Shandong within six or seven months. Mao even specified the tolerable casualty level at sixty to seventy thousand for this task. Therefore, Chen was expected to turn a largely offensive defense posture, suitable for interior lines, into active offense, usually for operating on exterior lines, in the next few months.[20]

But Chiang vowed not to allow the repetition of the same mistake made at Menglianggu. In June, Chiang adopted yet another new strategy through concentration of troops that would march in overlapped position. At the end of June, it appeared to Chen and Su that any attempt to isolate and destroy Chiang's large units would be futile. Continued concentration of large forces became a liability on the communist side. On June 29, the Party Central Committee pointed out in a telegram that Chiang's new strategy would leave his rear and wings in a vulnerable situation. It was high time for Chen and Su to change strategy and to split troops in order to seek opportunities to eliminate smaller government units one by one.[21]

This instruction in effect forced Chen and Su to start operating on exterior lines for the first time in the struggle for Shandong. One strategic reason for this decision was to indirectly support troops under Liu Bocheng and Deng Xiaoping, which, on July 1, began to cross the Yellow River, spearheading towards the Dabie Mountains in the Hubei and Anhui border area. This strategic march was Mao's favorite project. Under the circumstances, Chen Yi's task was doubled, for he had to foil Chiang's attack in Shandong and at the same time, to spare forces to divert enemy troops away from Liu and Deng. With limited resources, Chen and Su had to devise a strategy aimed at resisting government attack at the center while splitting their troops into two wings to strike at enemy's rear. Chen and Su personally led the center wing of four columns in strength. The left wing consisted of Ye Fei and Tao Yong's columns, the right wing of the former Shandong troops.

The result of splitting troops quickly turned into a major disaster. Lacking numerical superiority, the left wing under Ye and Tao were not able to take Zou and Teng cities in the enemy's rear as was planned in July. Seeing few results in battle, Chen and Su ordered the left wing to retreat to the south of Linqu and Nanma in southern Shandong where they were expected to collaborate with the other two wings who were waiting for opportunities to destroy government general Hu Lian's elite 11th Division which formed the main government attack column at the center position. This was similar to the strategy adopted at Mengliangu. It aimed to rip a strong enemy wing away from the main troop formation. This time, however, it could hardly work. Chiang deliberately allowed Hu Lian to jut out at Nanma in order to lure Chen and Su to attack him. As in the Battle of Mengliangu, the critical issue was whether or not Hu's 11th Division was able to hold on to its position at Nanma until the arrival of the other government forces. General Hu Lian, unlike Zhang Lingfu, was one of the best among the government generals in counter-siege warfare. From July 15 to July 22, Hu indeed succeeded in repelling Chen's attacks at Nanma until major government reinforcements closed in. Chen suffered heavy casualties and abandoned the attack in a hasty retreat.[22] During the communist attack on Linqu almost at the same time, the effect was also limited. For five days and nights, the government general held fast the city wall until the reinforcements arrived. This was perhaps the worst performance of the East China Field Army since the civil war started. The communists lost some 21,000 casualties in less than two weeks. In a gloomy report to Mao, Chen admitted that in the month of July, he "won only three battles among eight." And "at Nanma, for five days and nights, only one regiment was wiped out ......"[23]

The defeats at Nanma and Linqu were even more a disaster for Chen's best units, the left wing columns under Ye and Tao who were waiting to launch supportive attack on enemy troops from the south. They were suddenly left alone after Chen's hasty retreat and immediately isolated in the south of Nanma. Within days they were surrounded by overwhelming government troops. Chiang Kai-shek was all geared up. He personally directed the chase and encirclement of Chen's two elite columns in order to revenge for the demise of his beloved 74th Division. Ye and Tao's columns were code-named "bread" and "watermelon" during the government operation. Chiang ordered eight divisions to seek their complete destruction. Under desperate circumstances, Ye and Tao decided to send one division to divert the enemy toward the east, while the bulk of the forces moved to the west. The diversion succeeded only for a day. For the next seven days, the two columns were on the run through numerous rivers and swamps under heavy rain. Many were drowned in rivers and many killed during the chase. The casualties were so heavy that it was estimated that over a third of this elite force of Chen's perished during the escape. The remnants finally reached safety on August 1 and hooked up with Chen's right wing.[24]

The debacle at Nanma and Linqu shook the high command of Chen's East China Field Army. The troop morale was low and complaints were spreading among the rank and file. Since the campaign was launched under the slogan of "counterattack," as Mao had suggested before the operations, soldiers joked about it, saying, "counterattack means the loss of Shandong (*Fan Gong Fan Gong Fan Diao Shandong*." In his battle summary on September 3, Su painfully admitted that three major mistakes were made. First, they were too optimistic and therefore underestimated the enemy. Second, they lacked technique and experience in taking well protected fortresses. Third, the bad weather also delayed battle action. Su tried hard to dispel the pessimism in the troops who began to complain about Mao's decision to split their troops, and they were especially disappointed by the poor performance of Liu Bocheng and Deng Xiaoping's much publicized march to the Dabie Mountains.[25]

The defeat took an especially heavy toll on Su's mental status. Although part of the blame should be attributed to the Party Central Committee's erratic instructions, Su felt particularly ashamed. As the *de facto* battle organizer, Su was responsible for making and executing the operation plans. In a personal telegram to the Central Committee Su asked for official reprimand for his failure. To comfort Su, Chen sent a telegram pointing out that, "I think our party has not yet produced many outstanding military experts in the past twenty years. Recently Su Yu, Chen Geng and the others stand out, who will have a great future and will be in the same league as Peng (Dehuai), Liu (Bocheng), and Lin Biao are ...." Chen also accepted collective responsibility for recent failures.[26] Chen's praise of Su would turn out to be totally justified. Su's military brilliance would, in the next few months, help avoid many major mistakes by the supreme commander Mao whose penchant for guerrilla warfare could have cost the communists a great deal. Su's morale was boosted by Chen. Despite his military professionalism, Su had always been insecure about his status. Short and slim even by the Chinese standard, Su was by no means an imposing military hero. Always sensitive about his authority, Su more often than not encountered opposition and insubordination from his commanders. On many occasions, Su's orders were ignored or discounted by field commanders. During the Battle of Menglianggu, for example, one veteran column commander refused flatly to follow his instruction, and was only silenced by Chen Yi who took over the conversation over the phone to back up Su's authority.[27]

In early August, Mao sent a directive to Chen, urging him to reinforce Liu and Deng who were in the very dangerous position of being driven back to the north of the Yellow River. Su suggested that the East China Field Army be split into two parts---the East Corps and the West Corps. The main units, including the Ye-Wang-Tao columns would be put under his command, designated as the West Corps operating on the exterior lines, while a smaller East Corps under Xu Shiyou would remain in interior line. To reinforce his authority, Su asked Chen to stay with him to help command the West Corps. As a result, Chen and Su led the main forces across the Yellow River to connect with Liu and Deng.

From this time on, Mao began to return to his favorite guerrilla strategy of operating without a rear base as Liu and Deng had been operating since July. But the Liu-Deng mission was not a successful one. Since their march toward the Dabie Mountains in early July, the losses were exceedingly heavy and the troops, designated as the Central Plains Field Army, had little to show to justify this strategic move. Worse still, Mao did not really intend for Liu and Deng to reinforce Chen and Su in the Eastern China war theater, as the latter would have liked. But, much to Chen and Su's chagrin, they were simply going to replace Chen and Su so that the latter's forces could be sent across the Yangzi River to open up a new theater. For Chen and Su, large-scale mobile warfare without a strong rear and popular base for logistic support was a strategic anathema. But Mao's fantasy went further. To release enormous pressure the government forces brought upon the communist headquarters in Northern Shaanxi, Mao had been thinking of sending Chen's best units---the columns under Ye Fei and Tao Yong---to the south of the Yangzi River, as an expedition force, to directly threaten the heart of Chiang's power center in the Yangzi Valley. In late July, Mao instructed Chen to send Ye and Tao "out to Fujian, Zhejiang and Jiangxi to establish a base area." Chen and Su hesitated. Su, in particular, was quickly reminded of the disaster of 1935 when his troops advanced without rear support and perished in the mountains. Seeing no action on Chen's part for almost two months, Mao flared up and reprimanded Chen and Su on September 3, "You ... have had too strong a psychological reliance on rear support ... you should quickly change this attitude and adapt to new conditions."[28] Under Mao's heavy pressure, Su designed a battle plan aimed at convincing Mao of the necessity of retaining Ye and Tao. Su intended to eliminate a government division which was tailgating his West Corps across the Yellow River into Henan Province. Since Deng's troops were already in the nearby area, Su thought that it may be a good opportunity to show Mao the significance of the concentration of troops instead of splitting them. The two forces collaborated for the first time. Known as the Battle of Shatuji, the communist forces wiped out the government division in less than two days. Mao was not fully convinced. Yet, despite the enormous difficulty for Chen and Su to adapt to conditions on the exterior lines, this battle gave them some confidence that operation on the exterior lines, though risky, was viable.

By late September, a disgruntled Mao decided to transfer Chen and Su's command to Deng Xiaoping, apparently resulting from Chen and Su's reluctance to carry out Mao's new "Southern Strategy." On September 22, Mao sent a telegram specifying the new command structure: Chen's East China Field Army would belong to Deng's Jing-Ji-Lu-Yu Party Central Committee Sub-bureau (Shanxi-Hebei-Shandong-Henan Sub-bureau). Chen was appointed only the third in command. While the reasons remained unclear, Chen and Su apparently managed to resist this order. Throughout October, they continued to call their troops "East China Field Army" in defiance of Mao's instruction.[29] The difference in strategic visions between Chen, Su and Mao went still deeper. Mao's penchant for guerrilla war predicated a much longer struggle with Chiang during the course of the civil war. In 1946, Mao foresaw the possibility of defeating Chiang in a minimum of five years, the worst case scenario would be fifteen. Chen and Su had hoped to continue large-scale mobile warfare that they had mastered its craft by now, which would drastically shorten the course of the war. Mao was always in favor of building up mountain bases, as Deng was asked to do in the Dabie Mountains. Chen and Su preferred decisive showdown in open fields.

In November 1947, Chen was summoned to Northern Shaanxi for a Party Central Committee meeting. On his way, Chen was invited everywhere to give speeches, for his East China Field Army had achieved stunning successes in Shandong throughout 1946 and 1947. In one speech on November 9, Chen made a prediction that the victory might come in one, two, and at the most three years. It would turn out that Chen was not far off the mark. During the two-month travel, Chen was alarmed, however, by the widespread internal purge campaign in Northern China. In a personal telegram to Su, Chen warned him to avoid being "right-leaning" and that he should prepare for political purge campaigns as well, since, in the northern communist area, over forty percent of the party members were the potential targets of the purge. But Chen was soon disgusted by the purge method in the north, as it became increasingly farcical when a person's family background was considered the number one factor in the party's loyalty test. In some extreme cases, the troops were divided into different groups for serving meals. Thus there was a "poor peasant table" versus a "scum table"---the latter being the table seated by those who were from wealthy family background. Arriving at Northern Shaanxi, Chen was placed in a house neighboring Mao and Zhou, reflecting his growing importance in the eyes of the Party Central Committee. At the dinner banquet in honor of him, Chen startled his guests that included Mao and Zhou by making a joke that this luxurious dinner table was a "scum table," since none of the top communist leaders present was from poor peasant family![30]

The real purpose for Mao to summon Chen to Shaanxi was to discuss a top secret plan which was not even disclosed at the Central Committee meeting. This was Mao's favorite, and a clearly redefined new "Southern Strategy." It was not dissimilar to the original one invented by Xiang Ying, Mao's one time *bete noire*. Mao's idea was simple. He wanted to send Ye Fei and Tao Yong to southern China to establish a major guerrilla base area. Since Liu Bocheng and Deng Xiaoping were in trouble in holding on to the Dabie Mountains base, Mao hoped Ye and Tao could divert large part of the enemy troops to follow them across the Yangzi River so as to reduce pressure on Liu and Deng. Chen Yi was somehow converted into a "Southern Strategy" supporter by Mao's powerful persuasion. In late January of 1948, Mao's high command further decided to send three columns under Ye Fei, Tao Yong and Wang Bicheng, namely, Chen's original elite units south of the Yangzi. The task was specified as to "divert twenty to thirty enemy brigades back to the south." Moreover, "You should stay in Hunan and Jiangxi for half to one year ... then to adopt a hopping method to gradually reach the border area of Fujian, Zhejiang and Jiangxi." Mao stressed further the need for absolute secrecy, for this matter must not be made known to anybody "aside from Ye, Wang and Tao."[31]

Su Yu had never been enthusiastic about this type of plan which always reminded him of the ill-fated expedition in 1935. Besides, the rationale for this troop-splitting operation was by no means clear. Indeed, if Mao's purpose was to divert enemy troops away from Deng Xiaoping, the government may or may not take the bait. Moreover, Deng's difficulty in holding on to the Dabie Mountains base was largely self-made, for it was the result of the communist policies both in the past and at the present. The Dabie Mountains area was an old Red Army base that had produced Zhang Guotao's *Er-Yu-Wan* Soviet in the 1930s. The peasants had suffered a great deal throughout the bloody civil war in the 1930s. The communist land policy and the terror caused by constant purges had alienated the majority of the locals who did not want to be part of the communist war efforts against the government. Deng's troops encountered enormous difficulties in obtaining food and supplies. In most cases, the peasants even refused to smile and talk to the communists. The tension was heightened by the troops' forceful requisition of grains and other materials at the expense of the peasants. The result was disastrous. Deng admitted a few months later in an internal speech that his troops had committed numerous "mistakes." One was to destroy local economy through war measures to obtain supplies. Another was to implement "left-leaning" land policy. During the process of radical land reform in the Dabie Mountains area, the communists executed so many innocent people that in many cases, nine out of ten alleged "running dogs" of the landlords were verified to be poor peasants after their deaths. Deng had to put a stop to this nonsense.[32]

Because Deng could not hold on to the Dabie Mountains base anyway, Su thought it only logical to combine the strength of the two forces in the plain area for a major strategic showdown. In a telegram to Deng in January 1948, Su stated that he "is bold enough to make a straightforward suggestion" that he and Deng should begin strategic coordination, a suggestion that was apparently in contradiction to Mao's thinking. Su also made a humble gesture to allow Deng to command his troops if such coordination should occur.[33]

Through communication with Chen at Yanan, Su realized that Chen had been convinced by Mao's "Southern Strategy." He thus had no choice but to follow orders. But his military instinct told him that this strategy would not work. He began to devise plans for postponing the date of departure. In a carefully drafted telegram dated January 31, 1948 to Yanan, Su accepted the idea of sending his best troops to the south. But he also pointed out various practical difficulties, including the choice of route, the area for establishing a base, etc. The real purpose of this telegram was to delay the troop departure by suggesting that the earliest departure date would not be possible before March. Mao remained adamant. In a reply the next day, Mao urged Su to prepare for Yangzi River crossing and even specified a possible route. In early February, Chen began to leave northern Shaanxi for eastern China. Mao was afraid that Chen and Su might change their minds later. In a strange way, he wrote a handwritten note appointing Chen commander of a newly designated "Southeastern Field

Army," with Su and Ye as his chief deputies. The three designated columns under Ye, Wang and Tao were now called the First Corps. The "Southern Strategy" was thus finalized.

Chen was enthusiastic. Not only was his personal status becoming increasingly more important in the eyes of Mao, but also was he going to lead a force that would be his own original units---the units that had been under his direct command since 1938. He knew all the top commanders intimately well and was confident that the reunion of his elite troops would be a pleasant and successful experience. In a very upbeat poem he wrote in Northern Shaanxi, Chen declared that, "The final victory is in sight in the next five years, because we are sending Prince Su [Yu] to cross the Yangzi." Apparently, Chen at this point had changed his earlier, and more optimistic prediction that the war would end much sooner.[34] To appease Chen, Mao also agreed to tone down the internal purge campaign in northern China. Chen was given the unusual authority on his way back to the south to stop extreme actions and policies adopted by local party functionaries in that area. Although only partially successful, Chen was able to persuade some of the leaders to limit the purge targets, one of the most disagreeable leaders in audience was the dreadful internal security chief of the Central Committee, Kang Sheng.

In accordance with Mao's plan, the newly formed First Corps started preparation for the departure in March. But Mao was concerned about the political reliability of this force. In a directive to Su dated January 10, Mao pointed out that the "absolute importance" in maintaining troop discipline.[35] As usual, his best solution was to wage an ideological campaign of self-criticism, a constant process that had proved to be very effective in weeding out at any time those holding grudges against the party central authority. Having learnt the communist excesses in the north and the Dabie Mountains area, Chen and Su decided to modify Mao's request by waging a moderate campaign to concentrate on a theme of "eradicating warlordism" within this elite force.

While Chen and Su lacked a penchant for a political purge, they were concerned about troop discipline. Since the war against Japan, the units under Ye Fei, Wang Bicheng and Tao Yong had acquired an undisputed reputation as the best communist armed forces. The rank and file enjoyed enormous pride in their achievements, but they also became increasingly more arrogant. When encountering other communist troops on march, they tended to be overbearing and often showed obvious contempt towards the others and unabashedly declared themselves to be "number one," "invincible" and so on. During the narrow escape in Western Shandong in 1947, the troops under Ye and Tao alienated the local population through the forceful acquisition of food and shelter. It was rather unusual for a communist force to be accused by the peasants of being a "three-all" army, referring to forceful requisition of housing, fruit and chicken. Corporal punishment was also common within these elite communist troops. Tao Yong was known to have a temper that was extremely explosive. Wan Bicheng was a quiet man, but he had a penchant for court martial. Even Ye Fei, the best educated among the three, had his own share of "warlordism." During the self-criticism campaign, known as the "New Style Military Discipline"(*Xin Shi Zheng Jun*) campaign, Ye was under severe attack from his colleagues concerning a trivial 1945 incident of insubordination when Ye's temper exploded and he ordered the tying up of a communist Red Army veteran who was too slow to stop taking some unauthorized materials captured from the Japanese. The case became all the more embarrassing for Ye because the person in ropes used to be on an equal footing with Ye during the early New Fourth Army years. Such an incident was in fact reported directly to Mao.[36] Yet the campaign was heavily influenced by the purges in the north. Unexpectedly it went astray when some of the units imitated the cruel method as Chen Yi had witnessed in communist controlled northern China, such as excessive emphasis on family background and relentless personal attacks.[37] It became escalated day by day and its momentum seemed hard to be stopped.

It was fortunate that Mao could not wait any longer for the implementation of his strategic plan. He became impatient in April when he ordered Chen to finish the "New Style Military Discipline" campaign before May 15 in order to prepare for crossing the Yangzi River. Mao had been dreaming about this "Southern Strategy" for several years. In strict confidence, Mao had related to Chen in Northern Shaanxi a fully developed theory. According to Mao, only two approaches existed for the strategic shift of communist operation from enemy's interior to exterior lines: first, there was the "Northern Expedition" approach, which, as in 1927, required a strong rear base to support the troop's steady advance against the warlord enemy; second, there was a "hopping" approach, which required no rear support but could change strategic table far more quickly and dramatically. Mao apparently favored the latter, for he believed that, aside from Manchuria, the communist troops were not ready for large-scale mobile warfare in the open field.[38] Mao's decision was firm and elaborate. It would take a bold man who had to risk his career to challenge Mao's new fantasy.

During the two-month long "New Style Military Discipline" campaign, Su Yu was preoccupied with the pros and the cons of Mao's "Southern Strategy." After careful calculations, Su found this strategy totally devoid of logic and feasibility. First of all, Su would prefer to combine his troops and the troops under Deng Xiaoping's command to engage the government in the north of the Yangzi River, where the terrain was flat and ideal for a major strategic showdown. But Mao did not consider that the time had come for a showdown and seemed to have failed to grasp the fact that the strategic turning point had, in Su's view, arrived in Central and Eastern China in favor of the communists. Secondly, Mao's guerrilla tactics were no longer valid for the purpose of defeating the government troops. Some of the communist troops, especially Chen's forces, at this point had already acquired long experience and capability for large-scale mobile warfare. Only through modern war could Chiang Kai-shek be eliminated in a short period of time. Thirdly, it would be irrational to abandon Shandong which, after a two-year struggle for its mastery, had become a most reliable base area for the communist regulars. Fourthly, even for pragmatic reasons, Su considered it necessary to retain his best troops in the north of the Yangzi. Since a "hopping strategy" without a rear would cost him, as he calculated correctly, at least a half of his troops (totaled at over 100,000.) Given the fact that Mao seemed to have shown no scruples about wasting Chen and Su's elite units, it would still be better to sacrifice over half, i.e., 50,000 best troops in a major military showdown instead of losing the same number in a chasing game throughout Southern China. In a word, Su was convinced that Mao was completely wrong in his judgment.[39] All in all, Su's military professionalism ran counter to Mao's military amateurism.

While agonizing over the question whether or not he should tell Mao the truth, Su disclosed his thoughts to Chen. Chen and Mao had at least one thing in common. As passionately romantic poets, they were more dreamers than practical planners who had to deal with details. Chen was naturally shocked by Su's frankness in criticizing Mao's favorite project. But he knew that Su was such a cautious strategist and personality that under normal circumstances he would not do such a thing. After days of private conversations, Chen was finally won over by Su's powerful arguments. After all, Chen was never enthusiastic about Xiang Ying's old "Southern Strategy" in the early 1940s. Chen knew that Su's move would put Mao in a very awkward position, and if Su's bold plan for a strategic showdown should go sour under any circumstances, their entire military careers would be at risk. Nevertheless, Chen allowed Su to present his view to the Party Central Committee at once.

Before sending his dissenting view to Mao, Su was clever enough to first solicit opinions from Liu Bocheng and Deng Xiaoping whose support would carry enormous weight on Mao. Having had a poor showing since they had crossed the Yellow River in July 1947, Liu and Deng were anxious to win major military victories to justify their precarious existence in Eastern China. To Su's great delight, Liu and Deng fully supported Su's plan on April 18. In his long telegram to Mao on the same day, Su made his case forcefully but at the same time took all the responsibilities upon himself in order to extricate Chen Yi. In this extremely important telegram, the existence of which is only known in recent years, Su pointed out five reasons why the "Southern Strategy" would not work,

1. The war [in this area] has become a war of attrition .... It is very difficult for us to eliminate the main enemy forces.
2. Large numbers of troops entering a new area will encounter enormous difficulty in obtaining supplies and caring for the wounded. The morale will be low when the rank and file know that the wounded will have to be abandoned to the mercy of the enemy troops.
3. Guerrilla tactics [in Southern China] will require that heavy weapons and equipment be abandoned. Without them, any siege warfare will become impossible.
4. The number one issue is food .... During the battle of the Tianmu Mountain in 1945, we completely impoverished local population in less than three months ... not even the poorest peasants were exempted. Without a base area, it would be impossible to solve food problem for over 100,000 troops.
5. Chiang Kai-shek may not be willing to divert his best troops to chase us across the Yangzi River. If this were to be so, the [Southern] Strategy will be totally ineffective and we will be in a strategic stalemate in this area.

In conclusion, Su boldly suggested concentration of all troops in this area to prepare for a real showdown. The first step would be the attack on Jinan, the capital of Shandong Province. According to Su's plan, the capture of Jinan would result in a total communist victory in the struggle for mastery of Shandong and once Shandong was firmly secured, the communist troops would be in a position to wipe out bulk of the enemy forces along the Longhai Railway. Finally, a showdown may become inevitable from the government point of view.[40]

In April, the ever elusive Mao left his headquarters and arrived at Nie Rongzhen's base at Fuping city in Hebei province. Upon receiving this telegram, Mao was greatly alarmed. He immediately summoned Chen and Su to meet him. Mao and Su had not seen each other for over seventeen years. In the Jinggang Mountains days, Su once served as Mao's head of security detail. But they split in 1931 and never met again until now. While Su's arguments were very convincing, Mao refused to drop the "Southern Strategy" altogether. In a subsequent instruction, Mao reiterated that his old strategy was "correct, firm and unmovable." But he also agreed to delay Su's departure for Southern China for "four to eight months," citing the "problems related to the river crossing." The infallible Mao, of course, would not admit that his judgment was wrong.[41]

Meanwhile Mao apparently grew suspicious that Chen and Su, while rejecting his beloved "Southern Strategy," were becoming too powerful by clinging to their hold to a strong and large army group of the communist military. In a very clever move, he decided to transfer Chen to Deng Xiaoping's command for the second time in one year. This decision was prompted in part by Deng's demand for a major leader to strengthen his headquarters. Deng had asked for Chen's transfer in April. But Mao did not reply immediately. Deng tried again in May, mentioning three candidates: Peng Zhen, Chen Yi and Deng Zihui. Since Peng was serving Lin Biao as his political commissar in Manchuria, Deng asked Mao to assign Chen to be his deputy. Deng's opinion always carried enormous weight with Mao. Throughout his career, he had enjoyed a special relationship with Mao since the Jiangxi years. He was the only survivor of the pro-Mao faction known as "Deng-Mao-Xie-Gu Clique," which was brutally purged in the 1930s.[42] Deng was known to be an extremely sharp but reticent man, an ideal type for an effective political commissar. But Chen and Su had resisted a similar order a few months before. This time, Mao refused to budge an inch. Only at the end of the meeting with Chen and Su, Mao informed Su that Chen had to go to Deng's headquarters and that this was a final decision. Su was completely devastated. He knew that he must count on Chen's political authority to control troops so that he would be able to preoccupy himself with the beloved art of warfare. After repeated plea with Mao that "the East China Field Army cannot be without Commander Chen," Mao reluctantly approved Su's minimal demand that that Chen retain his nominal command and title with his old troops, even though his actual full-time duty was still to be with Deng's much smaller Central Plains Field Army.

Chen was more than frustrated by Mao's decision. Sensing that Mao intended to relieve him of military duties at this critical strategic moment, Chen made his melancholy sentiment known by getting rid of his treasured war mementos while preparing for departure from his beloved troops. He gave a metal folding table and a Browning pistol, both had belonged to the ill-fated government General Zhang Lingfu of the 74th Division, to his old colleague Zhu De, the communist commander in chief. He then sent a US-made radio transmitter to his fellow student in France, Zhou Enlai. In an interesting personal note to Zhou and his wife, a sentimental Chen expressed his feelings this way, "I will depart for the west [Deng's headquarters] tomorrow, and I have no intention to stay with the troops, and only wish to return to Sichuan together with them someday ......" Chen's rather gloomy note was read by all the top leaders and someone apparently found the last sentence significant enough to be highlighted with a marker.[43]

But for Su, the sacrifice of Chen's position was compensated with the temporary abandonment of the dreadful "Southern Strategy." This meant that there would be some possibility of continued concentration of communist troops in the north of the Yangzi River for a major strategic showdown with the government. One problem that worried Chen most was the supply system during large-scale warfare. The communists had by had a primitive logistics system. No unified logistics department or quartermaster corps ever existed. In guerrilla war or limited mobile war, the supply problem was not acute. Su had implied to Deng several months ago that there was a need for unified supply system. Deng showed little interest.[44]

Because the East China Field Army had mostly been engaging modern style mobile war for the past few years, Chen was also keenly aware of this problem. On his way to Deng's command, Chen began to study this problem which he considered to be of enormous importance. Logistics in large-scale military actions had never loomed large in peasant-based small-scale warfare. Despite the fact that in Jiangxi as well as in *Er-Yu-Wan*, the Red Armies through its land and economic policies had destroyed whatever material supporting base in the 1930s, the guerrilla-prone Mao had paid little attention to this problem in the past. Indeed, the communist troops by this time had not even established a regular logistics system. According to Mao's favorite "People's War" concept, any logistics problem could be solved by mass mobilization of the local population. The result was widespread waste of labor and materials. After careful observation of the communist practices in Deng's territory, Chen wrote a long telegram to Mao in June 1948, pointing out the need for a logistics system and transportation troops. To requisition peasant labors (*Min Gong*) for any large-scale warfare would "impose an enormous burden on the local population." Besides, "it is utterly ineffective if the peasant labors were not paid properly." Chen's suggestion was bold and somewhat "right-leaning" at the time, but he was strongly supported by Deng Zihui, who was another leader transferred to Deng's command and who was one of the very few communist leaders who possessed a sharp mind for economics and savvy for business.[45]

After Chen's change of job to join Deng Xiaoping's command, Su Yu became the *de facto* commander of the East China Field Army. Zhu De, the nominal communist commander in chief, was dispatched to Su's headquarters in May to boost the troop morale. Zhu specified a strategy that was favored by Mao: to eliminate General Qiu Qingquan's 5th Army. Qiu had been engaging the communists for several years now. He had a relatively successful record and his army was considered one of the strongest government units. Mao approved Su's plan to seek battle opportunities with the government in Eastern Henan. Aside from the troops under Su's command, Mao added two columns under Deng to reinforce Su's operation.

At the end of May, the well-rested troops under Su began to cross the Yellow River and to close in for engaging Qiu's army. One advantage for Chen Yi to join Deng's command was the better coordination between the two troops who had vast differences in history and style. Deng's Central Plains Field Army derived originally from the 129th Division of the Eighth Route Army during the war against Japan. But its battle record was far from glorious. Outshone by Lin Biao's 115th Division, its reputation was further tarnished by the ill-fated "hopping operation" in 1947 and the inability to hold on to a base in the Dabie Mountains. Troop morale was low and equipment poor. During the chase-and-run game with the government forces, Deng had to order abandoning heavy equipment and artillery pieces. Without artillery fire to cover infantry operation, casualties were bound to be high during the battle. Su's troops, however, had won most battles, and stood out among four communist military factions led respectively by Peng Dehuai, Lin Biao, Deng Xiaoping and Chen Yi. The East China Field Army had captured the best equipment, mostly US-made, and established strong a tradition in infantry-artillery synchronization, which was a rare symbol of modern warfare unsurpassed within the communist military establishment. The contempt towards Deng's Central Plains Field Army was widespread among the East China Field Army.

To clear the enemy of Southern Shandong in order to isolate Jinan, the capital city, Su Yu planned a major campaign in the border area between Henan and Shandong. While Mao preferred to strike directly at General Qiu's 5th Army stationing in Shandong, Su was not so sure about this idea since Qiu had a strong logistics base in this area. He suggested to lure Qiu out of Shandong by attacking Kaifeng, a major city of the Henan Province. The government defense at Kaifeng was very weak, for the bulk of their troops were concentrated in Shandong. The communists easily took the city on June 22. As expected, Chiang immediately ordered his elite troops to retake Kaifeng. Although General Qiu did not take the bait, one wing of the government troops led by General Ou Shounian quickly fell into Su's tactical pocket at Longwangdian. After the isolation of Ou had been achieved by swift troop deployment, Su used his best troops plus one of Deng's columns for the final kill. General Ou was captured alive a few days later.

Although Su's forces performed extremely well, Deng's columns seemed to have suffered a major setback during the battle when its position was broken through by government armored troops. It was a major humiliation for Deng's Central Plains Field Army. At the very beginning, Su thought that Deng's troop would be less useful in offensive operation, so he assigned the main force under Deng to perform the task of diversionary action. Even so, the latter did not do their job well, aside from slowing down government reinforcements spearheaded by General Qiu's Fifth Army. As a result, despite the fact that Chen Yi was with Deng's command, the relationship between the two filed armies was immediately strained. To make things worse, after the battle, the East China Field Army headquarters issued an official comment on the campaign. It made no mention of the role played by Deng's Central Plains Field Army. More embarrassingly, Su's chief of staff, Chen Shiju, alienated Deng's rank and file when giving a dramatic description of the battle in front of Deng's commander Liu Bocheng and his officer corps. Chen Shiju strongly believed in the decisive role played by artillery fire. He was so carried away with infantry-artillery synchronization that his audience turned silent, crestfallen and then agitated, since Liu and Deng had to abandon most of their artillery pieces during the march toward Dabie Mountains. Sensing that his officers were embarrassed, Liu asked them to stay after Chen Shiju's glowing presentation in a village square, even though it was already dark. Liu made a speech that pointedly criticized the "penchant for artillery fire" and stressed the role of throwing hand grenades during the battle. Chen Yi felt terribly awkward and instructed Su to avoid making similar mistakes in the future. In the end, Su and his chief of staff had to make an official apology to Deng and Liu.[46] After the battle in Henan, Su began to shift his attention to solving the problem in Shandong. He thought that the conditions had finally become mature for a major siege warfare against Jinan, the capital city of Shandong, and to put an end to the recent bid by the government to regain control of this strategically important corridor.

Chiang Kai-shek was deeply upset by the defeat in Eastern Henan. In a handwritten letter to General Qiu Qingquan, Chiang blamed him for the defeat and asked him to "redeem yourself with future success."[47] Chiang knew that the danger now lay with the isolation of Jinan. The fall of Jinan would mean the end of his two-year struggle for mastery in Shandong, which would expose his heartland in the Yangzi Valley to communist attacks. But General Qiu was not willing to "redeem himself" by sending his troops to reinforce General Wang Yaowu, the commander at Jinan. The communists organized a major attack on the capital city in September. Su's battle plan for taking Jinan was a risky one. Under normal circumstances, the communist siege strategy was characterized either as surrounding the city, but seeking destruction of enemy reinforcements (*Wei Cheng Da Yuan*), or attacking the city while blunting the enemy reinforcements (*Gong Cheng Zu Yuan*). The former was designed to lure enemy forces into a pocket, while the latter was aimed at taking the city. This time, Su decided to take the city and at the same time to eliminate the enemy reinforcements (*Gong Cheng Da Yuan*). In other words, he had to spend a much smaller force needed to take the city where General Wang Yaowu had at his disposal over 100,000 soldiers, since the bulk of Su's troops would seek destroying, instead of simply blunting, the enemy reinforcements. Because of General Qiu's hesitation, the communists were able to take Jinan in a battle that lasted eight days. General Wang became a prison of war.

The Battle of Jinan further whetted Su's appetite. During the course of battle, Su already began to ponder the possibility for a much bigger campaign aimed at wiping out Chiang's main force north of the Yangzi River in one swift strategic blow. The loss of Shandong would mean the concentration of the government troops in a very narrow strip along the Longhai Railroad, offering an opportunity for a showdown. This was possible especially since Chiang could never afford to give up this railway which was the last defense line north of the Yangzi River. Such a campaign, if successful, would guarantee the communist victory within a year. But Mao had not yet grasped the strategic turning point in lieu of the Battle of Jinan. In a telegram dated in September 22, Mao stated clearly that the Central Committee considered that the "defeat of Kuomintang within five years will be a sufficient possibility," since, for the first two years of the civil war, "we have eliminated over 189 regular brigades. Adding the irregulars to this figure, we have wiped out a total of 2.7 million enemy troops." Thus, Mao concluded that, if the communists could maintain the same pace, for five years "we will be able to finish off some 500 brigades at 7 million in strength."[48] Although he meant that the starting point of the five years was 1946, he still envisioned a final victory over the Kuomintang government no earlier than 1951!

Notes

1. *MZDJSWJ*, vol.3, p.649.
2. Ibid., p.651.
3. Quoted from *Biography of Chen Yi* (Official), p.362.
4. For detail of the Battle of Laiwu, see *Laiwu Zhan Yi Zong Jie* (Summary of the Battle of Laiwu), in *Military Works of Su Yu*, p.294-310.
5. Ibid., p.294, note.
6. Ibid., p.294-310.
7. *Memoirs of Ye Fei*, p.409-420.
8. Whitson, William, *The Chinese High Command* (New York: 1973), p.236.
9. *Memoirs of Ye Fei*, p.421.
10. *MZDJSWJ*, vol.4, p.1-2.
11. Guo, Rugui, *Guo Rugui Hui Yi Lu* (Memoirs of Guo Rugui, Chengdu 1987), p.244. General Guo was at the time the Operation Chief of Chiang's government.

12. *Biography of Chen Yi* (Official), p.368-369.
13. *MZDJSWJ*, vol.4, p.58-59.
14. Ye, Fei et al, *Hu Jiang Wang Bicheng* (Tiger General Wang Bicheng, Beijing 1992), p.352-356.
15. In the 1960s, Wang Bicheng's Propaganda Chief, Wu Qiang, published a highly acclaimed novel entitled *Hong Ri* (Red Sun), which inadvertently praised General Zhang Lingfu's 74th Division for its toughness. Wu had to pay dearly for this novel during the Cultural Revolution.
16. Sources from Taiwan and the West indicate that Zhang committed suicide. In fact, Zhang was killed by He Fengshan, a regimental commander of Wang Bicheng's Sixth Column. See *Biography of Chen Yi* (Official), p.376.
17. Whitson, *The Chinese High Command*, p.238.
18. *Zhong Guo Ren Min Jie Fang Jun Zhan Shi* (Battle History of the People's Liberation Army, Beijing 1987), vol.3, p.112.
19. *Biography of Chen Yi* (Official), p.376.
20. *MZDJSWJ*, vol.4, p.81-82.
21. *WJXJ*, vol.16, p.465-466.
22. For more detail, see Wang, Yuting, *Hu Lian Jiang Jun Ping Zhuan* (Biography of General Hu Lian, Taipei, 1987), p.76-79.
23. *Biography of Chen Yi* (Official), p.382.
24. *Memoirs of Ye Fei*, p.458-464.
25. *Military Works of Su Yu*, p.321-325.
26. *Biography of Chen Yi* (Official), p.382-383.
27. Ibid., p.375.
28. *MZDJSWJ*, vol.4, p.236.
29. *Biography of Chen Yi* (Official), p.388-389.
30. Ibid., p.393-396.
31. Ibid., p.402.
32. Deng, Xiaoping, *Deng Xiaoping Wen Xuan* (Selected Works of Deng Xiaoping, Beijing 1989), p.102-108.
33. *Military Works of Su Yu*, p.344-346.
34. *Complete Collection of Chen Yi's Poems*, p.217.
35. *WJXJ*, vol.17, p.8.
36. In his memoirs, Ye Fei still held grudges against these attacks and considered his action justified. See *The Incident of Wang Sheng*, in *Memoirs of Ye Fei*, p.364-366.
37. In Ye's First Division, such method was widespread. See *Fire Never Extinguishes*, p.261.
38. *Biography of Chen Yi* (Official), p.411-412.
39. Ibid., p.410-411.
40. For detail of this long telegram, see *Military Works of Su Yu*, p.353-356.
41. *MZDJSWJ*, vol.4, p.459.

42. Deng Xiaoping, Mao Zetan, Xie Weijun and Gu Bai. These were staunch supporters of Mao in the early 1930s. Mao Zetan, the younger brother of Mao, was Deng's best friend.
43. For impact of this unexpected job transfer, see Su, Yu, *War Memoirs*, p.542. *Biography of Chen Yi* (Official), p.415-419.
44. *Military Works of Su Yu*, p.345-346.
45. *Biography of Chen Yi* (Official), p.524.
46. Ibid., p.430-431.
47. *Memoirs of Ye Fei*, p.505-506.
48. *WJXJ*, vol.17, p.333.

Chapter 7

The Showdown

Chiang's fate was quickly sealed in 1948 and 1949 as a result of three major campaigns: *Liao-Shen* (Manchuria), *Huai-Hai* (Huaiyin, Huaian and Haizhou) and *Ping-Jin* (Beiping-Tianjin). The government lost altogether some 1.5 million troops. By 1948 the communists began to smash the government troops with dazzling pace. To the surprise of many outsiders, it seemed that the communists were not only adept at guerrilla tactics, but also skillful and decisive in mobile campaigns in a fashion that was typical during World War Two and on massive scale. In September 1948, as Su Yu was attacking Jinan, Lin Biao launched the Campaign of Manchuria. The communists already controlled over 97% of the territory and 86% of the population in Manchuria. The government forces at a half million strong had been effectively isolated in a few big cities, becoming "a turtle in a jar." Thus Lin Biao's task was simple: to cut off the connections between the government strongholds and to eliminate the enemy units one by one with massive siege campaigns. More importantly, Lin had some 700,000 regular troops plus over 300,000 irregulars at his disposal. His numerical superiority over the enemy was overwhelming. All in all, the conditions for the Campaign in Manchuria fitted like a glove with Mao's military thinking and instinct. In fact, Mao was at his best as the supreme commander. During the execution of the campaign, Mao was able to reject Lin's battle plans several times, usually with more sensible and sounder judgment. Mao's contribution to the victory in Manchuria was significant. After two months of prolonged battles, Lin ended the campaign with the elimination of 472,000 government troops.[1]

Among the three major campaigns that determined the outcome of the civil war, the Campaign of Huai-Hai was a unique one. It was the only campaign that ran against Mao's military belief and instinct, for there was neither numerical superiority, nor a unified command at the beginning of the campaign. Mao's performance as supreme commander was rather lackluster, his contribution was fuzzy. Nevertheless, the Campaign of Huai-Hai from November 1948 to January 1949 virtually destroyed Chiang's ability to fight north of the Yangzi River. Chiang could afford to write off Manchuria but not the area around Xuzhou in Eastern China.

Because it was the largest strategic showdown, which eliminated over a half million government forces, in communist military history, the Campaign of Huai-Hai has always been presented in the People's Republic of China as a showcase of Mao's strategic clairvoyance and tactical brilliance. Questions concerning who was responsible for the original idea and the actual execution of the campaign have always been a political taboo. In a blatant effort to rewrite history, editors of the "Selected Works of Mao Zedong" skillfully changed the context of the original telegrams between Mao and his field commanders to create the effect that it appeared that Mao deserved all the credit. The fact is that Mao's role was more often negative than positive. In the first place, he never wanted to fight the campaign the way it would actually turn out. In the second place, his directives during the course of action often appeared indecisive and showed a lack of direction.[2] As supreme commander, Mao was shaken under pressure during this military gamble of his life.

The original idea for the campaign came from Su Yu. With the success of the Battle of Jinan that had finished off some 100,000 government forces, the communists were now in full control of Shandong. On September 24, 1948, Su Yu sent a wire to the Party Central Committee, suggesting that the troops should not take a prolonged rest but seize the opportunity to wage a bigger campaign, the campaign of Huai-Hai. Afraid of a return to Mao's favorite "Southern Strategy," Su had been keen to continue engaging the enemy in the vast plains north of the Yangzi River. During the Battle of Jinan, Su had expected that major government reinforcements would come to rescue Jinan, thus falling into his waiting trap. But this did not happen, since government generals all decided to fold their hands and watch from afar. No one was willing to make efforts to relieve what appeared to be a hopelessly besieged city. As a result, after a two-year tug of war, Shandong was cleared of Chiang's troops. For Su, the next strategic step was naturally to push southwards to control the Longhai Railway, which was the only railway connecting the East China Sea with inland. Through this railway, it was very convenient for the government to transport troops from central China.

In fact, Chiang had already decided to merge his "Central China Pacification Headquarters" with "Xuzhou Pacification Headquarters." He appointed General Bai Chongxi, the key member of the "Guangxi Clique" to take over the combined command. General Bai, though a brilliant strategist, refused to accept what he considered to be a thankless task. Chiang's overall strategy was to hold on to Xuzhou to control the line of communication, while at the same time adopting an "offensive defense" posture through seeking opportunities for a showdown with the communists near the Longhai Railway. Although declining to take over the joint command, General Bai agreed to send some of his best units which formed the 12th Corps from his Central China Pacification Headquarters to reinforce Xuzhou. Thus the government was able to concentrate some 700,000 elite troops in the critical area along the railway.

Su's initial suggestion for the campaign of Huai-Hai was a modest one. According to Su, the objective of this campaign should be the seizure of Two Huai cities (Huaiyin and Huaian), both formerly served as Su's headquarters in northern Jiangsu before the communists were driven out of this area in 1947. If this operation were to be successful, they could push all the way to the port city of Haizhou, the eastern terminal station of the railway line, thus the name of campaign of "Huai-Hai" was born. At this stage, Su envisioned a "small Huai-Hai campaign" which would pursue rather limited objectives.

Mao liked the idea of controlling the line of communications, but he was more eager to eliminate the government troops that had already begun to secure the Longhai Railway. This was the 7th Corps commanded by a tough government general named Huang Baitao. After crushing this force, Mao suggested, Su should proceed to take over Huaiyin and Huaian. Mao also agreed that the final objective was to take control over Haizhou city.[3] The decision to eliminate General Huang Baitao's 7th Corps has often been presented as a key proof of Mao's strategic brilliance, for this step was said to have led to next steps towards a major strategic showdown. In reality, Mao did not have a clear idea about the next step and certainly showed no inclination at all for a showdown. His penchant for absolute numerical superiority at the battleground prompted him to request the elimination of as many government troops as possible. But he did not realize that this decision would dramatically enlarge the scope of the campaign, since it would force Chiang Kai-shek to prepare for a major strategic gamble in the area along the railway. This was a situation Mao did not really want. According to Mao's "Ten Major Military Principles" formulated in December 1947, no strategic showdown was yet called for in this theater of war. In fact, Principle Four specifically stipulated, "in every battle, concentrate an absolutely superior force (two, three, four, and sometimes even five or six times the enemy's), encircle the enemy forces completely, strive to wipe them out thoroughly, and do not let any escape from the net. In special circumstances, use the method of dealing the enemy crushing blows, that is, concentrate all our strength to make a frontal attack and an attack on one or both of his flanks, with the aim of wiping out one part and routing another so that our army can swiftly move its troops to smash other enemy forces." Mao added, "Strive to avoid battles of attrition, in which we lose more than we gain or only break even ......"[4] With inferior numbers on his side in this particular war zone, in sharp contrast to the conditions during the Campaign of Manchurian, Mao had no intention whatsoever of staking all he had at this time on one decisive campaign. His objective was simply to reconnect Jiangsu and Shandong, in order to lure the enemy into defending the Yangzi River line, therefore, his favorite "Southern Strategy"---the establishment of mountain bases in Southern China could finally be carried out.[5] It thus appears ridiculous to maintain that Mao had foreseen this strategic showdown coming and brilliantly executed the campaign that would drastically shorten the course of the civil war by an estimated two years.

In a way, the Campaign of Huai-Hai was to be almost a victory by default, because, from the very beginning there was no planned overall strategy from the top. Purely by coincidence, Mao's decision to first eliminate General Huang Baitao's 7th Corps created the momentum for a massive gamble of no return. It would transform beyond his own expectations Su's "small Huai-Hai campaign" into a gigantic engagement later known as the "big Huai-Hai campaign." It would end up to be enormously successful, not so much because Mao was right as because the field commanders resisted Mao's erratic instructions and wrong-headed interference in its execution on *ad hoc* bases, as battleground conditions changed so rapidly that many key decisions had to be made on the spot.

Mao's failure to realize the need for a large-scale mobile campaign in this area was even more clearly reflected in his most important directive issued on October 11, titled "The Operation Principle of the Campaign of Huai-Hai." The directive specifically pointed out that the purpose of this campaign would be the opening of Jiangsu and therefore, "the bulk of the troops could then be split into East and West Corps for operation in Henan and Anhui ... towards the Dabie Mountains area."[6] After that, "you can cooperate with Liu and Deng to push the enemy all the way toward the bank of the [Yangzi] River. Next fall, your main forces can probably start campaign of Yangzi crossing." This directive was undoubtedly consistent with Mao's "Southern Strategy" that had been delayed due to Su Yu's objection since March 1948. Although there was no evidence that Mao was prepared for risking all his forces in this area for a decisive war, the actual result of the Campaign of Huai-Hai would fulfill Mao's wildest dream of a quick victory at the national level and render his "Southern Strategy" meaningless.[7] It is thus not surprising that, the original context of this telegram, which would have indicated that Mao's real strategic calculation at the time was anything but a determination to seek a major showdown, was neatly cut out when the directive was published in the 1950s. Every trace leading to Mao's "Southern Strategy" was eliminated by official editors of the "Selected Works of Mao Zedong," undoubtedly with Mao's personal authorization, so as to distort the historical fact that Mao had by this time been bent on guerrilla warfare in Southern China. Some may argue that Mao did mention the possibility of a Yangzi Campaign. But the "Yangzi Crossing Campaign" envisioned by Mao in this directive was based on his original "Southern Strategy." It was completely different from the actual Yangzi Campaign which would become possible a few months later as a result of the Campaign of Huai-Hai. Thus, with the critical Point 4 in the directive missing, the whole document that was published later appeared to be a coherent instruction for a farsighted major strategic showdown.

There was another reason why Mao lacked enthusiasm for such a gamble. His confidence was further shaken by Chiang's simultaneous determination of seeking a showdown in the area through large-scale troop concentration, because three government army groups appeared to be converging rapidly in the wide plains near Xuzhou that was originally designated by Su for the "small Huai-Hai campaign." It was unusual, given Chiang's penchant for holding on to cities, that the government high command went as far as to order the abandonment of a few key cities along the Longhai Railway for the purpose of strategic retrenchment back to Xuzhou. when Mao issued his operation directive, General Huang Baitao had already begun preparing for withdrawal from the Haizhou city and had moved his headquarters to Xinanzhen station on the Longhai Railway. Such a move would inevitably block Su's movement towards the Two Huai cities which he originally had planned to seize. Under the circumstances, Su had to agree with Mao to concentrate his efforts on striking at General Huang's army group. Su realized that his burden was much heavier than he had initially envisioned. Except for the siege against Jinan, Su had no experience, nor had any other communist generals, in eliminating a whole army group, the 7th Corps, estimated at over 100,000 strong in one isolated battle. Besides, by following Mao's instruction, Su could not only expect no reinforcements but have to spare part of his forces to blunt government rescue operation. The reality that he lacked an adequate number of troops would render his task extremely difficult.

Aside from Huang Baitao's army group, the government deployed two other groups to coordinate their actions to defend the strategic railway and Xuzhou. Xuzhou was considered the gateway to Chiang's capital city of Nanjing. It was situated at the crossroads of the north-south running Jinpu and east-west running Longhai railways. Thus Xuzhou actually controlled the main artery of communication in Eastern and Central China. One army group was led by General Liu Zhi who was the commander of the Xuzhou Pacification Headquarters. Liu's forces were east of General Huang's position. Another was led by General Huang Wei, which was ordered to advance from the southwest towards the Longhai Railway. This was the newly formed 12th Army Corps designed specifically for the purpose of establishing a strategic connection with Huang Baitao's troops near Xuzhou.

The three government army groups were to form a triangular strategic posture, with Xuzhou as its base. From the very beginning, Chiang Kai-shek believed that Mao's objective was to take Xuzhou. Therefore, he ordered the three army groups to converge toward the city, seeking opportunities for a major engagement. But Mao's interest lay in opening up a corridor for carrying out his "Southern Strategy." He was not keen to seize Xuzhou at this time. Mao's objectives were limited. But he took full advantage of Chiang's miscalculation to confuse the government while guarding carefully his real strategic purpose of eliminating Huang Baitao's 7th Corps. Thus it was most unfortunate for General Huang Baitao's position, since the government did not have contingency plan to guarantee Huang's security on march during his badly organized withdrawal toward Xuzhou. But, since Huang's headquarters was within fifty miles of Xuzhou, it was not considered possible for the communist troops to isolate him in a very short period of time.

As a result, the communists were largely lucky that Huang's 7th Corps could be surrounded east of Xuzhou. But Mao was wavering as far as the overall strategic purpose was concerned at this critical juncture. In a word, he was shaken under pressure and afraid of a major showdown which would force him to gamble his best troops at 600,000 strong against the much larger concentration of Chiang's elite forces at this time, numbered at over 700,000. Another sign of Mao's unwillingness to engage the government in one decisive campaign was his insistence on separate operations by Deng's Central Plains Field Army and Su's East China Field Army, a fact that Su had often deplored. Apart from strategic coordination, Mao did not foresee the need for, nor consider it desirable of, combining the two field armies for a strategic showdown in this area. He merely intended for Deng's troops to take separate actions aimed at diverting government attention away from his true purpose of eliminating Huang Baitao. According to a directive dated October 14, Mao stated clearly that Deng should attack Zhengzhou, the capital city of Henan in the west of Xuzhou, so that the government could mistake it for a prelude to attack on Xuzhou, thus the real objective to surprise Huang Baitao in the east of Xuzhou could be concealed.[8]

A key reason that rendered Mao's strategy workable was that he had a superb espionage network within the government. Most of the government operation plans were quickly made known to the communist headquarters. Over the years, the widespread espionage activities were effectively organized by Zhou Enlai whose spies had penetrated deep into the government decision-making mechanism. One of the best known was General Guo Rugui who was none other than the Director of Operations at the government's Defense Ministry in Nanjing! By contrast, the government had no clues as to Mao's real intention. Compared with the faction-ridden, loosely knitted, and very ineffective organization of Kuomintang, the communist system was purified again and again with incessant political purges. There was little chance that the government spies could be able to hide for long within its organization, since each smallest atomic unit of the party had been thoroughly cleansed and brainwashed.

As late as on October 21, Su reported that throughout the quiet process of large concentration of his troops in the area near Huang's position, the enemy had not yet discovered the plan to attack this army group along the Longhai Railway.[9] Mao was delighted and instructed Deng Xiaoping and his deputy Chen Yi to attack Zhengzhou at once, and then to proceed to "wage a Xuzhou-Bangbu campaign." Bangbu was a city in the south of Xuzhou, far away from Su's operation area. There was thus little doubt that Mao continued to envision two separate battles operated by two field armies.

Deng and Chen easily took Zhengzhou on October 22, after the panicky government garrison force had fled the city without putting up serious resistance. Yet the two began to feel that Mao's idea of waging a "Xuzhou-Bangbu campaign" was neither realistic nor practical, since the Central Plains Field Army under their command was too small to independently perform such a task. More importantly, since Chen was now Deng's deputy commander, it would be logically much easier for the two field armies to stay in current region to cooperate not only strategically but also tactically. Therefore, they preferred to postpone the campaign against Xuzhou and wait for Su's move against Huang Baitao in the east of Xuzhou before taking further action. But Mao issued an erratic instruction three days later, ordering them immediately to move southward, to "cross the Huai River... and to hold on to the area between Xuzhou and Bangbu for two to three months" in order to fulfill the task of luring enemy into defending the Yangzi River area. Mao's intention became clear to Chen and Deng, because this troop movement would ensure that his "Southern Strategy" could be carried out while avoiding a final showdown. Typical of his style, the operation principle suggested by Mao would be guerrilla tactics, "a sudden concentration or sudden split of troops." Mao continued, "If overwhelming enemy troops should move towards you, you may consider scattering your twelve brigades along the Yangzi River, the Huai River, the Cao Lake and the Grand Canal to avoid the [frontal] pressure."[10]

Through this directive, Deng and Chen felt that Mao was out of touch with reality, and, as the government pressure mounting, his mind was becoming more and more irrational. They again insisted to Mao that it would be better for them to stay where they were for the purpose of combining troop strength under Deng and Su, after the attack plan against Huang Baitao started.[11] Mao remained adamant. In a stern directive dated October 26, he went so far as to order Deng and Chen to attack Xuzhou and Bangbu simultaneously.[12]

Mao's plan to split the troops would in fact fall into the trap of the government plan at this time. Chiang's strategy was to use whatever forces available to prevent Deng and Su from joining forces. The government operation plan called for concentrating troops to eliminate Deng's force first, because it was a much weaker and smaller field army compared with that of Su's. Should this operation be successful, the next step would be a major campaign aimed at crushing Su's main force in the vast area between Xuzhou and Bangbu.[13] Ironically, Chiang had in mind a major engagement that was also known to be the "Campaign of Xu [zhou]-Bang [bu]".

As Mao's high command continued to waver, the conditions in the battlefield became increasingly more severe. The elite government troops at 100,000 strong, fully equipped with US-made weapon systems under the command of General Huang Wei, began rapid movement from the southwest toward the Longhai Railway. Thus the government troops increased to 800,000 compared with 600,000 communist troops in the same area. Mao seemed to have reached a stage of nervous breakdown. It became painfully clear to Mao that this was no longer a campaign that could use his favorite strategy of concentrating superior troops against a weaker enemy, as was stipulated by his well-known "Ten Major Military Principles." Throughout his military career, Mao loathed any campaign with an inferior number of troops on his side. He was further convinced that he was right when the Campaign of Manchuria commanded by Lin Biao, which had been started a month earlier, had shown signs of winning a decisive victory. It appeared to be an example par excellence of applying this principle. The Huai-Hai Campaign was thus something totally alien to him: a war against the grain of his military thinking and experience.

Realizing that Mao's lack of direction would cost the communists dearly due to the failure of seizing the opportunity to gamble all troops in this area for another major victory on the Manchurian Campaign scale, Su Yu took a decisive personal step on October 31. In a wire from the party's

Central Military Committee one day earlier, Mao approved Su's attack plan against General Huang Baitao but pointed out the necessity of launching attack against Huang simultaneously with Deng's attack on government reinforcements. Su took the opportunity to suggest that, since this would be a large-scale campaign, it would be better to form a unified command under the overall control of Chen Yi and Deng Xiaoping.[14] Su sacrificed his own authority over his troops in exchange for a more effective commanding system. The Central Military Committee saw no reason to oppose this proposal, which would after all ensure better control of troops in the field. Moreover, Deng and Chen also seemed keen to cooperate with Su. This suggestion was immediately approved on the next day. Thus the idea of coordinated operation had become a *fait accompli*. Mao quickly realized that, from this time on, however, he could no longer avoid the fact that the original "small Huai-Hai Campaign" idea was to be abandoned and he could not back away from a "big Huai-Hai campaign" any more.

As a nod to military professionalism, the Party Central Committee on the same day issued a general directive to regularize all communist troops nation-wide. For the first time, each communist unit was given a coherent serial number for the designation of corps, army, division, regiment, battalion, etc.[15] But to avoid confusion in the battlefield that could be caused by such change, Mao decided to postpone its actual implementation until after the campaign.

Mao's approval of a unified command did not mean that he was clear about the overall strategy. Compared with the rather muddle-headed high command under Mao, once again, it was Su Yu who first demonstrated a farsighted vision about a possible strategic showdown. In an important telegram dated November 8, Su presented two possible scenarios. First, Chiang Kai-shek may continue to retain his troops north of the Yangzi River. Second, Chiang may decide to withdraw all his troops towards the Yangzi River to build strong defense line. "If Chiang should adopt the first option, it will provide us with opportunities to eliminate the bulk of his troops [in the north of the Yangzi]" and ... "after we cross the Yangzi, there would be no major battles to fight ......" But, Su continued, "If Chiang should adopt the second option, we may easily control the north of the Yangzi ... but it would be much more difficult for us after we cross the Yangzi." The key issue here, according to Su, was how long the communist-controlled areas could continue providing material and human support for a major prolonged campaign. If they could sustain the war for quite a while, then the best option was to force Chiang to engage a major showdown in the current area immediately. It was apparent that the newly unified command in this theater provided Su with a legitimate reason to think about a decisive campaign. But Mao was still not certain about this point. Shortly before Su began launching surprise attacks against Huang

Baitao, Mao appeared to be gravely concerned about the advance of Huang Wei's reinforcements and hurriedly ordered Deng's troops to cut off the Jinpu Railway in order to slow his movement. But he was frantic and unsure about the next move. Without being given a clear strategic purpose, Deng and Chen acted very slowly on this instruction. They suspected that Mao was still in favor of a "Xuzhou-Bangbu" campaign. They were certainly right. After Huang Baitao's 7th Corps was under siege a few days later, Mao from November 11 to 14 sent four telegrams making the same point that Deng should be prepared to take Xuzhou. But Deng and Chen continued to resist Mao's temptation for a premature and potentially disastrous move. In Xuzhou city alone, the government boasted over 200,000 elite troops. while Deng's poorly equipped units numbered some 120,000. Mao failed to explain clearly why he ordered Deng's troops to take such an action, because, according to Mao's vision for a "Xuzhou-Bangbu campaign," his purpose was just to prevent government forces from sending reinforcements to Huang Baitao. For Su, the convergence of a large number of government forces may not be a bad thing, yet the possibility for a major showdown would also require immediate severance of the north-south running Jinpu Railway in order to disconnect and retain the bulk of the enemy troops in the Xuzhou area, thus facilitating the preparation for one joint operation between him and Deng for the final kill. Therefore, Su's telegram provided Mao with a clear objective regarding the severance of the Jinpu Railway and at the same time helped Mao clarify the overall strategic purpose, i.e., to seek elimination of all government troops in the north of the Yangzi River. This was, of course, consistent with Su's original opposition to Mao's "Southern Strategy" in early 1948.[16] Under the circumstances, the course of the whole campaign was to be dramatically changed.

Mao was, however, quick to appreciate the value of Su's timely suggestion. In a directive issued the next day, Mao supported Su's argument and finally made up his somewhat unpredictable mind about the plan for one decisive strategic showdown in the north of the Yangzi River. One factor that convinced Mao of Su's cogency was the estimated feasibility of communist-controlled areas to provide the troops with enough logistics support for an extended period of time. The most important area was Shandong province, which, long under communist influence, proved to be one of the most reliable communist controlled logistics bases in Eastern China. This was, however, a province Mao had, ironically, decided to abandon but for Su's objection in early 1948. According to a report by Su during the course of campaign, the monthly supply of grain alone required over two million tons for some 600,000 troops, 600,000 "*Min Gong* (peasant laborers)" and 40,000 horses. The Shandong "liberated area" could single-handed manage to supply over fifty percent of that amount.[17]

Rather belatedly Yanan began to be concerned about the effectiveness of the communist logistics system, since the hasty merger of command of the two field armies was not matched by a unified logistics network, without which it could not ensure that war supplies would be sent to the troops on time. Since the beginning of the civil war, the East China Field Army had adopted a simple yet effective logistics system: each soldier's supply was taken care of by three peasant laborers, known as *Yi Bing San Fu* system. As the war becoming increasingly larger in scale, the communist leadership found it hard to organize effective operation to extract material supplies from the "liberated area," especially Shandong. As a result, peasant laborers were requisitioned at breathtaking speed. During the Manchuria Campaign, such requisition proved to be easy since Lin Biao had controlled over 97% of the territories and 86% of the population. Besides, the isolated enemy troops in Manchuria had all but relied on airlift supplies from the government. In the Xuzhou area, the communists did not enjoy such a luxury that the logistics problems were reserved for their enemy only. In fact, government troops were able to obtain direct supplies through railways and other modern transportation means. In other words, in Eastern China, the communists had to add another factor of inferiority to their list in logistics area. Yanan sent its logistics chief, Yang Lisan, to Eastern China shortly before the battle against Huang Baitao. It appeared that Yanan could not help very much the war efforts in this area where the logistics problems were mounting day by day. Nevertheless, it was remarkable that the communist organizers would pass the test with flying colors. It was estimated at the time that there would be over two million people who needed regular feeding for three to five months. Hospital facilities must accommodate some 200,000 wounded. Coordinating such an enormous task would inevitably encounter well-nigh insurmountable difficulties. But the communists quickly established a logistics command to control effectively all supply operations.

The key to the success was popular support. In a very short period of time, the communist cadres were able to mobilize some three million people for the war effort.[18] Most peasants benefited from a land policy and many were completely tired of the civil war, hoping that the government would be done with as quickly as possible. The transportation means were primitive, shoulder-poles and single-wheeled carts. But the communist organization was efficient. Each *Min Gong* team was quasi-militarized, complete with a political commissar and a chief of staff.[19] No less effective was the economic incentive given to the peasant laborers, as was suggested by Chen Yi a year before. Despite physical danger and stress, all peasant laborers fared much better than they would have at their war-ravaged homes. Most could not afford to have decent meals everyday at their villages. To join the war efforts, they were guaranteed a full stomach and various supplies including free tobacco, clothing, medical expenses and even a decent burial.[20] Without exaggeration, Chen Yi would insist years later that the Campaign of Huai-Hai was "pushed" to victory by the peasants' manually operated single-wheel carts.

Another factor that enhanced Mao's confidence was the enormous success of Su's troops in quickly assimilating captured government soldiers and using them effectively during battles. Su's East China Field Army suffered the most casualties during the first years of the civil war. But Su's troops continued to expand at a rapid pace. According to a contemporary report, for example, each of the columns that participated in the siege against Huang Baitao lost some 5,000 during the first week. The fighting strength had to be supplemented on the spot by captured government soldiers. Su's political officers invented the so-called "Capture, recruit and fight (*Sui Fu, Sui Bu, Sui Da*)" method to create a constant flow of the new recruits who were more willing to fight than they were on the other side. The political officers carefully provided a warm environment for the newly captured and made them feel at home and willing to sacrifice themselves for the war efforts. To ensure that they felt that they could have a future with their career, many captured soldiers during the Jinan Campaign two months ago had been boldly promoted to platoon or even company commander positions. This method of promotion did raise eyebrows with orthodox party leaders, for the question of political loyalty remained a major concern within the communist establishment. But Su boldly argued that, during the civil war in the Soviet Russia, the Red Army even had to pay high salaries to recruit officers who had served the Czar to enhance military professionalism, there was no reason that the Chinese communist troops should worry about promoting prisoners of war.[21] In fact, there were hardly any other alternatives but to use the POWs. It appeared that these soldiers carried out their duties very well. At the end of the Campaign of Huai-Hai, captured government soldiers consisted as much as 46% of the overall strength of the East China Field Army under Su's command.

At the time Su's strategic vision to break Chiang's backbone in the north of the Yangzi River was accepted by Mao, the carefully planned surprise attack on General Huang Baitao along the Longhai Railway started on November 8. General Huang was one of the very few government generals who did not belong to Chiang's "Whampoa Clique," but he remained intensely loyal to the Generalissimo. Sensing Su's movement shortly before the attack, Huang had already begun a rapid westward retrenchment back to Xuzhou. But, while on march, Huang made the fatal mistake of delaying his retreat for two days, only to wait

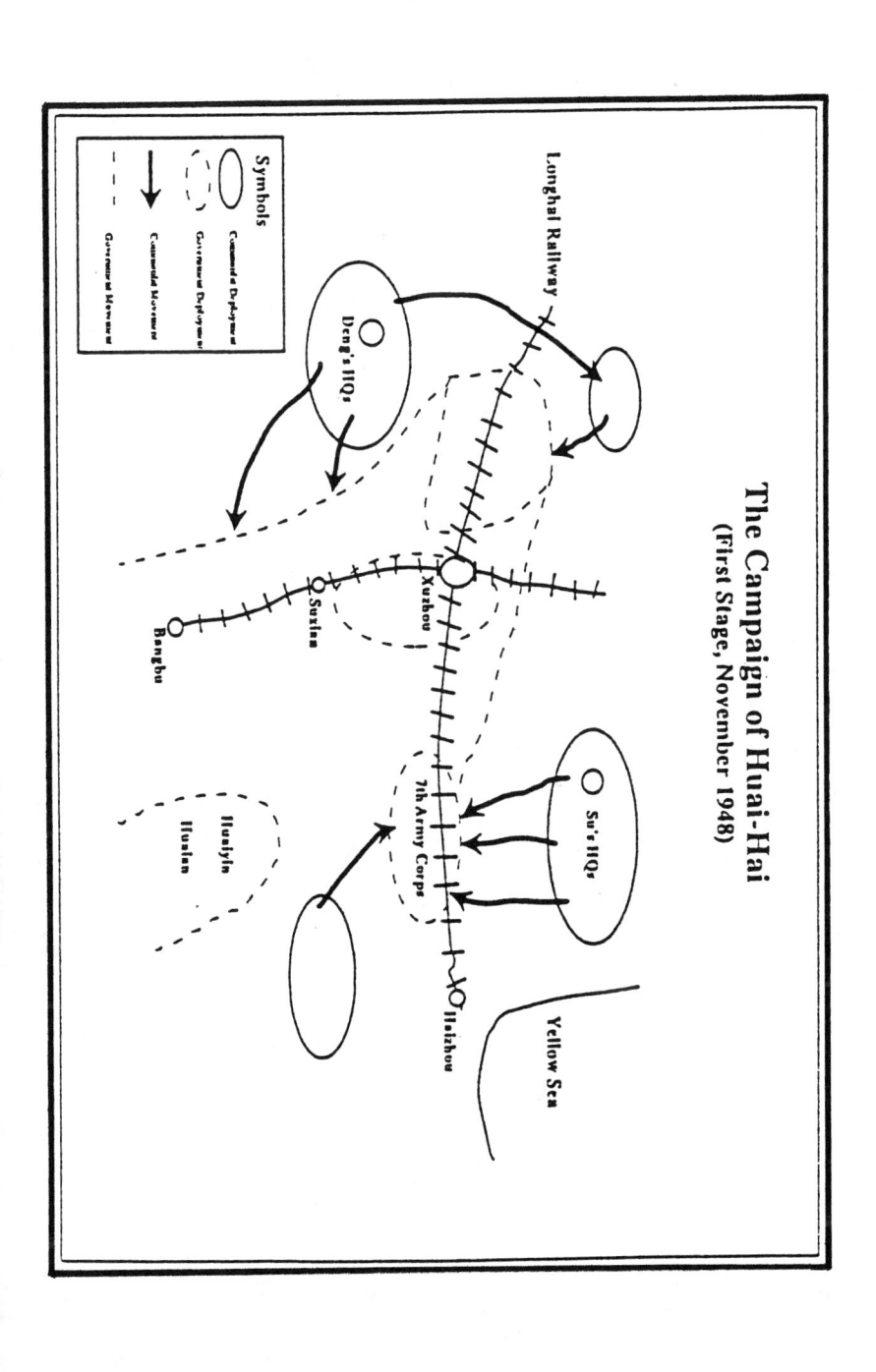

The Campaign of Huai-Hai
(First Stage, November 1948)

for one of his five armies that had just evacuated the port city of Haizhou to arrive and withdraw together. More disastrously, Huang's five armies had to cross the Grand Canal through only one iron-and-steel bridge. The passage process became extremely chaotic and every unit scrambled for the right of way, some times force was used to ensure their success. But, to solve the problem of the chaotic situation, Huang merely ordered construction of one pontoon bridge, thus precious time of retreat was further lost, a fact that Huang would regret deeply at the end of his life. At the time Huang moved his headquarters to Nianzhuang, a village less than thirty miles from the position of another government army group under General Liu Zhi at Xuzhou Pacification Headquarters, he discovered that it was already too late. His retreat route was immediately cut off when three and a half divisions led by Generals Zhang Kexia and He Jifeng belonging to Liu's command defected at the critical moment and on the critical spot between Xuzhou and Huang's headquarters. Zhang and He were both secret members of the communist party. Their timely defection allowed Su's attack troops to take a shortcut through the government position and advance directly toward Xuzhou to block Huang's westward movement. Without any alternatives, Huang decided to hold on to Nianzhuang to repel communist attacks while waiting for reinforcements.

The communist troops had been largely unsuccessful in taking strongholds where the government general had decided to put up a vigorous defense of his position and fight to a man, as the battles of Nanma and Linqu in 1947 had demonstrated. The communists had a penchant for avoiding prolonged siege battles, and they had excelled themselves in quick victory. Even though isolated, the troops under General Huang were well trained in countersiege warfare and vigorously prepared for the attack with the backing of a very sophisticated defense structure built by previous government troops. Su's original plan was to rip Huang's five armies apart and devour them separately. But Huang vigorously retained troop concentration and relied on a whole network of over a dozen villages complete with ramparts and trenches. The initial communist attack resulted in disaster. After enormous casualties were incurred, they hurriedly changed their tactics from mobile war to trench war without adequate time for preparing the transition. An exception was Ye Fei's First Column which managed to isolate one of Huang's five armies in a small town where it was prepared to cross the Grand Canal overnight. Ye's three divisions were able to wipe it out with a clean sweep.[22] It took almost two weeks and heavy losses for Su to overcome Huang's resistance. True to his words and character, General Huang Baitao held his position to the last minute and was killed in action.

During Su's attack on Huang, Deng's Central Plains Field Army finally moved to cut off the Jinpu Railway, according to Mao's instruction, to blunt General Huang Wei's Central China army group, the 12th Corps, which had advanced toward Su's battlefield. Huang Wei, unlike Huang Baitao, was rather a conceited government general and member of Chiang's Whampoa elite. He was recently appointed to the position of commanding the new 12th Army Corps consisting many best government units, among them was General Hu Lian's legendary 18th Army that had inflicted enormous casualties on Chen and Su during the battle of Nanma of 1947. From the very beginning, however, the troop morale was low since the rank and file would prefer Hu Lian instead of Huang Wei to command them. Huang had little experience in fighting the communists during the civil war in this part of China. Moreover, since Huang Wei's task was to rescue Huang Baitao at Nianzhuang, the troops were completely exhausted after days of nonstop travels over three hundred miles, during which they were the target of the constant harassment by communist guerrillas and small regular units tailgating them.

On the communist side, the next move remained unclear to the high command. Although the overall strategic vision had become clear after Su's telegram of clarification made on November 8, Mao was once again wavering about the next target. His desire for a "Xuzhou-Bangbu Campaign" remained strong. During the siege against Huang Baitao, Mao was thinking of taking Xuzhou after Huang's demise. He issued many erratic orders demanding the encirclement of Xuzhou to Deng and Chen's Central Plains Field Army, and Su's East China Field Army was expected, after eliminating Huang Baitao, to join the operation against Xuzhou.[23] Moreover, the lack of direction at the top began to affect Su's troop deployment, for it was important for Su to know, given Mao's deep worry about General Huang Wei's advancing forces in the southwest, what could be done if things should turn the other way around when General Liu Zhi may decide to abandon Xuzhou and withdraw to the south to link up with Huang Wei. To field commanders such as Su Yu, the delay in making such decisions would cost him precious time for redeployment of troops. It was not clear from Mao's directives whether a decisive step should be taken to prevent such eventuality.

Nonetheless, Mao's overall confidence seemed to have recovered by this time, perhaps because of the victory in Manchuria. In a very upbeat telegram, he told Lin Biao and the other commanders in confidence that he thought that there would no longer be a need for three more years to defeat the government. It would perhaps take only one year.[24] Boosted by this new confidence, on November 16, Mao issued a directive to approve the establishment of a "General Front Committee (*Zong Qian Wei*)" to control overall operations in the Huai-Hai area. Five members were appointed to the committee, which included Deng Xiaoping, Liu Bocheng, Chen Yi, Su Yu and Tan Zhenlin. Deng was appointed the secretary. This directive indicated that Mao and the communist high command had finally made up their minds to seek a gigantic showdown with the government in the whole area north of the Yangzi River. Although the General Front Committee could hardly function as one since Su and Tan were constantly at the other front, it finally provided a symbolic unified command that would prove especially critical during the next stages of the campaign.

But the question of determining the next target after General Huang Baitao's demise remained unanswered. Another rift between Mao and the commanders in the field became inevitable. Instead of attacking Xuzhou, Deng and Chen, in their new capacity as members of the General Front Committee, recommended a concentration of their efforts to eliminate Huang Wei first in the south. As early as on November 14, Deng and Chen already indicated the need for shifting the campaign focus from the north to the south. According to them a *coup de main* against Huang Wei would be "the best option." Mao's reply indicated that they had to wait. Mao had intended for Su's troops to join Deng to take Xuzhou. But the two-week gruesome battle against Huang Baitao totally exhausted Su's soldiers. Five days later, Deng and Chen reiterated their view. In a telegram dated November 19 to Mao, Deng and Chen pointed out that Su's troops were worn out and "their knife edge seems blunt." To allow Su's East China Field Army some time for a much needed rest, the next target should be Huang Wei in the south. The surprise quality of this plan would be superb. Mao continued to hesitate. On November 23, General Huang Wei began to launch fierce attack on a small town named Nanpingji, an operation that allowed his troops to dangerously jut out for the first time during the long march. Deng and Chen decided that they could wait no longer. They pushed Mao one more time to make a decision. Meanwhile, Yanan received telegrams from Su Yu who also supported the idea of eliminating Huang Wei in the south. Under the circumstances, Mao replied the next day, stating "We completely agree the plan to attack Huang Wei first."[25]

It is interesting to note that this was clearly Deng's idea. For Deng, the elimination of Huang Wei was to be one possible shining moment for his troops which had been rather lackluster in performance since 1947. Moreover, since the Central Plains Field Army had so far engaged no major battles, Deng hoped to carry out the task single-handed. More than once had Deng expressed his determination to win a major battle in the field, even at the "bankruptcy of the household (*Qing Jia Dang Chan*)." Chen Yi played the second fiddle during this decision-making process, since he, as deputy to Deng, was cautious enough to keep quiet and play a passive role in such a critical decision involving the future of Deng's troops. Although Chen knew that Deng's decision to gamble all he had would be a costly one, he avoided behaving like a rich man giving a handout to a poor vagabond. He wisely decided to help Deng only if asked. Chen knew in particular that Deng's Central Plains Field Army lacked heavy weapons and experience in modern siege warfare. For a major siege battle against the elite 12th Corps, which was U. S. equipped and trained, the cost and casualties were bound to be very heavy. After Mao had approved Deng's proposal to wipe out Huang Wei as the second stage of the campaign, Chen was asked to help in artillery support only, because Deng was keen to win a victory without much outside help. As a result, Chen ordered Su's artillery column to reinforce Deng's operation. Su could not, of course, refuse his old boss's request. As a nice gesture, Chen specifically instructed Su to "leave all the captured heavy weapons to Deng's troops."[26] Once again it was none other than Chen Shiju, Su's chief of staff and the artillery bug who made a gaffe and somehow mocked Deng's troops a year ago, who led the efforts to provide Deng with the much needed fire support.

After hasty preparation, Deng's troops launched a major attack on November 23. Within two days, they were successful in isolating and surrounding Huang Wei's 120,000 forces in a narrow area consisting a little town and a few villages. The victory and glory seemed within the reach. But they soon realized that the task of overcoming Huang Wei's tough defense would be well-nigh insurmountable. Huang possessed excellent artillery fire and air support. Moreover, the resistance was well organized. Once realizing the fact that he was besieged, General Huang quickly ordered construction of numerous concentric rings of strongholds and trenches, and deployed numerous tanks, trucks and heavy guns for performing the active forward defense function.

Deng's troops were not experienced in this kind of battle. Deng's chief of staff, Li Da, would admit years later that the Central Plains Field Army was not tactically prepared and they had relied too heavily on rifles and hand grenades. Besides, Deng's commanders had underestimated Huang's defense capability.[27] According to Su many years later, Deng's initial estimate was to finish Huang Wei's army corps within three days after complete encirclement was made. The Party Central Committee was also convinced of this estimate. Therefore, on November 27, Su was instructed to eliminate, through active frontal attack, another government army corps that was sent to relieve Huang Wei but was being held off by Su. Mao went so far as to suggest the completion of the whole campaign at the end of November. After the initial attacks were blunted, Deng had to extend the time frame to ten days. Yet this estimate would still prove to be too far from the battlefield reality.

Meanwhile Su's task was doubled as Deng's siege against Huang Wei seemed to be getting nowhere. Aside from performing the duty of

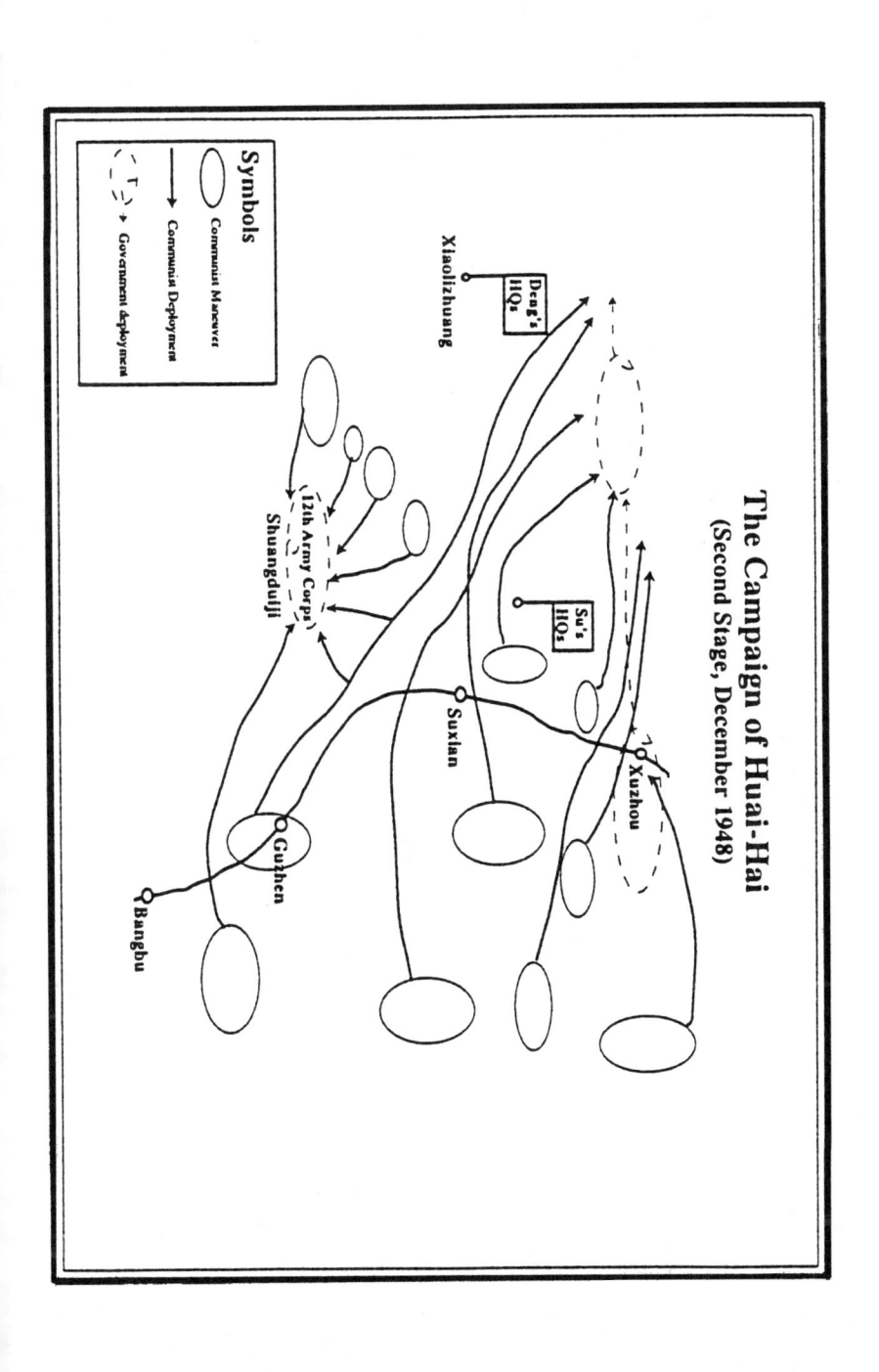

The Campaign of Huai-Hai
(Second Stage, December 1948)

blocking the enemy's reinforcements to Huang, Su's major concern was General Liu Zhi's group in Xuzhou because, given Huang's eminent demise, the next target was naturally the isolation and elimination of Liu's forces. Liu was an arrogant and slippery character within the government military establishment. Slow-witted and indecisive, he had excelled himself in internal political survival. Many of his colleagues considered his appointment at Xuzhou, the gateway to Nanjing, a major mistake by Chiang. There was a joke at the time within the government that Chiang should have sent a ferocious dog or a tiger to defend this gateway, instead, he had sent a pig. After the initial disaster with Huang Baitao, Liu's ineffectiveness was fully exposed. Chiang tried to remedy the situation by appointing Liu's deputy commander, General Du Yumin, a personal protege of the Generalissimo, to taken *de facto* control over the troops in early November. General Du was more farsighted and decisive. He immediately launched ferocious attack on the communist position in an effort trying to rescue Huang Baitao. But it was too late to be effective and the communists put up a persevering defense to prevent Du from marching more than a few miles a day.

After Huang Baitao's 7th Corps was wiped out, Chiang seemed to have two choices, either to hold on to an isolated Xuzhou city and watch Huang Wei in the south being eliminated bit by bit, or to give up Xuzhou and try to break through the communist encirclement. Because Huang Wei was able to defend himself so effectively, Chiang decided to abandon Xuzhou and ordered General Du Yumin to move toward Huang's position immediately. This would turn out to be a major disaster.

To Su's chagrin, Mao paid little attention to the Xuzhou direction. According to Mao's numerous directives, Su was expected to prevent Du's escape at any cost while at the same time eliminate one government army corps in nearby area. Under the circumstances, Su had no choice but to follow orders, knowing that no reinforcements would be forthcoming. Such a move would, however, require splitting his troops for separate functions. Fortunately, the government commander of the targeted army corps was extremely cautious. He refused to advance into Su's waiting pocket after Su retreated to lure him into taking the bait. Meanwhile, General Du Yumin began preparation for the troops at Xuzhou Pacification Headquarters to withdraw from the city. As Su recalled years later, he was lucky that the troops at his disposal were not entangled with that government army corps specified by Mao for annihilation, otherwise he would not have enough troops to prevent Du from joining Huang Wei in the south.[28] The outcome of the Huai-Hai Campaign could have been a very different one.

It soon became clear that Su's concern was totally justified, for Deng's fierce siege battle against Huang Wei began to show signs of disaster.

From November 25 to December 5, Deng's attack troops made little progress, and the casualties built up exceedingly heavily. While Deng was very single-minded in seeking glory for his troops, his tactics were rather old-fashioned---badly coordinated human-wave attacks from several directions instead of mobile and flexible tactics that could cut deep into enemy positions. After a few more days of futile operations, the impatient Mao became anxious and was compelled to instruct his protege that this old method of attack would not work this time, "Forceful isolation, reconnaissance, close-range attack, and artillery-infantry synchronization are all necessary."[29] These were, of course, characteristic of the style of Su's East China Field Army. While Deng remained keen to seek glory alone, he was forced to change tactics.

Since Deng's troops were tied down with Huang Wei for the unexpected long period of time, Su's burden became doubly heavy. According to Deng's original plan, Su's troops were supposed to take a rest while performing the function of blunting the enemy reinforcements to rescue Huang Wei. Now Su alone had to be responsible as well for surrounding Du's Xuzhou troops in retreat. Where would Du Yumin go? This was a question neither the government nor the communist side was clear about. At first the communist headquarters was confused by intelligence reports concerning Chiang's real intention. During a meeting attended by Chiang, Du Yumin and Guo Rugui---the communist spy and the government operation chief, it was decided to allow Du to withdraw to the eastern direction toward Northern Jiangsu. Guo had apparently sent this information to Mao's high command. But General Du, who was suspicious of Guo's character and loyalty, had decided to withdraw toward the west. Mao sent an intelligence report to Su, which, based on Guo's information, specified that Du would withdraw toward the east. Su was torn between the belief that Du would not rationally make that choice and the actual intelligence reports which had usually been accurate. Especially, the eastern retreat route would require crossing numerous rivers and swamps, a terrain that was impossible for heavily equipped government forces to march at fast speed. Pressured by time and space, Su had to spare some troops for guarding the reported route he did not believe in. But his main attention remained westward. Su's instinct proved to be right.

In fact, General Du had already abandoned the idea of eastward movement. Unbeknownst to Guo Rugui, Mao's spy, Du had met Chiang Kai-shek in private to secure his approval for the route toward the west.[30] On December 1, Du led three army corps at some 300,000 strong to move out of Xuzhou. The retreat was chaotic. But, since Deng Xiaoping could not finish Huang Wei in time, the East China Field Army under Su was especially under heavy pressure. Not only must they continue to blunt enemy reinforcements to save Huang Wei from all directions to ensure

Deng's victory, but also had they to chase and surround Du Yumin's much larger forces in flight. Worse still, Deng began to realize that, much to his chagrin, he had no choice but to swallow his pride to request more reinforcements from Su, in addition to the artillery units. Five of Su's sixteen columns had thus been sent to participate in Deng's attack troops against Huang. Under the circumstances, the troops for the chase outside Xuzhou were far from sufficient. Su would recall bitterly in his conversations years later, this was the worst and the most intense moment in his career, because the troop usage had reached its limits at this time. But Su brilliantly deployed his main forces from only one direction, the south, in order to prevent Du from linking up with Huang. Although he could not muster enough strength needed for a full encirclement, Su gambled with constant feint attack and bluffing. He boldly used scattered small units to form a thin net from all directions to chase and surround the enemy in a nonstop movement. It succeeded in deterring Du from splitting his troops for separate breakthroughs, which could have been successful given Su's rather thin troop deployment. Du's misfortune deepened when Chiang Kai-shek suddenly changed his mind. In an angry personal letter to Du dropped from an airplane, Chiang accused Du of abandoning Huang Wei in the south and "our nation and race will perish as a result." The heart-broken Du and his generals had no choice but to follow Chiang's order to turn around and strike at the south. Before any meaningful counterattack could be organized, Du found himself completely surrounded.[31]

By December 15, Deng was finally able to knock out Huang Wei's headquarters with the timely reinforcements from Su's columns. Huang Wei was captured alive. Deng, however, lost at a minimum over 30,000 soldiers, and probably more---this meant over twenty-five percent of all he had. According to Deng's daughter who wrote her father's official hagiography, what Deng regretted most was not so much the casualties but the fact that he had to share the glory of eliminating Huang Wei with Su's East China Field Army.[32] Deng's chief of staff, Li Da, would recall a telegram Deng sent to Mao shortly thereafter, it stated, "We ... have lost over twenty thousand before launching general attack, the morale was low. Only after adding two more columns from the East China Field Army, could we conquer the enemy ......" Deng added, "After the battle, we all feel that our troops were not sufficiently prepared, therefore we were unable to eliminate Huang Wei single-handed."[33]

By December 16, General Du's 300,000 forces were tightly surrounded at a village named Chenguanzhuang in the southwest of Xuzhou. It was fortunate that, due to the defeat of Huang Wei, Su no longer had to spare troops for blunting action against the government reinforcements which had fled to the south of the Huai River as soon as the news of Huang's demise was heard. The communists had by this time eliminated some 200,000 elite government forces. It must be pointed out that the role played by Su Yu and his East China Field army was decisive for the evolution of the campaign from a limited battle to a major showdown. During this period, Su was not able to fall asleep for straight seven days and nights, and collapsed shortly thereafter, suffering from a severe case of the Meniere's Syndrome.[34] The second, and the most difficult stage of the Huai-Hai Campaign was thus over.

The last stage was naturally the elimination of Du Yumin's besieged troops. But only at this time, the situation in the battleground had become clear. Squeezed into a twenty square-mile area, Du had no chance to escape. The communist headquarters were even able to give their troops a much needed twenty-day rest, since the winter snowstorm and the lack of food and shelter began to take heavy tolls on Du's soldiers day by day. There was also a strategic reason for this prolonged rest. After Lin Biao's success in Manchuria and the government's loss of Shandong, Beiping (Beijing) had become an isolated city. In order to provide the government garrison commander, General Fu Zuoyi, with a false sense of security and to retain his half million forces in the city, Mao decided to delay the final attack on Du in order to gain enough time for persuading Fu to surrender peacefully. One of the key negotiators on the communist side was the general's own daughter Fu Dongju, who, as a college student, had been a secret member of the communist party for some time. Thus the chance for success was very high.

Fu eventually did decide to surrender peacefully, but the besieged General Du in the south refused to give up. In desperation Du asked Chiang to provide him with US-made shells of poison gas. Du intended to fight to a man, but Chiang ordered him to try a breakthrough. Du refused to follow this order until January 6 when the communists finally launched a general attack. Within four days, Du's forces at over 200,000 were completely wiped out. Du tried to escape by wearing soldier's uniform but was captured and recognized through his erratic behavior and attempted suicide in the prisoner-of-war camp. The Huai-Hai Campaign thus ended with 555,000 casualties on the government side. The communists lost some 140,000.[35]

In sixty-six days, the communist commanders in the field proved to be extraordinarily innovative. The high command under Mao, by contrast, was more often than not confused and indecisive. Nevertheless, the unexpected success of this campaign had effectively eliminated Chiang's control over almost all the areas north of the Yangzi River. The capital city Nanjing was exposed to overwhelming communist forces that were moving rapidly towards the bank of the river. Ironically, the success of the campaign also killed forever Mao's favorite "Southern Strategy," which would appear ridiculous since Southern China would become what

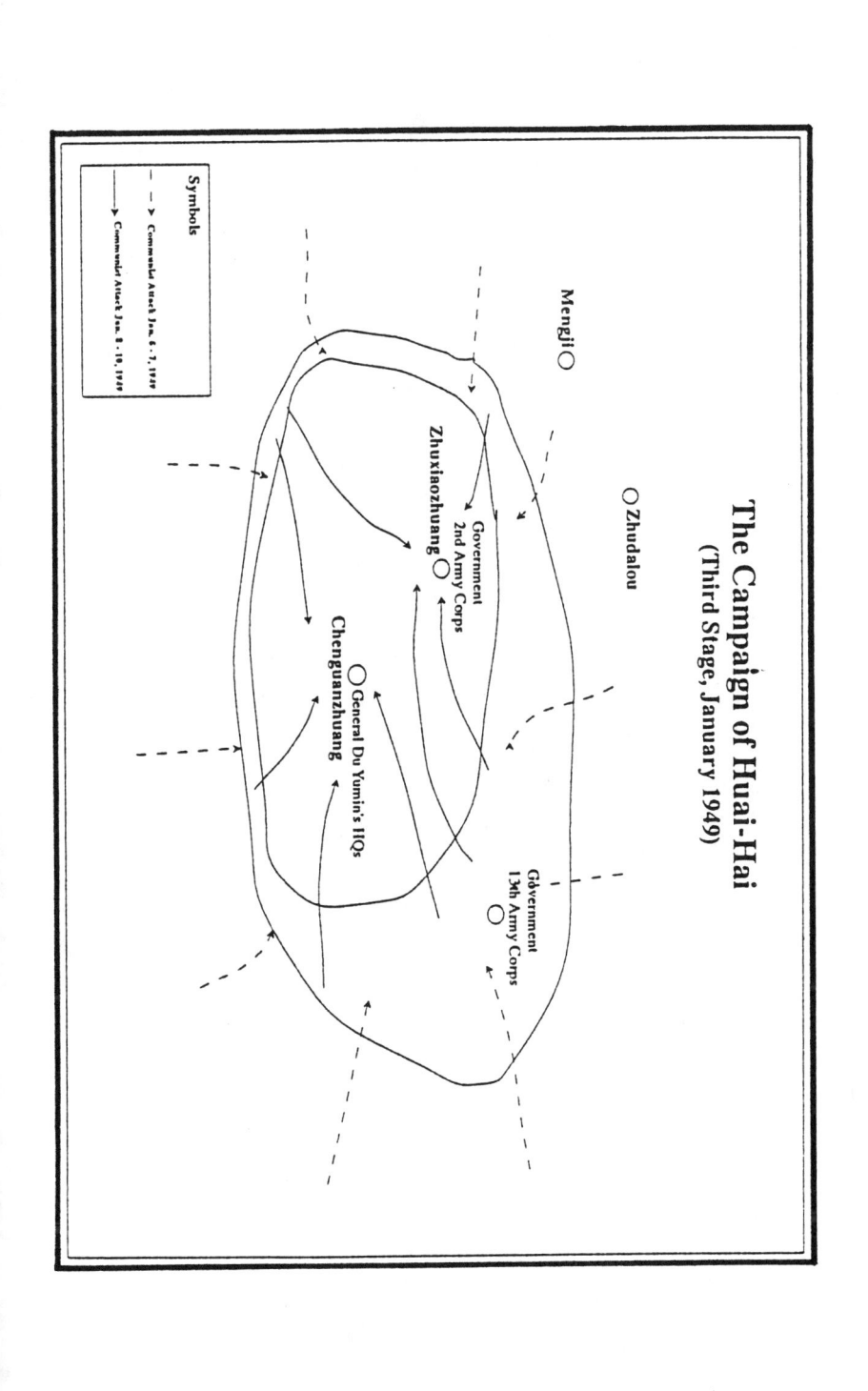

The Campaign of Huai-Hai
(Third Stage, January 1949)

was left in Chiang's control over China. A hot pursuit strategy, instead of strategic diversion, was the only effective one that was needed. As predicted by Su Yu during the campaign, the elimination of the main government forces north of the Yangzi River rendered the task of crossing the river much easier. Immediately after the Campaign of Huai-Hai, the communist high command began to implement its directive issued in November 1948 to regularize all the troops. Four field armies emerging from the civil war were now renamed by coherent serial numbers. Strictly along the original factional lines, Peng Dehuai's Northwestern Field Army became the First Field Army, Deng's the Second, Su's the Third and Lin Biao's the Fourth. The overall communist strength had now reached four million. Lin's troops were the largest, at 900,000 strong; Su's were the second at some 600,000; Deng's only half that number, while Peng's merely 150,000.[36]

Notes

1. *The Battle History of the PLA*, vol.3, p.246-263.
2. For detail, see *WJXJ*, vol.17, p.419-420.
3. It can be argued that Mao was unconsciously right about this point alone.
4. The gist of the Ten Principles had already been discussed by Mao in September 1946, see *Selected Works of Mao Zedong*, vol.4, p.103-107.
5. *MZDJSWJ*, vol.5, p.19.
6. Ibid., p.66-69.
7. *Selected Works of Mao Zedong*, vol.4, p.279-281. Here the editors conveniently omitted point 4, therefore the original point 5 became point 4.
8. *MZDJSWJ*, vol.5, p.77.
9. *Military Works of Su Yu*, p.404-405.
10. *MZDJSWJ*, vol.5, p.125.
11. *Cong Yanan Dao Beijing* (From Yanan to Beijing, Beijing 1993), p.394. This is a collection of some previously unpublished military documents. It also includes Su Yu's description of the Campaign of Huai-Hai.
12. *MZDJSWJ*, vol.5, p.131-132.
13. For detail, see *Kan Luan Jian Shi* (Short History of the War of Pacification, Taipei 1962), vol.3, p.184-187. See also *Biography of General Hu Lian*, p.94-99.
14. *Military Works of Su Yu*, p.416.
15. *WJXJ*, vol.17, p.446-451.
16. Ibid., p.419-420. This telegram destroys the image of Mao the clairvoyant. Because of the official efforts to revise history, Su Yu had never in his lifetime been given credit for his decisive contribution to the success of the Campaign of Huai-Hai. Su decided not to mention a word of this campaign

in his War Memoirs. Only through a recent publication of a series of interviews compiled by Su's wife Chu Qing, did we see a clearer picture at the time. See *From Yanan to Beijing*, p.408-424.
17. *Military Works of Su Yu*, p.442-443.
18. For an eyewitness account, see Liu, Ruilong, *Logistics Work during the Civil War in East and Central China*, in *Materials of the Party History*, vol.29, p.5-41. Liu was the logistics chief of the East China Field Army.
19. *Huai-Hai Zhan Yi* (The Campaign of Hai-Hai, Beijing 1988), vol.3, p.58-59.
20. Ibid., p.43-46.
21. *Military Works of Su Yu*, p.448-450.
22. *Memoirs of Ye Fei*, p.513-516.
23. *MZDJSWJ*, vol.5, p.195.
24. *WJXJ*, vol.17, p.473-474.
25. *MZDJSWJ*, vol.5, p.231-269.
26. *Biography of Chen Yi* (Official), p.437-438.
27. *The Campaign of Huai-Hai*, vol.2, p.14.
28. *From Yanan to Beijing*, p.418-419.
29. *MZDJSWJ*, vol.5, p.317-318.
30. Du, Yumin, *Huan-Hai Zhan Yi Shi Mo* (Origins and Results of the Campaign of Huai-Hai), in *Guo Gong Nei Zhan Mi Lu* (The Secret History of the Kuomintang-Communist Civil War, Taipei 1991), p.215-217.
31. Ibid., p.224-225.
32. Deng, Maomao, *My Father Deng Xiaoping* (New York 1995), p.431-432.
33. *The Campaign of Huai-Hai*, vol.2, p.22.
34. *From Yanan to Beijing*, p.420-421.
35. *The Battle History of the PLA*, vol.3, p.284.
36. Ibid., p.317-320.

Chapter 8

From Yangzi to Shanghai

During Deng's exhausting attack on Huang Wei, Mao and the Central Committee had already begun considering the strategy of crossing the Yangzi River. In a telegram to Deng and Chen dated December 12, 1948, Mao pointed out the need for the troops to rest for two months and prepare for the operation against Chiang's Yangzi River defense line. The campaign was planned to start in May and June of 1949. More importantly, Mao also specified that, after the Yangzi crossing, the task for the two field armies which fought the Campaign of Huai-Hai would be the "joint management of Southeastern China." Mao demanded that this telegram be read only by five members of the General Front Committee, and be burnt immediately.[1]

Mao's concern for uttermost secrecy was largely caused by the perceived possibility of military intervention by the American government, since the south of the Yangzi River had always been the hub of Anglo-American traditional interests in China. As Chiang Kai-shek seemed determined to defend the Yangzi River line, banking on rejuvenated support from Washington, Mao believed that a quick and decisive victory in cracking up Chiang's final defense along the river would deter the Americans who were known to have been agonizing over the unbearable cost for direct military intervention in China.[2]

In a Politburo directive titled "Current Situation and the Party's Task for 1949" dated January 8, 1949, Mao clearly pointed out that, "We have always included in our battle plans the possibility that the United States may directly send troops to occupy several coastal cities and engage war with us .... But the stronger [we] are, the more decisive we are, the possibility of American intervention will be less ......"[3]

Chen Yi, Deng Xiaoping and Liu Bocheng were invited to participate in a Politburo meeting held in Xibaipo in early January. It was decided at this meeting, much to Chen's delight, that he could go back to his old command at the now newly designated Third Field Army, especially since Su Yu was bedridden, suffering from severe Meniere's Syndrome due to the stress of the Campaign of Huai-Hai. More importantly, Mao decided not to deactivate the General Front Committee formed during the Huai-Hai Campaign and assigned it the additional task of overall control of the eminent Yangzi crossing campaign. The date of crossing was now set at April 10.

The Party Central Committee held an important meeting in March. Mao's report at the meeting destroyed any illusions about a "third road" between the government and the Communist Party, which had been popular among liberal intellectuals at the time. Mao made it clear that the military solution was the only one that would lead to complete victory of the Communist Party in China. Since the results of the Huai-Hai Campaign were far beyond original expectations, the communist high command began in great haste to shift its attention from war efforts to urban administrative takeover, a sphere that was totally new to them. During his private conversation with Mao, Chen Yi was overwhelmed by the latter's suggestion that he become the first communist mayor of Shanghai.[4] Shanghai was the biggest city not only in China, but also in the Far East. It was the center of the Chinese financial system, manufacturing industry and foreign trade.

Chen was awed by the heavy responsibility upon his shoulders. He had no experience in dealing with delicate issues such as foreign relations, financial management, legal system and foreign trade. Fortunately at this time, the Politburo had decided on a policy to drive all western influence out of China. This made Chen's task in the foreign policy area much easier. According to a directive concerning foreign relations of the new regime dated January 19, the communists "should not be anxious to reestablish trade relations with foreign countries." Although foreign missionaries were allowed to stay, no new missionary activities would be permitted to enter China. Moreover, contractual obligations between Chinese private employers and foreign employees would not be honored by the new regime.[5] Thus the efforts to rid foreign influence of Shanghai where foreign relations had dominated the city's activities became a relatively simple task. But the task of keeping this most prosperous city in China from going down the drain economically would turn out to be far more difficult than the communists expected.

After the Politburo meeting, Chen, Liu and Deng proceeded to participate in the Second Plenum of the Seventh Central Committee. At this plenum, Mao made a well-known speech titled "Carry the Revolution Through to the End," in which he mocked any lingering hope at home and abroad that the communists might be willing to stop at the Yangzi River line, seeking for peaceful settlement with the government. Mao's plan for 1949 was specified in a document which called for fulfilling seventeen tasks. Among them were the control of all southern provinces, the establishment of a "people's democratic republic" and the building of air force and navy. There was no mention of "peaceful settlement."[6]

Returning to Eastern China, Chen and Deng immediately began preparation for the campaign of the Yangzi crossing. By March, a detailed battle plan was worked out. Drafted by Deng Xiaoping, it was one of the very few detailed operation plans ever drafted by the communist command before a battle had started. Reflecting a new phase of military professionalism, it was formally titled "Nanjing-Shanghai-Hangzhou Campaign Operation Plan." The strategy was bold and innovative. It intended to launch the campaign of the Yangzi crossing simultaneously in three sections of the river. It is interesting to note that Deng at this time was not so single-minded in seeking glory for his Second Field Army, for the bulk of the task fell upon Chen's Third Field Army. According to the plan, Chen was responsible for crushing two most difficult sections of the river while Deng's section was a relatively easy one, since it was the farthest in distance from Shanghai where the government troop deployment was much thinner.[7]

Lacking modern transportation means was the number one problem. The million communist soldiers had to rely on wooden junks and sailboats to carry out the task. These were the same kinds of transport that were used during the Three Kingdoms period when frequent river battles were fought on the Yangzi. That was the condition for the Yangzi crossing, as Ye Fei remarked in his memoirs, more than a thousand years ago. Moreover, most of the new recruits were from Northern China where the terrain was typically flat and dry. They hardly knew how to swim. Weather conditions were another problem. It was estimated that the best time to cross the river was before April when the rainy season had not started. After April, the water level would rise very rapidly on the river, a condition that could hinder the military operation based on primitive transportation means. Deng and Chen were naturally inclined to launch the campaign as soon as possible.

But the political situation in China took another twist. In January, as a result of the Huai-Hai Campaign, Chiang Kai-shek announced his resignation as president of China. His vice president Li Zongren became the acting president and immediately sent out olive branches for peace. Li was the leader of Chiang's arch rivals within the government, the "Guangxi Clique." The unexpected peace negotiations that ensued forced

Mao to put his plan for the Yangzi Campaign on hold. But the delay was not a total disaster from Mao's perspective, since, the communists had proven quite unprepared for taking over city administration, as was clearly indicated by their experience in Manchuria, Beiping and Tianjin. From the Party Central Committee down to regional party bureaus, there was a general lack of understanding and experience in urban affairs. Lin Biao's relatively smooth takeover of Manchuria was facilitated by the Soviet Red Army authorities as well as the concentration of the best economic minds of the Communist Party, such as Chen Yun. But even in Manchuria, the administrative task proved to be much heavier than was originally envisioned. Lacking clear direction and instructions from the top, any controversial issue could trigger major internal debates among the cadres. For incidence, the takeover of government-owned enterprises seemed much easier than the task of keeping their businesses running. When entering a city, the communists typically established a "military control committee" in charge of all administrative affairs. But the communists were often at loss in comprehending the complicated organizations and personnel labyrinth of various manufacturing enterprises. In many cases, they adopted rigid military approaches to manage business, which more often than not turned into disasters. As a result, the Party Central Committee made a major concession by issuing an internal directive in January, which specified that the task for the communist "military representative" at any enterprise to be "supervising," not replacing the old personnel network. "Even if the old managers have fled," according to the directive, the new managers "should be promoted from the existing organizations."[8]

In Eastern China, where cities were considerably bigger and more complicated, the communists admitted a Party Central Committee directive dated February 3, were "not yet competent" for taking over administration of cities such as Shanghai. An interesting incident involved the inquiry by the East China Party Bureau concerning the salary level for employees working at public utilities companies in Jinan after the communist takeover. Since the communists had long eliminated the concept of salary within its internal mechanism, no one knew what to do. The Party Central Committee realized that it would set a precedent for the whole country in the future. It cautioned against setting any new policy at this stage, except for retaining the old salary system.[9]

Another issue involved policies towards the private Chinese enterprises, or the "national capitals" according to the official communist classification. The official policy was to allow these businesses to continue operating. But many problems occurred when the communist representatives were asked to make decisions in such sensitive issues as labor disputes between the employer and the employee. The communists by definition were supposed to take the position against employer. But if they should do so, the employer might simply decide to close down the business altogether. Moreover, issues involving foreign trade, currency exchange and inflation controls all proved to be well-nigh insurmountable in communist-controlled areas. Under the circumstances, Mao welcomed with certain enthusiasm a short respite before the Yangzi crossing campaign in order to prepare adequately for the administrative takeover of urban affairs.

Meanwhile, the military preparation for the Yangzi Campaign continued. In the face of the Li Zongren government's peace initiative, Mao had no choice but to respond positively to his gesture. Yet political and propaganda value aside, Mao did not from the outset take the negotiations too seriously. As early as in January, Mao pointed out in a directive that Chiang Kai-shek would not accept the "Eight Conditions" for peace listed by the communists, which included prosecution of Chiang and over forty "war criminals." Therefore, "the war must be carried through to the end."[10] With the same attitude in dealing with Li Zongren, Mao proceeded to ask for *de facto* unconditional surrender on the government side.

Mao issued another directive in February, indicating two possibilities: one, the government may continue to organize its defense along the Yangzi River line, so that the communists should prepare carefully for crossing the River in April; two, the government may give up the Yangzi line altogether, in which case, the communist troops must cross the river a month earlier, since there would be little resistance and the fall of the capital city of Nanjing would produce an "extremely favorable impact at home and abroad." Mao was inclined to believe that the second possibility was increasingly more probable.[11]

But Mao was gravely concerned that the news of possible agreement between the communists and the government may slacken the fighting spirit of the soldiers who had already shown signs of fatigue and dreaded for the idea of dying in the last battle before the total communist victory. The troop's morale was, indeed, the cause for major apprehension. Mao was especially alarmed by a report at the end of the Huai-Hai Campaign, in which the author, Su Yu, pointed out frankly that there was widespread fear of death among officers who "are pessimistic that they might get killed before the end of the civil war .... Especially when they observe those officers who have been assigned to take over city administration [in communist-controlled areas] are now living in big houses, riding cars ... and with splendid furniture and interior decoration. [They] are always having an entourage around, appearing very contented. [Their] families are also living a good life. Therefore, many officers want to save themselves during the campaign."

During the Campaign of Huai-Hai, Mao's response to this fear of death was rather cruel and straightforward. He simply kept on increasing allowed casualty numbers for the troops in the field. During the first stage of the campaign, many field commanders complained loudly about the exceedingly heavy casualties and asked for a respite. Mao sent a wire warning them to be prepared for a casualty figure of over 100,000, i.e., some twenty percent of Su's East China Field Army. It thus destroyed any hope for a short rest. In the second and third stages of the Huai-Hai Campaign, Mao increased the permitted number to 200,000. Few dared to complain any more.[12]

Realizing that the old trick of increasing projected casualty numbers may not work this time, since the enemy morale had sunk so low that the communist soldiers were more anxious to get it over as quickly as possible, Mao instructed Chen and Deng "not to tell the rank and file that the reason for delaying [the Yangzi Campaign] is the possibility of success in negotiations with the government." Mao added, "Just tell them that the other troop units have not yet been fully prepared." Chen and Deng differed with Mao on this issue. They suggested telling the truth to the officers while at the same time they could explicitly warn them that they must not slacken their fighting spirit.[13]

The field commanders were even more anxious to launch the campaign, because the low river tide would be most favorable for the operation before May. On April 10, however, Mao sent a wire to the General Front Committee under Deng and Chen, stating that the agreement with the government might be signed on April 15, thus it would be better to delay the crossing for another fifteen to thirty days. The General Front Committee strongly disagreed, proposing "crossing first, peaceful takeover later." Su Yu personally sent another wire, asking for no delay. On April 16, Mao informed Chen and Deng that the communist proposal had been presented to the government, but "you should still prepare for the breakdown of the negotiations and for waging the campaign." Because even if "Nanjing decides to sign it, many reactionary generals such as Tang Enbo may refuse to carry it out, we must use military means to cross the Yangzi River."[14]

Despite his resignation from the government, Chiang Kai-shek continued to exert direct control over the Yangzi defense. In appearance Chiang's defense plan was an impressive one. Twenty-four armies at some 450,000 strong were deployed along the river from Shanghai to Hubei. While General Bai Chongxi commanded another quarter million troops to guard the river section from Hubei to Sichuan. The government navy sent 133 warships to cruise the Yangzi together with some 300 airplanes. The American and the British warships were also anchoring near Shanghai and the mouth of Yangzi.[15] Behind the scenes, however,

Chiang decided in uttermost secrecy to abandon the defense of the capital city of Nanjing, not only because it was indefensible, but also because he had no desire to help Acting President Li Zongren, his long-time political *bete noire* at Nanjing. According to General Guo Rugui, the government operation chief and the communist spy, Chiang vehemently rejected a plan designed by the Ministry of Defense to deploy main force at the city of Wuhu where the river condition was rough and the chance of beating back the communists was the highest. Instead, Chiang ordered a concentration of defense at Yangzhong in Jiangsu, which was between Shanghai and Nanjing. This was apparently an effort to hold on to Shanghai while at the same time writing off Nanjing.[16]

The final peace protocol proposed by the communists was tantamount to an ultimatum. It was rejected by the government on April 20. In the same night, communist troops started massive crossing of the river from three sections of the river bank. The major task of crushing the government defense fell on Chen's Third Field Army because Chiang Kai-shek was seriously prepared for defending the river section between Nanjing and Shanghai. Deng's troops were deployed in an easier section for the purpose of cutting off Zhejiang-Jiangxi railway line to secure Chen's right wing, in case the United States should decide to intervene.

Since the Campaign of Huai-Hai, the communist troops were further regrouped into large units of army corps to befit the scale of battle. The communists were prepared for encountering the American troops. But they did not expect problems with the British. The commander of Chen's Tenth Corps, General Ye Fei, was responsible for taking the important Jiangyin Fort across the river. This was the closest landing point that could make a short cut directly to Shanghai. Ye's operation was smooth and facilitated by the work of communist spies within the government fortress. But in the afternoon of April 20, Tao Yong, now commander of the 23th Army under Ye, suddenly telephoned his superior, telling him that there were several warships blocking the route of the waters where they had planned for crossing. Ye asked Tao what kind of flags on these ships, since the communists had been successful in persuading a government fleet to surrender as soon as the crossing would start. Tao, the uncouth peasant boy, simply said "colorful ones." Ye thought that they might be specially designed signals from those government warships intended to defect, he therefore ordered sending warning signals to them. These ships reacted by turning guns towards Tao's position. Tao immediately ordered to open fire. A major gun battle erupted and was ended with heavy casualties on both sides. The communists admitted a loss of 252 soldiers. The unknown warships were also damaged heavily. It soon turned out that these were British ships sent by the Admiralty to bring supplies to and take British personnel from Nanjing. One of the ships named *Amethyst* lost its captain and the British had on the whole suffered over 100 casualties. The Amethyst Incident, as it was later known, was totally unexpected from both the communists and the British. The communist headquarters immediately realized that this was a mistake. Ye Fei was reprimanded for this action. But Tao Yong refused to accept any responsibilities, for one of his best artillery commanders was killed in action. Ye decided to stick with his old friend Tao. Reporting to the communist headquarters, Ye insisted that it was the British who opened fire first. In private they both laughed about this incident for years to come.[17] On the British side, Parliament was outraged by the incident. Fueled by belligerent rhetorics of the opposition led by Winston Churchill, various threats were made by the British government. But behind the scenes, the Labour cabinet also realized that it was a mistake, since the communists had made clear their intention to cross the river on April 20, but the information did not reach the ships which were "well up the river." Under the circumstances, the Attlee government was, tough talk notwithstanding, very cautious and refrained from overreaction to the incident, especially because the British were pondering the question of diplomatic recognition of the new regime.[18] The communist authorities, on their part, considered this incident, though undesirable, a good opportunity for propaganda. The communist-controlled media fully utilized this incident to declare the end of the imperialistic gunboat diplomacy and the dawning of a new era. Ye was ordered to exert artillery control of *Amethyst* stranded on the Yangzi. The stalemate on the river was finally ended with *Amethyst*'s daring escape during the night of April 30.

According to Deng's original Operation Plan, the Yangzi Campaign was to be carried out in three stages. First, they should crush the government defense line on the southern bank of the river, then the three attack army corps would converge towards Nanjing; second, they must take over Nanjing and the control of Zhejiang-Jiangxi railway in order to isolate Shanghai; and third, they would seize Shanghai, the biggest and the most prosperous city in China. The crossing of the river proved to be much easier task than they had expected. In fact, Acting President Li Zongren simply abandoned the city and fled to Guangzhou to set up a provisional government. In only two days, the communist forces at a million strong overwhelmed the government defense in three sections of the river. Ironically, it was not due to the effectiveness of the wooden junks and sailboats carrying the communist soldiers, which were not much an improvement from 200 A.D. It was the government abandonment of the Yangzi defense that had prompted the fall of Nanjing on April 23.

After the government ordered general retreat towards the coastal area, the speedy chase by the communist soldiers began. Many government forces had by this time had lost the will to fight. By early May, Hangzhou, the capital city of Chiang Kai-shek's home province, Zhejiang, in the south of Shanghai, fell. Shanghai thus became an isolated city. Meanwhile, Deng's Second Field Army had secured control over Zhejiang-Jiangxi railway. Although the American military intervention did not materialize, Deng's move had severed the connection between General Tang Enbo in charge of defending Shanghai and General Bai Chongxi in Central China. Because the communists did not have a navy, there was still a viable retreat line for General Tang Enbo's garrison command at Shanghai through the East China Sea.

Encouraged by the low morale and utter ineffectiveness of the government defense forces at the Yangzi River line, Mao was somehow carried away. He began to take Tang Enbo lightly. On May 6, Mao's high command ordered the General Front Committee to cut off Tang's sea exit through seizing the Wusong port "between May 10 and 15," so that "most of the assets at Shanghai will not be shipped out." It appeared to Mao that that the fall of Shanghai was just a matter of one easy knockout.

But it was easier said than done. The communist headquarters apparently under-estimated Tang's will to fight. In fact, the government defense plan for Shanghai was personally controlled by Chiang Kai-shek, who, although resigned from his post as the president of China, continued to exert tight control over most of the elite forces. Chiang considered the defense of Shanghai a major gamble. His purpose seemed two-fold. On the one hand, the tenacious defense of Shanghai would allow General Tang enough time to ship out most of the valuable assets in Shanghai where almost all the major Chinese banks were located. On the other, Chiang hoped that the devastation of Shanghai caused by a prolonged war might trigger major international incidents that could draw the Western Powers into the conflict.

Assuming that Shanghai would easily fall on his lap, Mao began to change his mind. Instead of a rapid seizure of Shanghai when the government troops were still in chaotic frenzy for preparing trench battles, Mao decided to stop operations for as long as a month. It seemed incomprehensible to the commanders in the front. Several factors affected Mao's considerations. The first and the most important one was the mistakenly perceived possibility of the peaceful surrender of Shanghai. The communists had been secretly working General Tang's mentor Chen Yi, a former provincial governor of Zhejiang (not to be confused with Chen Yi, the communist) who had agreed to persuade General Tang to give up. Strangely enough, Mao was also convinced that the "Shanghai Bourgeoisie class are not in favor of a battle inside the city, therefore a peaceful solution is extremely probable." Thus, Mao suddenly ordered Chen and Su to halt attack on Shanghai on April 27. Secondly, Mao was delighted by the indication that the American intervention may not occur during the seizure of Shanghai, since the American warships had been ordered to withdraw from Shanghai and were merely waiting near the port of Wusong. Thirdly, the administrative takeover of the capital city of Nanjing proved to be a terribly stressful task for the communists who were deeply rooted in rural conditions, but very limited in governing big cities. Not only the administrative duties, but diplomatic protocol and international law all seemed beyond the immediate ken of these seasoned soldiers who, for incidence, would forcefully enter a foreign embassy to "check out and engage a harangue in order to teach the 'imperialists' a lesson."[19]

Seeing the difficulties at Nanjing, Chen Yi, the communist mayor-designate for Shanghai, reported to Mao on April 30 that "We might fall into an awkward position if we should enter Shanghai in a great hurry and without adequate preparations." Chen suggested delay for a half to one month to take over the city. Since he had been convinced that General Tang might flee the city in about a week without putting up a vigorous defense, Mao readily approved Chen's plan.

For communist commanders in the field, the delay proved to be a disaster. As Ye Fei complained bitterly in an article published in 1990, after General Tang arrested his mentor Chen, all the hopes for peaceful solution had been crushed in early May. Yet the communist headquarters continued to discount Tang's ability to fight and did not even hold an operation meeting before it directly issued orders for launching the attack.[20] General Tang had 200,000 of the best troops at his disposal. More important were over 3,000 cement strongholds which were the legacies before World War Two and were built with the American and German technology. These strongholds were further connected by 4,000 concrete trenches. Such a defense structure was unsurpassed in any place China. General Tang boasted that his defense network was "stronger than Stalingrad by 1/3."[21]

Chen Yi was not directly involved with military operation against Shanghai. The mayor-designate was at Danyang, a small town near Nanjing, where he was busy gathering over three thousand communist cadres who knew something about economy for a crash course on city administration. But the news in the battlefield was not encouraging. The communist headquarters under Su Yu launched a hasty attack on May 12, but the troops were quickly met with persevering defense efforts on the government side. Su's battle plan for Shanghai was based on Mao's order earlier to directly spearhead towards the port of Wusong in order to cut off Tang's retreat sea route. Su himself also seemed to have taken General

Tang a bit too lightly. According to Su's one-time rival Ye Fei who was responsible for taking Wusong, Su told him that there would be little difficulty in taking Shanghai and that he could easily reach the port of Wusong in two days. But when Ye's Tenth Corps approached the suburbs of the city, their troubles immediately began to mount. It soon appeared to Ye that the idea of reaching Wusong in two days was totally unrealistic, unless there was no active government resistance. After heavy casualties were incurred during the first hours, Ye asked for abandoning the plan and changing tactics.

Su also slowly began to realize the severity of the situation. After encountering a long and stalemated battle for a few days, Su sent a report to Mao on May 16, stating that " ... in two days we have to suffer a thousand casualties for eliminating each government battalion." Some of the government positions "changed hands for as many as five times." Therefore, the siege of Shanghai was not an easy task, because of the permanent defense structure at the government's disposal. The unexpected cost during the battle forced the commanders in the field to change their attack tactics constantly. Since Mao had instructed Su not to enter Shanghai without the Party Central Committee's specific approval, Su asked the high command to remove any fixed time frame and space limits for the battle of Shanghai and urged for faster preparation for administrative takeover.[22] It turned out that General Tang was more than capable of inflicting major pains on the communist troops. After a 15-day prolonged and gruesome trench warfare with enormous death tolls, the communists were finally able to overwhelm Tang's defense on May 27. Mao's original plan of cutting off Tang's sea exit did not have any chance of being carried out. General Tang and over 50,000 best government troops were allowed to flee to the high seas.

Meanwhile Chen Yi continued careful preparation for taking over the administration of Shanghai. In a very short period of time, three thousand future communist economic administrators were gathered and were given a crash course to acquaint themselves with some two hundred pamphlets compiled from numerous almanacs, books, and intelligence reports about this most prosperous city. The task seemed enormously heavy. The urgent issues involved policies towards government-owned enterprises, private businesses, the organization of municipal Shanghai, public utilities, etc. Chen initially summarized the most pressing task to stabilize the Shanghai life as to be securing "Two Whites and One Black," meaning cotton, rice and coal. But through intensive readings, he soon realized the scope of administrative task was far beyond his earlier imagination. As he warned the future administrators in May that Shanghai "is very complicated, there are many problems that we do not understand. We should not brag and adopt a complacent attitude. Shanghai needs

200,000 tons of coal a month, and its six million population need be fed everyday .... [The breakdown] of the sewage system alone will create so many insurmountable problems and difficulties for our administration."[23] The most difficult problem for Chen was limited policy options he had to choose from in dealing with the previously propertied class. It was in this area many communist administrators were treading a dangerous political tightrope. They risked becoming either "right-leaning" or "extreme-leftist," because the Party Central Committee had never outlined a clear policy towards the so-called "national bourgeoisie [i.e., Chinese capitalists]." As late as in May when the communists were entering Shanghai, the party central authorities finally decided to focus on avoiding the "extreme-leftist" tendency. It was triggered by a letter to Liu Shaoqi from a communist administrator in Manchuria named Zou Dapeng. In the letter, Zou pointed out the fact that the party's policy toward "national capitalists" had been debated for years but had not been resolved by the Party Central Committee yet. Liu Shaoqi himself went to Tianjin for an inspection, where his new bride and the fourth wife, Wang Guangmei's family was well-known in Tianjin capitalist circles. Liu discovered at Tianjin that the communist administrators went so far as to refuse to talk to property owners for fear of being labeled right-leaning by their colleagues and superiors. The result, according to a Central Committee directive written by Liu, was the lack of enthusiasm on the capitalists' side to keep their business operation going, a result that seriously hurt local economy. The directive, for the first time, explicitly warned against "extreme-leftist views."[24]

The problem with the labor-capital dispute was no less stressful. In most cases, the communist-controlled trade unions performed the function as arbitrator. But they were always on the workers' side. According to one Party Central Committee directive dated in July, many industrial workers complained "wherever there is a trade union, we will suffer," because its unreasonable demands often resulted in the loss of jobs. Therefore, the directive ordered return to some form of labor-capital co-determination in wage control.[25]

Although the Party Central Committee's timely turn to the right was a welcome news to Chen, nowhere was the administrative task more heavier than in metropolitan Shanghai. Its six million residents had long enjoyed modern life unsurpassed by anywhere else in China. It boasted a complete trolley and bus transit system. It had led the nation in almost all manufacturing industries, trading activities, shipping business and entertainment industries. But, the Shanghai economy was wrecked by the civil war. According to one estimate, among 12,000 manufacturing plants, only 30% were still operating at the time Chen Yi took over the mayor's office. The Shanghai textile industry used to have an enormous share of 40% in overall national production. Shanghai had also long been the leading trade center for China. Its two-way trade with foreign countries was some 50% of the volume of the national foreign trade. The Shanghai economy was thus crucial for the economic well-being of the new communist regime.

In the short-run, Chen's problem was compounded by the more urgent issue of food and fuels, since the city's existing food supplies were sufficient for fifteen days and coal only seven. Besides, there were refugees, vagabonds, prostitutes and beggars everywhere, estimated at 600,000.

Chen Yi arrived at Shanghai on May 26. When entering the city hall, Chen could not help but recall his first arrival at Shanghai some twenty-nine years ago when he and his brother were preparing for departure for France. At the age of 48, aside from commanding some 600,000 troops, Chen became the mayor of the city he had always admired. A French correspondent interviewed Chen at the time, asking him "when is the best moment in your life?" Chen answered unequivocally, "The day I entered Shanghai."[26]

By all accounts, Chen proved to be one of the most effective communist administrators after 1949. He was also lucky in that Shanghai was not devastated by the battle. Before the fall of Shanghai, the underground communist agents led by Liu Changsheng had been able to organize massive preservation activities to ensure that key public utilities would still function after the communist takeover. Electricity, telephone and running water facilities were, in particular, kept intact during the ferocious battle that raged for fifteen days.

Although Chen had always been criticized for having a "rightist tendency" throughout his career within the party, he was supported by Mao and the Party Central Committee at the time when the need for keeping the Shanghai economy afloat outweighed the need for political conformity. Chen was at his best in winning the "Bourgeois" elements in Shanghai. During a speech in front of top intellectual leaders of the city, Chen made a sensational statement that brought the house down. He said: "I was not a natural born communist. I am an intellectual, too. I have translated poems by de Musset, published novels and poems. I have gone through three stages in my life: first I was born in a landlord family, believing in Confucianism. Then I accepted the new thinking and was converted into a believer of Mr. D[emocracy] and Mr. S[cience] .... Finally, after study abroad in France, I went through self-contradiction, depression, and failure, and eventually became a revolutionary ......"[27] Chen's warm and positive attitude towards the intellectuals created strong echo in educated Shanghai and was enormously popular. While most of the other communist leaders were not in the same position to make the similar statement that would create a sense of empathy with China's most modern intellectual society, Chen was able to speak their language with ease. He even made a few genuine friends with the top-notch academics. While Chen was sincere in stressing the importance of gaining intellectual support, it was an attitude that often ran foul of Mao's hatred for the well-educated, whom Mao often labeled "hairs [intellectuals] on the skin [the masses]." But Chen would never abandon this attitude in his life time. Already in 1942 he was accused by Rao Shushi, the party boss of the New Fourth Army, of possessing a "right-wing Bourgeois spirit." As it would turn out, his pro-intellectual attitude would continue to create political problems for him in the years to come.

The Shanghai economy began to boom very quickly, which prompted many foreign observers to reconsider their attitude toward communist leaders who were said to know nothing about administration. Through skillful alternation between persuasion and coercion, Chen at first succeeded in fighting inflation. Within a week after the communist authorities started "Renminbi" (People's Currency) circulation, the new currency was devalued as much as fourteen times because of an active speculative run on the silver dollar. Chen's solution was simple: to eliminate East Asia's famous Shanghai Stock Exchange. Two battalions and 400 plainclothes policemen were dispatched to the Exchange building. They arrested 250 people and closed down the business until the late 1980s! Although it sent shock waves abroad, it was effective in eliminating speculators and regaining Shanghai residents' confidence.

Another burden for Chen was to reduce the impact caused by the trade embargo imposed by the U.S. government. Chiang Kai-shek, with Washington's tacit approval, began a naval blockade of Shanghai on June 23. Many manufacturing industries that had relied on raw materials and markets abroad were in serious trouble. Worker layoffs were increasing day by day. Chen was very innovative in solving the unemployment problem. Instead of coercing the employers into re-hiring the unemployed, as was practiced in many other cities under the communist control, Chen adopted a method that was characteristic of modern Keynesianism. He hired 100,000 jobless workers to start public projects such as dams on the coast to create arable land, while at the same time requested a one percent "voluntary" deduction of each worker's pay. The party cadres would then collect the sum and distribute it to a relief fund for the unemployed.

Severe gasoline shortage also threatened to shut down the city's sprawling public transportation system. Chen immediately organized a massive campaign of adaptation. Within months, 99.7% of the motor vehicles began to use coal-powered engines. According to one contemporary estimate, from July to November, Shanghai's textile production increased 90%; machinery industry saw increase in operation capacity from 20% to 60%.[28]

Aside from his mayoral duties, Chen, of course, remained the commander of the Third field Army. His elite troops on the other hand, continued to carry out the task of wiping out Chiang's remnants in Southeastern China. Su Yu was appointed Chen's deputy at the military control committee of Shanghai. He was forty-one years old. Ye Fei was ordered to lead his Tenth Corps to enter Fujian, his native province to which he had not returned since 1938. Ye was thirty-five, and would become a young governor of Fujian. After several battles in Southeastern China, Tao Yong and Wang Bicheng, both in their mid-thirties, were soon to be sent to the Korean front to fight General Douglas MacArthur's UN troops. The friendship and factional loyalty within Chen's original elite troops remained strong, but their troubles also began to mount, as the new emperor Mao Zedong would soon start incessant political campaigns to purge the party and the military. Year after year, the romantic poet Chen Yi would find his free spirit, deeply rooted in the French Enlightenment, become increasingly out of the place in the People's Republic he had helped create. It would turn out, however, that few of Mao's old colleagues, free-spirited or not, were able to escape the ever closing net of political suspicion and purges.

Notes

1. *MZDJSWJ*, vol.5, p.382-383.
2. For detail of the American policy during this period, see Xiang, *Recasting the Imperial Far East---Britain and America in China, 1945-1950*, Chapters 5 and 6.
3. *MZDJSWJ*, vol.5, p.471-474.
4. *Biography of Chen Yi* (Official), p.442-443.
5. *WJXJ*, vol.18, p.44-46.
6. Ibid., p.16-22.
7. *Selected Works of Deng Xiaoping*, p.131-134.
8. *WJXJ*, vol.18, p.31-33.
9. Ibid., p.23-24.
10. Ibid., p.30.
11. Ibid., p.105-106.
12. *Military Works of Su Yu*, p.446-448.
13. *Biography of Chen Yi* (Official), p.445-446.
14. *WJXJ*, vol.18, p.226-227.
15. Zhang, Zhen, *San Ye Zai Du Jiang Zhan Yi Zhong* (The Third Field Army during the Yangzi Campaign), in Materials of the Party History, vol.36, p.44-45.
16. *Memoirs of Guo Rugui*, p.352-353.

17. *Memoirs of Ye Fei*, p.538-543.
18. For detail of the British attitude, see Xiang, *Recasting the Imperial Far East*, p.190-191.
19. *WJXJ*, vol.18, p.246-247.
20. Not only did General Tang refuse to listen to Mr. Chen's advice, but he turned his mentor over to Chiang Kai-shek. Chen was executed shortly after.
21. *Biography of Chen Yi* (Official), p.451.
22. Zhang, Zhen, *The Third Field Army during the Yangzi Campaign*, p.49.
23. *Memoirs of Ye Fei*, p.557.
24. *WJXJ*, vol.18, p.317-319.
25. Ibid., p.359-362.
26. *Biography of Chen Yi* (Jiang), p.643.
27. Ibid., p.642.
28. *Biography of Chen Yi* (Official), p.461.

Concluding Remarks

The basic conclusion of this study is that Mao did not deserve as much military credit as he has had and they must be restored to his generals. and above all, Chen Yi and his colleagues. Another implicit conclusion deriving from the original materials is that cause of the victory in the Chinese communist revolution is both political and military. Communist military efficiency has been underestimated in the past, in contrast to the sociopolitical aspect of communist work. The military nature of the People's Republic after 1949, which was present at its birth as well as now, has been all but ignored by experts and practitioners alike. The obvious result is that, many studies on the "political system" in China lack historical empathy and appear to scratch the itch from outside the boots, as a Chinese saying goes. It may be argued that, without adequate understanding of the communist military history, any study of contemporary China is tantamount to studying the Manchu Dynasty without knowledge of the elite Bannerman caste in Beijing. This kind of study is all the more urgent in view of the fact that the second generation of the Chinese military elite, the contemporary Bannerman descendants, have been quietly and decisively taking over the country at all levels. The study of the Chen Yi faction is nothing but a starting effort to comprehend one of the most important topics of the history of twentieth century China. The task ahead remains enormous, for each of the three other military factions would deserve one volume of its own.

The success of Chen Yi and the New Fourth Army elite was a decisive factor in communist victories in Eastern China. What are the characteristics of this elite group? First of all, the New Fourth Army officers could truly be called the most diversified group within the communist officer corps. The other three military factions led respectively by Lin Biao, Peng Dehuai and Deng Xiaoping, had grown more or less from common roots that dated back to the Red Army years. Chen Yi's faction was based on cooperation and friendship formed during the war against Japan. It was thus a unique faction. Its factional loyalty and pride derived from Chen Yi's ability to absorb the best and brightest elements from the most developed regions in China, socially as well as economically, and they were from various backgrounds and from all walks of life. In a sense it was the most open faction whose guiding principle was genuinely founded on meritocracy within the communist establishment.

Secondly, proportionally speaking, it represented the best-educated communist leaders in the history of the party. The officer corps under Chen were typically high school diploma holders. A contemporary report indicated that over 60% officers of Chen's elite troops were either educated at high school and above or schooled with private tutors at home. One reason for this high literacy rate was that most of the members of the officer corps were recruited during the war against Japan from prosperous southern China, from provinces such as Zhejiang, Jiangsu and Fujian where education, even during the imperial time, had long occupied leading positions in the country.

Thirdly, from the institutional point of view, the New Fourth Army elite had little in common with the Eighth Route Army elite who were always directly under the control of Mao's high command. The original members of the Chen Yi faction were either the "dumpees" by the escapist Party Central Committee in 1934, or the founders of independent guerrilla base areas of their own. The spirit of independence and the courage to differ from the party central authorities had been an asset instead of a liability of this military faction. Commanders such as Su Yu and Ye Fei had always been apathetic toward the center. They longed for freedom from the shackles imposed from Yanan, a place they had never visited and had no sentimental attachment to in their careers. Under the circumstances, their penchant for independence was undoubtedly a major reason why the troops under Chen Yi proved to be the most effective and innovative in strategy and tactics.

Last but not the least, military factional loyalty was and continues to be sustained by a distinctive geographical distribution of power among four factions in regional affairs of the People's Republic. In early 1949, Mao assigned the task of "joint management of southeastern China" to Deng Xiaoping and Chen Yi. But Deng's Second Field Army was soon ordered to take over Southwestern China. Lin Biao's Fourth Field Army was in control of Manchuria and southern China, while Peng Dehuai's First Field Army controlled western China, managing places like Gansu and the Turkish region of Xinjiang. In southeastern China, Chen's faction has always been in firm control. Despite the fact that Chen was soon to be promoted to the position of Vice Premier and Foreign Minister of China, the party bosses of the six provinces and the city of Shanghai, which was directly controlled by the central government, were mostly chosen from Chen Yi's old power base. Among whom, Ye Fei (Fujian), Tan Qilong (Shandong), Chen Pixian (Shanghai) and Jiang Weiqing (Jiangsu) were the most prominent soldiers of Chen's original elite units in the New Fourth Army. After 1949, Su Yu was soon to be appointed chief of staff of the People's Liberation Army. Tao Yong would become the commander of the East China Sea Fleet based in Shanghai, and Wang Bicheng would assume the deputy commander position at the important Nanjing Military Region. Apart from assignment to Beijing, few of the original members of the New Fourth Army would leave the east China region to make a successful career elsewhere. This geographical distribution of the factional power base was strongly maintained until the Cultural Revolution. Yet, despite the effort by Mao to dilute factional loyalty during the Cultural Revolution, the intra-party relationships are still by and large divided along the original factional lines up until today. Even the second generation of the People's Liberation Army officer corps are still living with the factional ghosts of the past. This phenomenon will undoubtedly affect China's future, since the military, as the powerful "state within the state," has always been decisive in intra-party power transition at every turn of events of the People's Republic's history.

Epilogue

One day in August 1965, Marshal Chen Yi, Vice Premier and Foreign Minister of the People's Republic of China, attended a banquet in honor of Tao Yong, deputy commander of the Chinese navy, who had recently sunk two of Chiang Kai-shek's warships on the waters between the mainland and Taiwan. Politically, Tao was in trouble, for his opponents, supported by Lin Biao, the vice chairman of the communist party, were bent on relieving him of his duty. Chen sighed heavily during a toast, "Ye [Fei], Wang [Bicheng], Tao [Yong], Ye, Wang, Tao, now nobody cares about them any more." Chen was prophetic. Less than a year later, the Cultural Revolution began.

In October 1966, Chen held a last banquet with his best generals who were party bosses in provinces in East China and who were all panicky in front of the massive Red Guards movement against them encouraged by Mao. Among the attendees were Ye Fei, Chen Pixian, Tan Qilong and Jiang Weiqing. Chen toasted them, "This might be the last toast; I can no longer save you. You should try to save yourselves this time. If you do, we may toast again, if not, this will be our last meeting." A few months later, Ye, Tan, Jiang and Chen were all arrested by Mao. Tao Yong threw himself into a well. Wang Bicheng was lucky to survive the Cultural Revolution but was severely criticized within the party for being right-wing. Among Chen's best generals, only Su Yu survived without a scratch this time. But Su had already in the 1950s been deactivated by Mao, after being abruptly removed in humiliation from the position of the People's Liberation Army chief of staff in 1958, because of his obssession with military professionalism. During the Cultural Revolution, Su was merely serving as a deputy Minister of Defense and a deputy superintendent of the Chinese Military Science Academy. Since 1958, the heartbroken Su had vowed never to get involved in any power struggle. Mao had no reason to purge him. Chen Yi himself soon ran into trouble with Mao and lost his position in the government and the party. Due to medical neglect, Chen died from colon cancer on January 6, 1972. He was 71.

Shortly before his death, Chen was resurrected by Mao to start participating in active military and diplomatic affairs of the party, because Mao's hand-picked successor and a key initiator of the Cultural Revolution, Lin Biao, had crashed his plane in Mongolia a few months before while fleeing his mentor's purge. Chen's death was devastating to Mao. According internal funeral protocol, Chen was to be given a small service, since his only title was as a member of the Central Committee. Luminaries such as Mao, Madame Sun Yat-sen or Prince Norodon

Sihanouk of Cambodia were not included in the guest list. On January 10, the day of the funeral, Mao suddenly woke up from his routine nap, and decided to go to Chen's funeral. He had not attended anyone's funeral since 1963 when Marshal Luo Ronghuan, another veteran of the Jinggang Mountains days, passed away. Premier Zhou Enlai quickly realized its significance and immediately enlarged the guest list while Mao's limousine was already on the way. Wearing only a pajama, Mao had to put on an overcoat to conceal it at the funeral. Chen's wife Zhang Qian was overwhelmed when shaking Mao's hands. Her first words were "How could you come? Chen was against you in the past." Mao apparently was emotional, tears falling down his cheek. No one knew what was really in his mind. True emotion for a lost friend or simply a guilty feeling?

In the Byzantine politics of China at the time, the picture of Mao's participation at the funeral in the official People's Daily meant a lot. It rehabilitated Chen's reputation completely. It also helped rehabilitate those top lieutenants associated with Chen, such as Ye Fei, Wang Bicheng, Tao Yong, Chen Pixian and Jiang Weiqing shortly thereafter. The Chen Yi faction had survived Chen Yi. History thus seemed to have come full circle.

Notes

1. Ye, Fei, *Huai Nian Wang Bicheng Tong Zhi* (In Memory of Comrade Wang Bicheng), in *Hu Jiang Wang Bicheng* (Tiger General Wang Bicheng), p.13.

2. *Biography of Chen Yi* (Official), p.600-601.

Appendix:
Evolution of the New Fourth Army

1938

Commander Ye Ting
Political Commissar[1] Xiang Ying
Chief of Staff Zhang Yunyi
Political Director Yuan Guoping
Deputy Political Director Deng Zihui
Deputy Chief of Staff Zhou Zikun

1st Column: Commander Chen Yi

1st Regiment
    Commander Fu Qiutao
    Political Commissar Jiang Weiqing
    Chief of Staff Hu Fajian

2nd Regiment
    Commander Zhang Zhengkun
    Political Commissar Liu Peishan
    Chief of Staff Wang Bicheng

2nd Column: Commander Zhang Dingcheng
          Deputy Commander Su Yu

3rd Regiment
    Commander Huang Huoxing

---

[1] Until January 1941, the position of political commissar was deceptively designated as "deputy commander."

Political Commissar Qiu Jinsheng

4th Regiment
    Commander Lu Sheng
    Political Commissar Ye Daozhi[2]

3rd Column: Commander Zhang Yunyi

5th Regiment
    Commander Rao Shoukun
    Political Commissar Zeng Shaomin
    Chief of Staff Zhao Linbo

6th Regiment
    Commander Ye Fei
    Political Commissar Wu Kun
    Chief of Staff Huang Yuanqing

4th Column: Commander Gao Jingting[3]

7th Regiment
    Commander Yang Kezhi
    Political Commissar Cao Yufu
    Chief of Staff Lin Yingjian

8th Regiment
    Commander Zhou Junming
    Political Commissar Lin Kai
    Chief of Staff Zhao Qimin

9th Regiment
    Commander Gu Shiduo
    Political Commissar Gao Zhirong
    Chief of Staff Tang Shaotian

Handgun Regiment
    Commander Zhan Huayu
    Political Commissar Wang Shaochuan

1940

---

[2] Ye was executed soon after the concentration of troops.

[3] Gao was executed in 1939.

1. The New Fourth Army Headquarters

Commander Ye Ting
Political Commissar Xiang Ying
Political Director Yuan Guoping
Chief of Staff Zhang Yunyi
    New 1st Column[4]: Commander Fu Qiutao
    New 2nd Column: Commander Zhou Guisheng
    3rd Column: Commander Zhang Zhengkun

2. Northern Jiangsu Command

Commander Chen Yi
Deputy Commander Su Yu
Political Director Zhong Qiguang

    1st Column: Commander Ye Fei
    2nd Column: Commander Wang Bicheng
    3rd Column: Commander Tao Yong (alias Zhang Daoyong)

3. The North of the Yangzi River Command

Commander Zhang Yunyi
Deputy Commanders Xu Haidong and Luo Binhui
Political Director Deng Zihui

    4th Column: Commander Zhang Yunyi (concurrent)
    5th Column Commander Luo Binhui (concurrent)

1941

The Newly Established New Fourth Army Headquarters

Commander Chen Yi[5]
Political Commissar Liu Shaoqi

---

[4] The so-called New Columns were formed at the heAdquarters to deceive the government because the old columns were sent to Jiangsu. The 3rd Column maintained its original form since only one regiment, i.e., Ye Fei's 6th Regiment was in Jiangsu.

[5] From 1941 to 1945, Chen Yi retained "Acting Commander" title, for the purpose of honoring the imprisoned commander Ye Ting, who died in a flight accident upon release by the Nationalist Government on August 7, 1945.

Deputy Commander Zhang Yunyi
Political Director Deng Zihui
Chief of Staff Lai Chuanzhu

1st Division
    Commander Su Yu
    Deputy Commander Ye Fei
    Political Commissar Liu Yan[6]
1st Brigade: Commander Ye Fei
2nd Brigade: Commander Wang Bicheng
3rd Brigade: Commander Tao Yong

2nd Division
    Commander Zhang Yunyi (concurrent)
    Political Commissar Zheng Weisan
    Deputy Commander Luo Binhui
    Political Director Guo Shushen
    Chief of Staff Zhou Junming
4th Brigade: Commander Liang Congxue
5th Brigade: Commander Cheng Jun
6th Brigade: Commander Tan Xilin

3rd Division
    Commander and Political Commissar Huang Kecheng
    Political Director Wu Faxian
    Chief of Staff Peng Xiong
7th Brigade: Commander Peng Mingzhi
8th Brigade: Commander Tian Shouyao
9th Brigade: Commander Zhang Aiping

4th Division
    Commander and Political Commissar Peng Xuefeng
    Political Director Xiao Wangdong
    Chief of Staff Zhang Zhen
10th Brigade: Commander Liu Zhen
11th Brigade: Commander Teng Haiqing
12th Brigade: Commander Rao Zijian

5th Division
    Commander and Political Commissar Li Xiannian
    Political Director Ren Zhibin

---

[6] Though a Jianggang Mountains veteran, Liu Yan was constantly in poor health. He died in 1945.

Chief of Staff Liu Shaoqing
13th Brigade: Commander Zhou Zhijian
14th Brigade: Commander Luo Houfu
15th Brigade: Wang Haishan

6th Division
    Commander and Political Commissar Tan Zhenlin
    Chief of Staff Luo Zhongyi
    16th Brigade: Commander Luo Zhongyi
    18th Brigade: Commander Jiang Weiqing
7th Division
    Commander Zhang Dingcheng
    Political Commissar Zeng Xisheng
    Political Director He Wei
    Chief of Staff Li Zhigao
    19th Brigade: Commander Sun Zhongde

1945

Commander Chen Yi
Political Commissar Rao Shushi
Deputy Commander Zhang Yunyi
Political Director Shu Tong
Chief of Staff Chen Shiju

1. Shangdong Field Army

Commander Chen Yi (concurrent)
    1st Column: Commander Ye Fei
    2nd Column: Commander Luo Binhui
    7th Division: Commander Tan Xilin
    8th Division: Commander He Yixiang

2. Central China Field Army

Commander Su Yu
    6th Column: Commander Wang Bicheng
    7th Column: Commander Ji Pengfei
    8th Column: Commander Tao Yong
    9th Column: Commander Zhang Zhen

1947

East China Field Army

Commander and Political Commissar Chen Yi
Deputy Commander Su Yu
Political Director Tang Liang
Chief of Staff Chen Shiju
Deputy Political Director Zhong Qiguang

>   1st Column: Commander Ye Fei
>   4th Column: Commander Tao Yong
>   6th Column: Commander Wang Bicheng[7]

1949

The Third Field Army

Commander Chen Yi
Deputy Commander Su Yu
Political Commissar Rao Shushi
Political Director Tang Liang
Chief of Staff Zhang Zhen
Deputy Political Director Zhong Qiguang

The Original Ye-Wang-Tao troops
>   20th Army (Ye Fei's 1st Column)
>   23rd Army (Tao Yong's 4th Column)
>   24rd Army (Wang Bicheng's 6th Column)

---

[7] Other columns which were not part of the original New Fourth Army in 1938 are omitted here.

BIBLIOGRAPHY

Since this work is primarily based on documents, I choose to list only a partial selection of the secondary sources. Many documents are published and circulated internally (or Nei Bu) in China. The most important document collections are Mao Zedong, Chen Yi and Su Yu's military works. These documents are usually in telegram form, most of which were not available in the past. The advantage of using the telegrams is that they are often more accurate and precise in timing than post-battle reports.

Another important source of information is a large number of "private" collections of reminiscences, usually for the purpose of commemorating a particular general. They are compiled by the general's old comrades and families, who typically chip in financially for their publications. These materials are not allowed for sale but only for limited internal circulations. Many of these materials are very candid and detailed.

For other published sources, there are enormous amount of biographies, memoirs and battle histories concerning the New Fourth Army. Compared with the other military factions of the People's Liberation Army, the number of publications of the New Fourth Army faction is rather unusual. This is largely due to the fact that the New Fourth Army veterans are typically better educated. Among the vast number of personal memories, General Ye Fei's memoirs deserve particular attention, because it broke with the traditional party history method of recording only successes but not failures. Ye was very candid and straightforward in pointing out mistakes and internal power struggles. Ye's memoirs have inevitably raised eyebrows of the orthodox party historians. Su Yu's War Memoirs was published posthumously. Due to the circumstances, it was by no means a complete memoirs. The most notable omission in this important memoirs is the Campaign of Huai-Hai, an event that contributed a great deal to the final victory of the Communist Party in 1949. The reason for this omission is clear: General Su Yu, who re-directed Mao's thinking on this campaign, had never been given credit till the last day of his life. Mao had stolen all the credits by re-writing the history of this campaign through changing the contents of the original military telegrams. Fortunately, we are able to see a glimpse of Su's mental status during his campaign through an internal oral history project, compiled by Mrs. Su Yu. General Huang Kecheng's memoirs are important for its candid criticism of Mao and the other party leaders. Unfortunately, a sequel to Huang's memoirs, which were originally planned for two volumes, never has the chance to see the light.

As far as biographies are concerned, the official biography of Chen Yi is, to a surprising degree, much superior to many other unofficial ones. Published in 1992, this biography was written by a group of writers based in the Nanjing Military Region where the New Fourth Army veterans are mostly concentrated, with an editorial board consisting of people historically associated with Chen Yi and the New Fourth Army. The authors had apparently done a lot of research and had had accesses to many sensitive documents. The Biography of Chen Yi by Jiang Hongbing, though perhaps the best of its kind, suffers from being more a literary than history work. Nonetheless, Jiang had conducted many important interviews with high-level New Fourth Army veterans, such as Su Yu, which had enabled him to present many important facts that were hitherto unknown. Chen Yi has left a lot of poems throughout different stages of his life. These poems have become a complete collection thanks to Chen Haosu, the oldest son of Chen Yi. The importance of this collection lay in the fact that it is the key to understanding Chen Yi's state of mind.

I. Primary Sources (* denotes internal circulation or "Nei Bu.")

1. Document Collections

The Central Archives of the Chinese Communist Party, *Zhong Gong Zhong Yang Wen Jian Xuan Ji* (Selected Documents of the Chinese Communist Party Central Committee, referred to as WJXJ), 18 Volumes. The Party Central School Press: Beijing 1989.

---------.*Wan Nan Shi Bian* (The Southern Anhui Incident). The Central Archives Press: Beijing 1982.

---------. *Cong Yanan Dao Beijing* (From Yanan to Beijing), a collection of previously unpublished military documents. The Central Archives Press: Beijing 1993.

---------. *Zhong Gong Dang Shi Zi Liao* (Materials of the Chinese Communist Party History), serial, 1979-1995. Beijing: China

Chen, Yi, *Chen Yi Jun Shi Wen Xuan* (Selected Military Works of Chen Yi). The PLA Press: Beijing 1996.

---------. *Chen Yi Zi Liao Xuan** (Selected Materials on Chen Yi). Shanghai People's Publishing House: Shanghai 1979.

Deng, Xiaoping, *Deng Xiaoping Wen Xuan* (Selected Works of Deng

Xiaoping), 3 Volumes. The People's Publishing House: Beijing 1989.
Jiangsu People's Publishing House, *Xin Si Jun Zai Maoshan* (The New Fourth Army in Maoshan. Nanjing 1982.
---------. *Xin Si Jun Chong Jian Jun Bu Yi Hou* (The New Fourth Army After Reestablishing Its Headquarters). Nanjing 1983.
---------. *Su Zhong Si Fen Qu Fan Qing Xiang Dou Zheng* (Anti-Pacification Struggle at the Fourth Zone in Central Jiangsu). Nanjing 1985.
Jiangsu Provincial Archives, compiler, *Su Nan Kang Ri Geng Ju Di* (The Southern Jiangsu Anti-Japanese Base Area). The Party History Press: Beijing 1987.
---------. *Su Zhong Kang Ri Geng Ju Di* (Documents of the Central Jiangsu Anti-Japanese Base Area). The People's Publishing House: Beijing 1990.
Li, Xiannian, *Li Xiannian Wen Xuan* (Selected Works of Li Xiannian). The People's Publishing House: Beijing 1989.
--------. et al, *Xin Si Jun Di Wu Shi Kang Ri Zhan Zheng Shi Gao* (Draft History of the Fifth Division of the New Fourth Army). Hubei People's Publishing House: Wuhan 1989.
Liu, Shaoqi, *Liu Shaoqi Xuan Ji* (Selected Works of Liu Shaoqi), 2 Volumes. The Party Central Committee Document Compilation Commission, The People's Publishing House: Beijing 1981.
Mao, Zedong, *Mao Zedong Jun Shi Wen Ji** (The Military Works of Mao Zedong), 6 Volumes, referred to as MZDJSWJ. The PLA Press: Beijing 1992.
---------. *Mao Zedong Xuan Ji* (Selected Works of Mao Zedong), 5 Volumes. The People's Publishing House: Beijing 1981.
The Military Science Academy, *Jun Shi Zi Liao* (Historical Materials of Military History), series. Beijing 1981-1997
The New Fourth Army Battle History Compilation Committee, *Xin Si Jun Kang Ri Zhan Zheng Shi Zi Liao Xuan Bian** (Selected Historical Materials of the New Fourth Army during the Anti-Japanese War). Beijing 1964.
Number Two Archives of China, *Min Guo Dan An* (Archives of the Republic of China), Serial, 1985-1995. Nanjing.
Shanghai People's Publishing House, *Xin Si Jun Ji Hua Zhong Kang Ri Geng Ju Di Shi Liao** (The Historical Materials of the New Fourth Army and the Central China Anti-Japanese Base Area), 7 Volumes. Shanghai People's Publishing House: Shanghai 1984.
Su, Yu, *Su Yu Jun Shi Wen Ji** (Military Works of Su Yu), edited by General Sun Keji et al. The PLA Press: Beijing 1989.
---------. *Su Yu Lun Su Zhong Kang Zhan* (Su Yu on Anti-Japanese War in Central Jiangsu), edited by General Sun Keji. The Jiangsu People's

Publishing House: Nanjing 1993.
Ye, Fei, ed., *Xin Si Jun* (The New Fourth Army), documents, memoirs and reference materials, 6 Volumes. The PLA Press: Beijing 1988 - 1995.
Zhang, Aiping, *Zhang Aiping Jun Shi Wen Xuan* (Military Works of Zhang Aiping). Long March Press: Beijing 1994.

2. *Diaries, Memoirs and Other Reminiscences*

Bao, Houchang, *Si Xia Jiang Nan* (Four Trips to the South of the Yangzi---Memoirs of Bao Houchang). Wuxi People's Publishing House: Wuxi 1959.
Chen, Geng, *Chen Geng Ri Ji* (Diaries of Chen Geng). The Soldier Press: Beijing 1982.
Chen, Pixian, *Gan Nan San Nian You Ji Zhan Zheng* (Three-Year Guerrilla War in Southern Jiangxi). The People's Publishing House: Beijing 1982
---------. *Su Zhong Jie Fang Qu Shi Nian* (Ten Years of the Central Jiangsu Liberation Area). Shanghai People's Publishing House: Shanghai 1988.
---------. et al, *Hui Yi Tan Zhenlin* (In Memory of Tan Zhenlin). Zhangjinag People's Publishing House: Hangzhou 1992.
Chen, Yi, *Chen Yi Zao Nian Hui Yi Yu Wen Gao* (Chen Yi's Early Reminiscences and Writings). Sichuan People's Publishing House: Chengdu 1981.
---------. *Chen Yi Shi Ci Xuan Ji* (Selected Poems of Chen Yi), edited by Zhang, Qian (Mrs. Chen Yi). People's Literature Press: Beijing 1977.
---------. *Chen Yi Shi Ci Quan Ji* (Complete Collection of Chen Yi's Poems), edited by Chen, Haosu (the eldest son of Chen Yi). Huaxia Publishing House: Beijing 1993.
Du, Yuming et al, *Huaihai Zhan Yi Qing Li Ji* (Personal Experiences during the Campaign of Huai-Hai). Wenshi Press: Beijing 1983.
---------. *Guo Gong Nei Zhan Mi Lu* (The Secret History of the Kuomintang-Communist Civil War). Babylon Press: Taipei 1991.
Gong, Chu, *Hui Yi* (Memoirs), 2 Volumes. Minpao Monthly Press: Hong Kong 1978.
Guan, Wenwei, *Guan Wenwei Hui Yi Lu* (Memoirs of Guan Wenwei), 2 Volumes. The People's Publishing House: Beijing 1985 and 1988.
Guo, Rugui, *Guo Rugui Hui Yi Lu* (Memoirs of Guo Rugui). Sichuan People's Publishing House: Chengdu 1987.
Huang, Kecheng, *Huang Kecheng Hui Yi Lu* (Memoirs of Huang Kecheng), The PLA Press: Beijing 1989.
Jia, Qinglin and Yuan, Qitong ed., *Hui Yi Zhang Dingcheng* (In Memory of Zhang Dingcheng). Fujian People's Publishing House: Fuzhou 1991.

Jiang, Weiqing, *Jiang Weiqing Hui Yi Lu* (Memoirs of Jiang Weiqing), Jiangsu People's Publishing House: Nanjing 1996.
Jiangsu People's Publishing House, *Hui Yi Pan Hannian* (In Memory of Pan Hannian). Nanjing 1985.
Jin, Ye, *Zai Tong Zhan Bu de Ri Zi Li* (My Days at the Headquarters), Jiangsu People's Publishing House: Nanjing 1993).
Lai, Chuanzhu, *Lai Chuanzhu Ri Ji* (Diaries of Lai Chuanzhu). 3 Volumes, The PLA Press: Beijing 1988.
Li, Weihan, *Hui Yi Yu Yan Jiu* (Memoirs and Study), 2 Volumes. Party History Press: Beijing 1986.
Li, Yimang, *Mo Hu De Ying Ping* (The Fading Screens---Memoirs of Li Yimang), The People's Publishing House: Beijing 1992.
Li, Yimin, *Li Yimin Hui Yi Lu* (Memoirs of Li Yimin). Hunan People's Publishing House: Changsha 1986.
Liu, Zhen, *Liu Zhen Hui Yi Lu* (Memoirs of Liu Zhen). The PLA Press: Beijing 1990.
Liu, Bocheng, *Liu Bocheng Hui Yi Lu* (Memoirs of Liu Bocheng), 3 Volumes. Shanghai Literature Press: Shanghai 1981.
Liu, Hengyun, *Zhe Dong Kang Ri You Ji Dui* (The Anti-Japanese Guerrilla in East Zhejiang), Zhejiang People's Publishing House: Hangzhou 1987.
Liu, Ruming, *Liu Ruming Hui Yi Lu* (Memoirs of Liu Ruming). Biography Literature Press: Taipei 1966.
Liu, Shufa, *Chen Yi Nian Pu* (Chronology of Chen Yi's Life). People's Publishing House: Beijing 1995.
Liu, Zhi, *Wo De Hui Yi* (Memoirs of Liu Zhi), Rong Yuan Press: Taipei 1966.
Lu, Sheng, *Lu Sheng Hui Yi Lu* (Memoirs of Lu Sheng). Dongfang Press: Beijing 1992.
Nie, Fengzhi, *Zhan Chang---Jiang Jun De Yao Lan* (Battlefield---Cradle for Generals, Memoirs of Nie Fengzhi). The PLA Press: Beijing 1989.
Nie, Rongzhen, *Nie Rongzhen Hui Yi Lu* (Memoirs of Nie Rongzhen), 3 Volumes. The Soldier Press: Beijing 1983.
Pi, Dingjun, *Pi Dingjun Ri Ji* (Diaries of Pi Dingjun). The PLA Press: Beijing 1991.
Rao, Zijian, *Cong Zhan Shi Dao Jiang Jun de Zheng Cheng* (From Soldier to General---Memoirs of Rao Zijian). Jiangsu People's Publishing House: Nanjing 1992.
Shanghai People's Publishing House, *Zhan Jiang Tao Yong* (Fighter Tao Yong), a collection in memory of Tao Yong. Shanghai 1990.
Su, Yu, *Zhan Zheng Hui Yiu Lu* (War Memoirs). The PLA Press: Beijing 1988.
---------. *Qian Wan Li Zhuan Zhan* (Campaign Life for Ten Thousand

Miles). The PLA Press: Beijing 1984.
Xu, Shiyou, *Xu Shiyou Hui Yi Lu* (Memoirs of Xu Shiyou). The PLA Press: Beijing 1986.
Xu, Xiangqian, *Xu Xiangqian Hui Yi Lu* (Memoirs of Xu Xingqian). The PLA Press: Beijing 1991.
Wang, Daming, *Wang Daming Ri Ji** (Diaries of Wang Daming). Jiangsu People's Publishing House: Nanjing 1988.
Wang, Hao, *Tie Jun Xiao Jiang** (Brave General of the Iron Army, a collection in memory of General Liao Zhengguo). Deqing Press: Deqing 1992.
Yang, Fan, *Yang Fan Zi Shu* (Autobiography of Yang Fan), Mass Press: Beijing 1989.
Ye, Fei, *Ye Fei Hui Yi Lu* (Memoirs of Ye Fei). The PLA Press: Beijing 1988.
--------. et al, *Hu Jiang Wang Bicheng* ('Tiger General' Wang Bicheng), a collection in memory of General Wang Bicheng). The PLA Press: Beijing 1992.
Yue, Shiming et al, *Hao Zhu Ren Zhong Qiguang* (Good Director Zhong Qiguang), a collection in memory of Zhong Qiguang. The Military Science Press: Beijing 1993.
Zhang, Kexia, *Pei Jian Jiang Jun---Zhang Kexia Jun Zhong Ri Ji* (The Dagger General- Zhang Kexia's Diary in Army). The PLA Press: Beijing 1988.
Zhou, Gucheng et al, *Ji Nian Ji Fang* (In Memory of Ji Fang). Wenshi Press: Beijing 1990.
Zhou, Ze et al, *Jue Huo Bu Xi** (The Fire Never Extinguishes, a collection in memory of General Zeng Ruqing). Navy Academy Press: Nanjing 1992.

3. Biographies

Chen, Xinren, *Luo Binghui Jiang Jun* (General Luo Binghui). China Youth Press: Beijing 1986.
Cui, Xianghua and Chen, Dapeng, *Tao Yong Jiang Jun Zhuan* (Biography of Tao Yong). The PLA Press: Beijing 1989.
Deng, Maomao, *My Father Deng Xiaoping*. Basic Books: New York 1995.
Deng, Liqun et al, *Chen Yi Zhuan* (Official Biography of Chen Yi). Modern China Press: Beijing 1991.
Duan, Yusheng et al, *Ye Ting Jiang Jun Zhuan* (Biography of General Ye Ting). The PLA Press: Beijing 1989.
Feng, Wengang et al, *Yi Dai Ming Jiang---Peng Xuefeng Zhuan Ji* (A Famous General---Biography of Peng Xuefeng). Henan People's

Publishing House: Zhengzhou 1991.
Jiang, Boying, *Deng Zihui Zhuan* (Biography of Deng Zihui). Shanghai People's Publishing House: Shanghai 1986.
Jiang, Hongbin, *Chen Yi Zhuan* (Biography of Chen Yi). Shanghai People's Publishing House: Shanghai 1992.
Jiang, Weiqing et al, *Tan Zhenlin Zhuan* (Biography of Tan Zhenlin). Zhejiang People's Publishing House: Hangzhou 1992.
Jin, Chongji, *Zhou Enlai Zhuan* (Biography of Zhou Enlai). Party History Press: Beijing 1988.
--------, and Huo, Xiguang, *Zhu De Zhuan* (Biography of Zhu De). The People's Publishing House: Beijing 1993.
Li, Liangmin, *Xiang Ying Ping Zhuan* (A Critical Biography of Xiang Ying). Economic Daily Press: Beijing 1993.
Liu, Puqing, *Cai Huiwen Jiang Jun Zhuan* (Biography of General Cai Huiwen). The PLA Press: Beijing 1987.
Lu, Xingdou, edited, *Liu Shaoqi He Ta De Shi Ye* (Liu Shaoqi and His Career). Party History Press: Beijing 1991.
Luo, Yingcai, *Tie Jun Dang Dai Biao* (Party Representative of the Iron Army). The People's Literature Press: Beijing 1992.
The Military Science Academy, *Ye Jianying Zhuan* (Biography of Ye Jianying). The Military Science Press: Beijing 1987.
The New Fourth Army Research Committee, *Ming Jiang Su Yu* (Famous General Su Yu). Xinhua Press: Beijing 1986.
Wang, Fuyi, *Xiang Ying Zhuan Lue* (A Brief Biography of Xiang Ying), *Materials of the Chinese Communist Party History*, vol.37, Beijing 1991.
-------. *Xiang Ying Zhuan* (Biography of Xiang Ying). Party History Press: Beijing 1995.
Wang, Yuting, *Hu Lian Ping Zhuan* (A Critical Biography of General Hu Lian). Biography Press: Taipei 1987.
Xiang, Lanxin, *Recasting the Imperial Far East---Britain and America in China, 1945 - 1950*. Sharpe: New York 1995.
Zhang, Lin and Ning, Fan, *Xu Haidong Da Jiang* (General Xu Haidong). Haiyan Press: Henan 1987.
Zheng, Naizang and Wang, Nan, *Su Yu Da Jiang* (General Su Yu), Haiyan Press: Henan 1987.
Zhu, Yuanshi, *Liu Shaoqi Chun Qiu Lu* (The Career of Liu Shaoqi). Sichuan People's Publishing House: Chengdu 1992.
Zuo, Lin and Zhou, Hang, *Huang Kecheng Da Jiang* (General Huang Kecheng). Haiyan Press: Henan 1987.

4. Battle Histories

The Central Committee's Commission for Collecting Party History Materials, compiled, *Huai-Hai Zhan Yi** (The Campaign of Huai-Hai), 3 Volumes. Party History Press: Beijing 1988.
Jin, Ye ed., *Su Zhong Qi Zhan Qi Jie* (Seven Victories in Central Jiangsu). Jiangsu People's Publishing House: Nanjing 1986.
Lianshui County Party History Office, *Lianshui Bao Wei Zhan** (The Defensre of Lianshui). Jiangsu People's Publishing House: Nanjing 1989.
The Military Science Academy, *Zhong Guo Ren Jie Fang Jun Zhan Shi* (Battle History of the People's Liberation Army) 3 Volumes. The Military Science Press: Beijing 1987.
Taiwan Defense Ministry, *Kan Luan Zhan Shi* (Battle History of the Pacification War). Taipei 1962.
--------. *Kan Luan Jian Shi* (A Brief Battle History of the Pacification War). Taipei 1965.
The Twentieth Army Corps, *Di Er Shi Jun Zhan Shi** (Battle History of the Twentieth Army Corps). Mimeograph.
Yang, Guoyu et al, *Liu-Deng Da Jun Zheng Zhan Ji* (The Battle History of the Liu [Bocheng]-Deng [Xiaoping] Troops), 3 Volumes. Yunnan People's Publishing House: Kunming 1984.

II. Secondary Sources

1. Books

Benton, Gregor, *Mountain Fires: The Red Army's Three-Year War in South China, 1934-1938.* Berkeley: California 1992
--------. *At the Brink: Xiang Ying and Mao Zedong: Countdown to the Wannan Incident, March 1939 - January 1941.* Leeds: Department of East Asian Studies 1996.
Bullock, Alan, *Hitler and Stalin---Parallel Lives.* Knopf: New York 1992.
Central Party School, *Zhong Gong Zhong Yang Zai Xiang Shan* (The Central Committee at the Fragrance Hill). Party History Press: Beijing 1993.
Chassin, Lionel Max, *The Communist Conquest of China; a history of the Civil War, 1945-1949.* Cambridge: Harvard 1965
Chen, Yung-fa, *Making Revolution---The Communist Movement in Eastern and Central China, 1937-1945.* Cambridge: Harvard 1986.
Ding, Xing et al, *Xin Si Jun Ci Dian* (Encyclopedia of the New Fourth Army, Shanghai Dictionary Press: Shanghai 1997)
He, Li, *Kang Ri Zhan Zheng Shi* (The History of the Anti-Japanese War). Shanghai People's Publishing House: Shanghai 1985.

Johnson, Chalmers, *Peasant Nationalism and Communist Power.* Stanford: California 1962.
Li, Ruqing, *Wan Nan Shi Bian* (The Southern Anhui Incident, a very controversial novel). The PLA Literature Press: Beijing 1989.
Luo, Huanzhang and Zhi, Shaoceng, *Zhong Hua Min Zu de Kang Ri Zhan Zheng* (The Chinese Nation's War Against Japan). The Military Science Press: Beijing 1987.
Ma Hongwu et al, *Xin Si Jun Zheng Tu Ji Shi* (A Chronology of Events of the New Fourth Army). Jiangsu People's Publishing House: Nanjing 1988.
Tong, Zhiqiang, *Wan Nan Shi Bian Yan Jiu Yu Zheng Ming* (Study and Debate over the Southern Anhui Incident). Anhui People's Publishing House: Hefei 1990.
Wang, Fuyi, *Xin Si Jun Shi Jian Ren Wu Lu* (The New Fourth Army: Events and Personnel). Shanghai Publishing House: Shanghai 1988.
Wei, Pu et al., *Xin Si Jun Zu Zhi Fa Zhan Shi Lu* (True History of the Organizational Development of the New Fourth Army). Jiangsu People's Publishing House: Nanjing 1992.
Whitson, William, *Chinese High Command.* Praeger: New York 1974.
Zhang, Zhen et al, *Lun Su Yu de Jun Shi Li Lun Yu Shi Jian* (On Su Yu's Military Theory and Practice). National Defense University Press: Beijing 1991.
Zhong Guo Jun Shi Shi Lun Wen Ji (The Symposium of the Chinese Military History), University of Henan Press: Zhengzhou 1989.

2. *Magazines and Newspapers*

Chen Bao (The Morning News), Beijing 1919 - 1925.
Da Jiang Nan Bei Magazine, Shanghai 1985 - 1997
Dang Shi Wen Hui (Party History Literature). Taiyuan 1979 - 1997
Min Guo Ri Bao (The Republic Daily), Beijing 1919-1926.
Ta Kung Pao, Hong Kong 1949.
Wen Hui Yue Kan (The Wen Hui Monthly), Shanghai 1978 - 1995
Xin Wen Bao (The News), Shanghai 1938.
Zhong Gong Dang Shi Yan Jiu (Studies of the Chinese Communist Party History), Beijing 1981 - 1997
Zhong Gong Dang Shi Zi Liao (Materials of the CCP History). Beijing 1985 - 1997

INDEX

AB Clique, 20-23, 26

Bai, Chongxi, 87, 162, 188
Bo, Gu, 24, 37, 38, 49
Braun, Otto, 24
Bukharin, Nikolai, 17, 19

Cai, Hesen, 5, 6, 7, 8
Cai, Huiwen, 22
Chen, Duxiu, 4, 7, 10, 51
Chen, Geng, 41, 145
Chen, Mengxi, 3, 6, 12
Chen, Pixian, 79
Chen, Shiju, 157
Chen, Yi, 8, 9, 10, 12-14, 26-28, 33-36, 39, 46, 56-58, 64, 73, 122, 184
   Childhood, 1-3
   in France, 4-7
   marriage, 20, 22-23, 25, 61, 70
   Red Army period, 16-23, 43
   conflict with Rao, 114-117
   drafting military report, 119
   return to central China, 124-125
   and Battle of Laiwu, 136-137
   and Battle of Mengliangu, 140-143
   and debacle at Nanma and Linqu, 144
   trip to Yanan, 147-148
   join Deng's command, 154-155
   designated Mayor of Shanghai, 184
Chen, Yi (a KMT official), 191-192
Chiang, Kai-shek, 11, 12, 13, 15, 20, 27, 48, 161, 177, 179, 183, 185, 188, 196
   with New Fourth Army, 35, 37, 45
Churchill, Winston, 190
Clausewitz, Karl von, 74
Comintern, 17, 19, 24, 48
Communist International, 44, 49
Communist Party Congress,
   First, 16
   Sixth, 17

Deng, Xiaoping, 23, 46, 184
   Deng-Mao-Xie-Gu Clique, 23
   and the strategic march, 146
   against Huang Wei, 175-176
Deng, Zihui, 40, 154
Du, Yumin, 177-180
Duan, Qirui, 9

Eighth Route Army, 34, 46, 48
Er-Yu-Wan Soviet Regime, 41, 43

Fan, Shisheng, 15
Fang, Zhimin, 40
First United Front, 9, 10, 11

Gao, Jingting, 37, 41, 45-46, 51, 95
Gu, Bai, 23
Gu, Zhutong, 45
Guan, Wenwei, 58

Han, Deqin, 63-64, 67
Harvest Uprising, 15
He, Changgong, 15, 16
He, Long, 12, 24
He, Shuheng, 25
He, Yi, 25, 34
He, Yingqin, 87
He, Zizhen, 22
Huang, Baitao, 163, 172-173
Huang, Gonglue, 20, 22
Huang, Kecheng, 43-44, 70, 84, 89, 101, 114, 212
Huangqiao Battle, 78-83
Huang, Wei, 168, 176-179

Hugo, Victor, 6

Ji, Fang, 80
Ji, Zhengang, 57
Jin, Mancheng (alias Qiu Yang), 9
Jiangxi Soviet Regime, 19-26, 28
Jinggang Mountains, 14-15, 16-.9

Kang, Sheng, 111, 150

Lai, Chuanzhu, 99
Leng, Xin, 78
Lamartine, Alfonse de, 6
Li, Hongzhang, 3
Li, Da, 176
Li, Dazhao, 9, 10
Li, Lisan, 19, 20
Li, Shaojiu, 21-22
Li, Shouwei, 83-84
Li, Xianzhou, 138
Li, Xiannian, 70, 95
Li, Zongren, 187, 189
Liao, Zhengguo, 96
Lin, Biao, 14, 18-19, 48, 161
Liu, Bocheng, 128, 157, 184
Liu, Shaoqi, 44-45, 50, 59, 66-69, 84, 98-99, 103, 194
Liu, Ying, 36, 37, 40
Liu, Zhi, 173, 177
Long March, 24, 25, 27, 41, 43

Mao, Zedong, 15, 43-44
  Jiangxi Soviet Regime, 19-24
  Jinggang Mountain, 16-17
  New Fourth Army, 36-39, 67-68
  and Shandong, 109-110
  and purge campaign, 110-111
  letter to Chen Yi, 118
  order to take cities, 121-123
  and Southern Strategy, 148
  rewrite history, 166-168
  wavering during battle, 166-168
  and the Yangzi Campaign, 183
  and peace settlement, 191-192
  at Chen Yi's funeral, 203
Mao, Zetan, 15, 23, 25, 34
Marshall, George, 127

May Fourth Movement, 4, 5, 8
Mountain-Toppism, 43, 45
Musset, Alfred de, 6, 195

Nanchang Uprising, 12, 13, 15, 18, 35
New Fourth Army, 33, 35, 37, 42
  early period, 45-48
Nishio, Juzo, 97
Northern Expedition, 10, 11, 13, 20, 35

Peng, Dehuai, 17, 22, 48, 50, 97
Peng, Xuefeng, 70, 101-102, 115
Pingjiang Uprising, 17

Qu, Qiubai, 25

Rao, Shushi, 93, 103-104, 114-117, 120
Red Army, 15, 17, 20, 23, 25, 34
Red Fourth Army, 16-19
Ren, Bishi, 117
Rectification Campaign, 103

Second United Front, 28, 34, 49, 64, 93
Service, John, 118
Southern Anhui Incident, 84, 88-93
Stalin, Josef, 19, 85
Su, Yu, 14, 24, 40, 42, 46, 61-62, 65, 113, 116, 211
  in Northern Jiangsu, 72
  and Battle of Huangqiao, 79-84
  and Battle of Cheqiao, 120
  and Battle of Xiaofeng, 121-123
  and Battle of Suqian, 130
  and Battle of Laiwu, 136-139
  and Battle of Menglianggu, 140-143
  and debacle at Nanma, 189-190
  objection to Mao, 152-153
  and Huai-Hai Campagin, 162-164, 170-173, 177-180
  redirect Mao's thought, 169
  and Battle of Shanghai, 191-193

Sun, Yefang (alias Song Liang), 98
Sun, Yat-sen, 9, 10

Tan, Yubao, 39
Tan, Zhenlin, 40, 46, 61, 66, 95, 114
Tang, Enbo, 101, 191
Tao, Yong, 65, 72, 73, 81, 96
  And the Amethyst Incident, 189-190
Tojo, Hideki, 96
Two Lis, 63, 64

Wang, Bicheng, 72, 73, 96
Wang, Jingwei, 11, 12, 97
Wang, Ming, 38, 48, 49, 58-59
Weng, Da, 82
Whampoa Academy, 12, 41, 46
Wu, Kun, 47-48
Wu, Peifu, 11
Wu, Yuzhang, 3-4
Wu, Zhihui, 3, 6, 9

Xian Incident, 27-28
Xiao, Wangdong, 101
Xiang, Ying, 22, 23, 25-26, 28
  death, 94
  conflict with Mao, 36-37, 43, 51-52, 55-56, 84-94
  with New Fourth Army, 38-39, 45
  with Ye Ting, 59-60
Xie, Weijun, 23
Xu, Shiyou, 146
Xu, Xiangqian, 41

Yamamoto, Isoroku, 102
Yang, Hucheng, 27
Yang, Lisan, 171
Yang, Sen, 8, 10-11
Yangzi River Bureau, 38, 45, 49, 59
Ye, Daozhi,
  Execution of, 47
Ye, Fei, 41-42, 62, 96, 127, 211
  Secret talk with Liu Shaoqi, 68-69
  and Battle at Guo Village, 70-72
  and Battle of Suqian, 130
  and Battle of Laiwu, 138-139
  narrow escape, 144-145
  criticized, 151
  and Amethyst Incident, 190
  and Battle of Shanghai, 192
Ye, Jianying, 37
Ye, Ting, 12, 13, 35, 36-38, 45, 59-60, 88, 93

Zeng, Ruqing, 77-78, 96
Zeng, Shan, 78
Zeng, Xisheng, 95, 114
Zhang, Dingcheng, 36, 37, 40, 46
Zhang, Fan, 71
Zhang, Guotao, 9, 41, 43, 46, 47
Zhang, Qian, 61, 70, 135, 203
Zhang, Wentian (Lo Fu), 44, 50
Zhang, Xueliang, 27-28
Zhang, Yunyi, 115
Zhong, Qiguang, 95
Zhou, Enlai, 5, 6, 7, 10, 11, 12, 13, 19, 23, 24-25, 37, 38, 49-50, 59-60, 154
  Xian Incident, 27-28
Zhu, De, 10, 11, 12, 13-19, 20, 22, 23, 40, 44, 50
Zou, Dapeng, 194
Zunyi Conference, 25, 44

Lanxin Xiang teaches international history at the Graduate Institute of International Studies in Geneva, Switzerland. A graduate of Fudan University in Shanghai, he obtained graduate degrees from the Johns Hopkins University and taught for five years in the United States. He was an Olin Fellow at Yale University and a MacArthur Visiting Fellow in Germany. He has published a book, *Recasting the Imperial Far East*, and a number of articles in *Journal of Contemporary History*, *Orbis* and others. He is completing a study on the origins of the Boxer War.